The Age of Wit

D. JUDSON MILBURN

The Age of Wit

1650–1750

If Faith itself has diff'rent dresses worn,
What wonder Modes in Wit should take their turn?

—Alexander Pope, *An Essay on Criticism* (1711)

The true wonder of Poesy is, That such contraries must meet to compose it . . . the Fire, the Hammer, the Chizel, and the File.

—Sir William Temple, *Of Poetry* (1690)

THE MACMILLAN COMPANY • *NEW YORK*

COLLIER–MACMILLAN LTD • *LONDON*

Library of Congress Catalog Card Number: 66–15026
SECOND PRINTING 1966

The Macmillan Company, New York
Collier-Macmillan Canada Ltd., Toronto, Ontario

Printed in the United States of America

TO

MY MOTHER, MY FATHER,

MY MOTHER-IN-LAW, AND

MY FATHER-IN-LAW

whose help, each in his own way during those trying years which made this book possible, was nothing—

short of indispensable.

Contents

Preface

THE intellectual framework of the century from 1650 to 1750 is vast and complex—but it has one center in wit. Wit in itself is a subject which causes confusion, and to bring some order out of what has seemed to be great disorder, I have reexamined the century for a new view of its rationale. As the basis for the study, I have identified and described in some detail certain contexts for meanings of wit by which the age understood itself. Of these contexts (enigma, rhetoric, psychology, truth, grace, republic, caricature, and stigma), only rhetoric and psychology have received much attention heretofore by students, rhetoric being the only one developed with some thoroughness. Because of the exhaustless and involved nature of the subject not only in England but on the Continent, this study is compendious, a kind of outline, suggestive rather than complete or final, concentrating primarily on phenomena in England.

I am gratified, after the labor of many an hour, pleasant and engrossing though most of it has been, to see my study in its present form. Its value lies not only in illuminating a period in great contrast to ours but in reaffirming a crucial and valuable intellectual force in human society—wit. The significance of the designation "Age of Wit" has dimmed before other meaningful names for parts of the years: "Seventeenth Century," "Eighteenth Century," "Age of the Restoration," "Augustan Age," "Age of Dryden," "Age of Pope," "Age of Swift," "Age of Johnson," etc.

Of the various names, "Neoclassical Age" and "Age of Reason" most nearly parallel the Age of Wit in time. In a real sense, the unifying spirit of these years was wit. It was recognized as such then and needs to be so recognized more generally again.

While the study is my own, it was not begun or continued without the influence and assistance of others. My interest in the seventeenth and eighteenth centuries began with my first graduate studies at Oklahoma State and Harvard Universities. My attention was attracted to this subject by some passing remarks of Dougald MacMillan in class lectures at the University of North Carolina. Original research was begun as a project in the classes of John M. Raines and John Paul Pritchard at the University of Oklahoma, who became subsequently the co-advisors of my dissertation on certain aspects of wit.

In the tedious progress of this study, I have been encouraged by my good friend and fellow student, James R. Wilson, now of Central College in Iowa. He urged me often to keep to my task and not only offered to help but did so, reading the manuscript at three crucial stages and making valuable contributions.

In its later stages, the study has been improved by several of my colleagues: Samuel R. Woods, who helped substantially with troublesome chapters; George H. White, who read the completed manuscript carefully and objectively; and others who either read a portion critically or gave considered opinions on specific problems: Hans H. Andersen, Richard C. Bailey, Harry M. Campbell, Loyd Douglas, M. H. Griffin, Daniel R. Kroll, and Geoffrey Pill. I appreciate the numerous services and conveniences afforded by the Oklahoma State University Library under the excellent direction of Edmon Low. I thank Robert B. Kamm, Vice-President for Academic Affairs, formerly Dean of the College of Arts and Sciences, for his help in providing for two complete typings. And very important, I am grateful to Cyclone Covey for a most thoughtful and timely suggestion.

There is one other indebtedness I would not forget—that which I owe to my wife, Vera Pritchard Milburn. She has invested untold hours in this study:—constant contact with its progress which led to much sound advice, peripheral reading in primary sources which I should never have gotten around to, and the very important close examination without which no manuscript can be brought to its final stage of completion.

Jud Milburn
Oklahoma State University
Stillwater, Oklahoma

The Age of Wit

What is this wit, which must our cares employ?
The owner's wife, that other men enjoy:
Then most our trouble still when most admir'd,
And still the more we give, the more requir'd;
Whose fame with pains we guard, but lose with ease,
Sure some to vex, but never all to please;
'Tis what the vicious fear, the virtuous shun,
By fools 'tis hated, and by knaves undone!

—ALEXANDER POPE, "An Essay on Criticism" (1711)

1
The Enigma of Wit

IN 1704, DANIEL DEFOE, a lower-middle-class journalist, novelist, and poet, related in his periodical *Review* (VIII, No. 180) an incident dating back to the Restoration involving the Duke of Buckingham and John Dryden, a gentleman poet and wit. The duke had been party to the attempts by the first Earl of Shaftesbury to supplant James II, the Roman Catholic king, with Charles II's illegitimate but Protestant son, the Duke of Monmouth. Dryden had written *Absalom and Achitophel* (1681), a poetic satire on this treachery. In it Dryden had flayed Buckingham audaciously and delightfully, but had resorted also to mere name-calling with such words as "fiddler" and "buffoon." When the duke, a Court wit and accomplished writer himself, chanced to meet Dryden in a London coffeehouse, he scored the poet as no gentleman—for the duke believed name-calling a breach of manners out of place in satiric wit—and caned him for it: "There, Sir, is for your ill manners." He then handed Dryden a purse of thirty guineas, adding, "And here, Sir, is for your wit."

This account is of more than passing interest to the student of wit, for it reveals that wit was a subject of urbane conversation which interested all men of intelligence. It was one subject which aroused strong feelings since it meant very different things to different people.

"Wit" is one of the more interesting words in the English language. A common term in Old English, it continued to signify "mind" or "intellect" for approximately a thousand years. Then, in the intellectual whirl of the English Renaissance beginning in the sixteenth century, it acquired complications of meaning arising primarily from its new (fifteenth- and sixteenth-century) association with two ancient traditions—rhetoric and faculty psychology. Thus enriched, it continued to acquire an even greater variety of meanings in the seventeenth and early eighteenth centuries. Scholarly studies have helped to clear up some aspects of this development,[1] but our understanding of wit and of the century in which it flourished in all its complexity has remained fragmentary. Eight separate contexts for the meaning of wit developed from the late Renaissance through the Augustan Age. The hundred years from 1650 to 1750 was indeed the Age of Wit.

That century was distinguished by brilliant conversation and scintillating literary accomplishment in satire, in humorous raillery, and in spirited criticism. Men of letters prided themselves in these and other displays of wit. John Dryden, the prophet of the new Age of Wit, wrote in his Epilogue to the Second Part of *Conquest of Granada* (1672) of the supreme achievement:

> Wit's now arriv'd to a more high degree;
> Our native language more refin'd and free
> Our ladies and our men now speak more wit
> In conversation, than those poets writ.

"Those poets" were Ben Jonson and John Donne of the preceding age. Since a common metaphor in Dryden's day for comparing contemporary writers with those of the past was the image of a dwarf standing upon the shoulders of a giant, here was indeed praise of the dwarf at the expense of the giant.

So high were wit's attainments at this time that many men were drawn to emulate its posture, some of the greatest minds and a multitude of lesser ones. So while it encouraged major literary efforts by men of genius, its irresistible attraction as a fashion turned many a fop into a scribbling, would-be wit, and the resulting deluge of wit was not only diverting, but extraordinarily mixed. Each in its own way—the ingenious neoclassical couplet of John Dryden and Alexander Pope, the vituperations against man and the misery of his reason of Jonathan Swift, the sophisticated correspondence of Lady Mary Wortley Montagu, the fatuous histrionics of Etherege's Sir Fopling Flutter, the libelous and obscene broadsides hawked in every street, the nonsense whispered in milady's ear by a pretentious coxcomb, the Nickers' nocturnal pastime of throwing halfpennies through glass windows—all passed for wit. Little wonder that wit became, almost literally, all things to all people.

Conditions for the Age of Wit

The Age of Wit cannot be dated precisely, though one could argue that it began with the Restoration in 1660 and continued through the publication of the *New Dunciad* in 1742. But these dates are arbitrary. The word wit itself is as difficult to define. Whatever wit is, it has been used for a variety of aims: personal display, enjoyment, enlightenment, and chastisement. Two basic conditions were necessary: the knowledge and sophistication of an urbane society and the stimulus of a dynamic environment, alive with intellectual, social, and political movement. And London was rich in these conditions in the seventeenth and eighteenth centuries.

A polished and civilized society had been developing in London for some two hundred years. Until the early fifteenth century English culture was predominantly rural, the largest centers of population being cathedral towns. Education was conducted in monasteries, priories, and other church institutions; Oxford and Cambridge were there, but as ecclesiastical foundations. For entertainment, each town enjoyed its mummers and folk festivals. Miracle plays were presented in annual pageants from Aberdeen to Cornwall. Trade guilds produced in the town streets elaborate cycles of mystery plays, manuscripts of which have survived at York, Coventry, Chester, Norwich, Newcastle, and elsewhere. Poetry, history, and philosophy were written throughout the kingdom wherever learning happened to meet genius. Of the major literary figures in the fourteenth century, only Geoffrey Chaucer spent his literary career in London, partly because he was employed there in an assortment of public services for the government but partly because he happened to have been born there. Although John Gower owned large holdings in Norfolk and Suffolk, he was buried at the priory of St. Mary Overy in Southwark, in London; Richard Rolle lived the life of a recluse in and about Hampole; and John Wycliffe lived the years of his maturity at the rectory of Lutterworth in Leicestershire. In the fifteenth century Thomas Hoccleve lived at the priory of Southwick in Hampshire, and John Lydgate wrote at Bury St. Edmunds.

With the one notable exception of the new merchant class, traditional English life did not vary in its basic social structure from the fourteenth century through the Renaissance to the Age of Wit. This life was centered in the country, where for a great part of the year, if not all of it, the English lived. At the crest of this society was the royal family, whose estates in the country outnumbered those in London. Next came the lords: dukes, marquises, earls, viscounts, and barons, all with castles and large country mansions standing in vast estates. Below these the country gentry—baronets, knights, and esquires—kept busy at their agricultural pursuits. Finally, and most numerous, were the rural folk—the yeomen and tenant-farmers.

But a significant change was occurring in London. The centralized power enforced by Tudor monarchs, particularly Henry VIII and Elizabeth in the sixteenth century, led to an increase in the military strength and wealth of England, which were naturally concentrated in London, the center of trade and money. Foreign trade and local business were expanding to new wealth only dreamed of by the landed aristocracy and gentry. The new middle class of merchants, bankers, and tradesmen was developing rapidly, most of them urban in habits and Protestant in views. London was the center of this new class.

This affluence, and the ensuing interest in more education, influenced an unparalleled literary efflorescence which began about the middle of the sixteenth century. In Elizabethan London there were such literary figures as Edmund Spenser, Sir Philip Sidney, William Shakespeare, Ben Jonson, Francis Bacon, John Donne, and the "University Wits": Christopher Marlowe, John Lyly, Robert Greene, and Sir Thomas Lodge.

The scions of nobility and gentry thronged to London in ever greater numbers to enjoy all its advantages and pleasures: the opportunity for ready fame and fortune; the availability of diversion and revelry; the enjoyment of superior entertainment; the spectacle of the Court and Parliament; even merely the excitement of crowds and activity. The achievement of the Elizabethan and Jacobean theaters and Court life, the brilliant displays of the pulpit oratory of Lancelot Andrews, John Donne, Thomas Fuller, and Hugh Latimer, the atmosphere of scientific enquiry which was to lead to the foundation of the Royal Society of London—all these made London one of the most intellectually stimulating centers in all of Europe.

But in spite of all of its great cultural advantages London was a place of dramatic contrasts: crime in churchyards, brutality in face of emergent sensibility, starvation amid wealth, and profligate immorality in defiance of Puritan rigor. When about 1650 the Age of Wit began, London was a rowdy, disordered town, chafing under the restrictions of the Puritans. The theaters, taverns, and pleasure gardens were closed; the festival of the Maypole and even the celebration of Christmas were proscribed; bear baiting and cock fighting had been suppressed; and all public dancing was strictly forbidden.

With the restoration of the Stuarts to the throne in 1660, all of these pleasures were quickly resumed. In the tradition of Mediterranean cities, most activities of the citizenry were carried on in the streets: business, fairs, feasts. Victories were celebrated by lighting bonfires, opening barrels of wine, and roasting oxen on spits. These streets were still medieval in character—crooked and narrow, always congested with people, and with the waste water, ordure, and garbage habitually thrown into them. Orders were issued periodically by the Lord Mayor for daily cleansing of the streets and gutters, but the citizens were not impressed with the need for any rigorous health measures.

These deplorable conditions encouraged the famous outbreak of the plague, which began slowly in the fall of 1664 and increased during the following months to fierce proportions. During August and September of 1665, there were more than 4,000 dead a week. The plague continued, though somewhat abated, to the outbreak of the Great Fire in 1666, which destroyed much of the old town within the medieval wall. The remaining citizens, too exhausted from the plague for any sustained battle with the flames, simply watched the conflagration.

Rebuilding was done hastily along the pattern of the old streets, so that within a few years the streets were as filthy as ever, especially during heavy rains when heavy cascades of water poured from the roofs into the central street-gutters to form offensive quagmires. In 1710, Jonathan Swift gave in his poem "A Description of a City Shower" many of the grim details:

Now in contiguous Drops the Flood comes down,
Threat'ning with Deluge this Devoted Town.
To Shops in Crouds the daggled Females fly,
Pretend to cheapen Goods, but nothing buy.
The Templer spruce, while ev'ry Spout's a-broach,
Stays till 'tis fair, yet seems to call a Coach.
The tuck'd-up Sempstress walks with hasty Strides,
While Streams run down her oil'd Umbrella's Sides.
Here various Kinds by various Fortunes led,
Commence Acquaintance underneath a Shed.
Triumphant Tories, and desponding Whigs,
Forget their Fewds, and join to save their Wigs.
Box'd in a Chair the Beau impatient sits,
While Spouts run clatt'ring o'er the Roof by Fits;
And ever and anon with frightful Din
The Leather sounds, he trembles from within.

. . . .

Now from all Parts the swelling Kennels flow,
And bear their Trophies with them as they go:
Filth of all Hues and Odours seem to tell
What Street they sail'd from, by their Sight and Smell.

They, as each Torrent drives, with rapid Force
From Smithfield, or St. Pulchre's shape their Course,
And a huge Confluent join at Snow-Hill Ridge,
Fall from the Conduit prone to Holborn-Bridge.
Sweepings from Butchers Stalls, Dung, Guts, and Blood,
Drown'd Puppies, stinking Sprats, all drench'd in Mud,
Dead Cats and Turnip-Tops come tumbling down the Flood.

A few years later John Gay wrote his *Trivia, or the Art of Walking the Streets of London* (1716) describing the same old confusion and smells:

Who would of Watling Street the dangers share,
When the broad pavement of Cheapside is near?
Or who that rugged street would traverse o'er,
That stretches, O Fleet-ditch, from thy black shore
To the Tower's moated walls? Here steams ascend
That, in mix'd fumes, the wrinkled nose offend.
Where chandlers cauldrons boil; where fishy prey
Hide the wet stall, long absent from the sea;
And where the cleaver shops the heifers spoil,
And where huge hogsheads sweat with trainy oil,
Thy breathing nostril hold.

Gay, a distinguished wit and member of the Scriblerus Club, was one of the country boys come to town. Born at Barnstaple in 1685, he first arrived in London to be an apprentice to a silk mercer. He soon tired "of either the restraint or the servility of his occupation, and easily persuaded his master to discharge him," as Dr. Johnson commented in his *Lives of the Poets.* Gay returned home but in a few years was back in London, where he persisted to literary fame and the ultimate honor—burial in Westminster Abbey. Gay enjoyed London and in *Trivia* wrote of his favorite city:

Happy Augusta! law-defended town!
Here no dark lanthorns shade the villain's frown;
No Spanish jealousies thy lanes infest,
Nor Roman vengeance stabs th' unwary breast;

Here tyranny ne'er lifts her purple hand,
But liberty and justice guard the land;
No bravos here profess the bloody trade,
Nor is the church the murd'rer's refuge made.

This eulogy to a "law-defended town" cannot obscure the fact that early eighteenth-century London was not much improved in public demeanor from the riot of the previous century. There may have been some surface refinement in language and manners, but "men and women were rude in a more elegant way; they said lewd things with a finer accent, and kicked citizens with a touch of polish."[2] Violence and immorality still flourished, but Londoners habitually defended their city against all criticism—and for good reason. Terrible as city life might be, it was better than life in the country. With their poised manner, Londoners looked upon their rural counterparts as unspeakably crude and dirty. Dr. Samuel Johnson, a country boy from the town of Lichfield, had come to London fired with ambition and a zeal for knowledge, and had stayed to become the most respected scholar and writer of the mid-eighteenth century and one of the wittiest of men. He would not suffer criticism of his adopted city. Once, upon hearing a lady from the provinces complain of how she disliked London because there her fingernails were always dirty, he remarked, "Perhaps, Madam, you scratch yourself!"

The culturally enriched community which nurtured such minds as Swift, Gay, and Johnson provided also a dynamic environment for wit. The intellectual, social, and political developments of London were so unsettling during the Age of Wit that their very rapidity commanded public attention. Changes in politics alone, to select just one area, were prodigious.

Although the ruler of England set the tone for the Court circles and almost all English society, forces developed early in the age which wrought a complete transformation in the status and prestige of the king. In fact, England in 1650 was in the midst of an experiment in republicanism, having executed the Stuart king Charles I in 1649 and instituted the Commonwealth. The rule of the Protector, Oliver Cromwell, lasted to his death and a few months after.

When in 1660 Charles II was joyously welcomed to the throne, the king's prestige was temporarily restored. The licentious pace of the Restoration was set by the Court wits who circulated about the town, assisted by the town gallants attracted to the Court; the galleries at Whitehall were packed with awed spectators. John Evelyn vividly recreates the scene in his diary:

> I can never forget the inexpressible luxury and profaneness, gaming, and all dissoluteness, and as it were forgetfulness of God (it being Sunday evening) which this day se'nnight I was witness of, the King sitting and toying with his concubines, Portsmouth, Cleveland, Mazarin, etc., a French boy singing love songs in that glorious Gallery, whilst about twenty of the great Courtiers and other dissolute persons were at basset round a large table, a bank of at least 2,000 pounds in gold before them. . . . Six days after, all was in the dust!

For Charles II died on Friday, February 6, 1685.

At his death, his brother became King James II. Although a Roman Catholic, he began his reign in an unusually strong position, created by Charles' extraordinary political astuteness. However, public and private intrigue over the continuance of a Roman Catholic on the throne threatened his authority. A crisis arose when a son, born in June, 1688, assured a Catholic succession if James remained. Parliamentary leaders invited William of Orange and his wife Mary, eldest daughter of James, to the throne. A swift and bloodless exchange of kings, called the Glorious Revolution of 1689, placed Protestant rulers permanently on the throne. Mary died in 1694, but William continued to rule until 1702. He was succeeded by Anne, a younger daughter of James and also a Protestant. Queen Anne died without heirs in 1714, the last of the Stuarts.

By the Act of Settlement in 1701, Parliament granted the right of succession to Sophia, the granddaughter of James I and the nearest Protestant relation to the English royal house. In 1714, Sophia, the Electress of Hanover, was already dead, so her eldest son George Lewis, the fifty-four-year-old Elector of Hanover, became George I of England. Thoroughly German and unable to speak English, the first Hanoverian king reigned until his death in 1727, when he was succeeded by his eldest son, George II. By the time George II died in 1760, the Age of Wit was over.

In an autocratic society, the fate of the autocrat is everyone's fate. But fate was soon to be centered elsewhere. Another institution was developing which was destined to surpass in power the office of king—the modern political party. Before the Puritan Revolution and for a few years thereafter, political life was largely confined to intrigues among the favorites of the king and to struggles between contestants for the throne itself. But during the reign of Charles II, the first political groups developed and quickly divided the court. Under the leadership of the first Earl of Shaftesbury in the House of Lords and of William Sacheverell in the House of Commons, a loosely knit group known as the Country Party was formed in the mid-seventies and became known as the Whig Party in 1679. It stood for parliamentary supremacy against the king and for religious toleration. The Tory Party, created to oppose the Whigs, supported the position of the Crown. Early Whig leadership carried that party to power through the Glorious Revolution and into the eighteenth century. Queen Anne hated the Whigs but was dominated by a girlhood intimate, Sarah Jennings, wife of John Churchill, the Duke of Marlborough, and a Whig. During the eighth year of her reign, however, Anne was able to throw off the influence of Lady Churchill and thence appointed Tory ministers. This was the change in Court politics, incidentally, which spurred Jonathan Swift to his greatest gamble with fortune: he paid court to royalty in hopes of a high church appointment. His hopes and those of the Tory leadership were short-lived, for upon the death of Anne in 1714, George I appointed Whig ministers. Whig leadership continued to be dominant throughout the century. These two parties (not really parties in the modern sense but two groups of leaders with politically influential followers[3]) divided London society into contending camps. As John Dryden wrote in "To the Reader," a preface to *Absalom and Achitophel* (1681), "Wit and Fool, are Consequents of Whig and Tory: And every man is a Knave or an Ass to the contrary side."

A significant development within this formation of political parties was the emergence of the prime minister. The Stuarts, like the Tudors before them, were usually too astute to permit the centering of power in the office of one man outside the throne. However, with the beginning of the Hanoverian rule, the monarchy was weakened by kings unaccustomed to English customs and politics. As a result, the Georges relied upon English leadership in Parliament, and parliamentary leaders assumed more and more responsibility. In 1720 Sir Robert Walpole was appointed chief minister (later called "prime" minister by his enemies), an office he was to retain until 1742. The prestige and power he gave to the office were retained and later increased.

These developments in government, political though they were, provided a framework in several ways for men of wit and for the writing of wit. Literature was not a means of livelihood in these centuries; indeed, it was not to become a means of financial independence, generally speaking, until the nineteenth century. Poets, playwrights, philosophers, and others who spent most of their time in study and composition had to be subsidized in some manner. One means was royal patronage; another was government or church sinecure. Regardless of the means of support, the recipient was dependent on it. Thus, John Dryden, brilliant essayist, poet, literary critic, and friend of Tories, was poet laureate (with an annual stipend), but lost the honor (and honorarium) to the inferior playwright Thomas Shadwell, a Whig. Jonathan Swift entered his first literary war in defense of his patron Sir William Temple, himself a man of letters and wit, in the Phalaris controversy and in 1697 wrote *The Battle of the Books* (1704). Later, Swift played politics with the Tory leaders during the last years of Anne's reign, only to obtain a secondary preferment, the deanery at St. Patrick's, Dublin—not at all what he had hoped for. Swift's friend Alexander Pope was fortunate, for his father, a linen draper, was able to support him until some of his publications, notably his translations of Homer's *Iliad* (1715–20) and *Odyssey* (1725), made him financially independent.

"What Is This Wit?"

One cannot read much of the literature of these years without perceiving the all-pervasive influence of wit. It was the word à la mode; the quality which insured literary, social, and intellectual recognition; the prerequisite to acceptance in an age caught up by the very spirit of the word. But always present was the baffling question of Pope: "What is this wit, which must our cares employ?" The Age of Wit was beset by the extremely perplexing problem of defining itself, of clarifying its own nature. The period was never satisfied with any of its answers. Thus, the first context for meaning of wit is its perplexity, its enigmatic quality.

The men of learning understood this context well. The nearest that they came to common agreement was that there were certain aspects of wit too elusive to define. If the fact of enigma was not explicitly stated, it was at least a crucial reservation, conditioning succeeding remarks. But this enigma did not indicate meaninglessness; it revealed the complexity of the term. There were several reasons for the enigma.

The Age of Wit found the word wit more confusing than had any other period in English history. This confusion resulted from an intense search for new values amid outworn values not yet discredited in public thinking—basically a search for a revised view of the world like that in our own twentieth century. The forces defending each point of view—the old versus the new, often called the "ancients" and the "moderns"—were powerful. In the endless arguments, various key terms were not only used in traditional ways but also forced into new meanings. Such terms as reason, nature, sense, taste, and imagination were made to conform in meaning to both the old and the new views. The word wit was particularly sensitive to these changes.

Wit had a great diversity of associations, each revealing only part of its meaning and often clashing with other interpretations. Wit entered the age in 1650 attired, as it were, in time-honored rhetoric, but it was at the same time crowned with excessive ornamentation. It had the good fortune to be identified with the inestimable "Act of Reason," i.e. judgment, but it had the simultaneous ill fortune to be linked popularly to "the Wantonness of an extravagant Fancy." Wit was thought to be the expression of nature, as embodied in the universal "rules" of the ancients, yet some argued that it was a "Grace beyond the reach of Art," the inexplicable product of individual genius. It was praised in the conversation of gentlemen for its sprightliness and elegance, but it was viewed with alarm by the conservative middle class as the source of "noisy mirth," which, as Richard Steele remarked apprehensively in his *Tatler,* No. 252, "has something too rustic in it to be considered without terror by men of politeness." Again, wit became the stock-in-trade of the men of wit, who used it as a means of discovering truth, undermining vice, and laughing folly out of existence; but its detractors dismissed it for distorting, counterfeiting, and otherwise confusing not only vice and folly but also truth itself.

These meanings thrived in an atmosphere of contention in which each man of learning thought himself a wit and each wit by this very fact considered himself a critic. The resulting criticisms and definitions were plagued with semantic complications. The word wit accumulated a score or more of synonyms, including ingenuity, invention, imagination, fancy, extravagancy, epigrammatic conceit, humor, raillery, satire, irony, criticism, and ridicule.[4] Further complication resulted from the equation of the word with foreign terms: *εὐφυΐα, scientia, engenium, engegne,* and *esprit.*

Another difficulty lay in the variety of its manifestations. The numerous results can be indicated briefly by a list prepared by Dr. Isaac Barrow, a seventeenth-century divine who as a mathematician at Cambridge was second only to his pupil Isaac Newton:

> Sometimes it lieth in pat allusion to a known story, or in seasonable application of a trivial saying, or in forging an apposite tale: sometimes it playeth in words and phrases, taking advantage from the ambiguity of their sense, or the affinity of their sound: sometimes it is wrapped in a dress of humorous expression; sometimes it lurketh

under an odd similitude: sometimes it is logged in a sly question, in a smart answer, in a quirkish reason, in a shrewd intimation, in cunning diverting, or cleverly retorting an objection; sometimes it is couched in a bold scheme of speech, in a tart irony, in a lusty hyperbole, in a startling metaphor, in a plausible reconciling of contradictions, or an acute nonsense; sometimes a scenical representation of persons or things, a counterfeit speech, a mimical look or gesture passeth for it; sometimes an affected simplicity, sometimes a presumptuous bluntness giveth it being; sometimes it riseth from a lucky hitting upon what is strange, sometimes from a crafty wrestling obvious matter to the purpose.[5]

This list is part of a discussion of wit in a sermon preached about 1677 on the subject of foolish talking and jesting. One can well ask, as Dr. Barrow does in effect, if it is all these things, then what is it?

One is prepared, therefore, to understand the enigma of the word. While meaning many things, it often meant nothing in essence. Frustration accompanied efforts to define it. Some men who refused to describe the term positively were satisfied to identify it merely by what it was not. Abraham Cowley in his "Ode: Of Wit" (1650) asked the question,

> What is it then, which like the Power Divine,
> We only can by Negatives define?

William Congreve, the most brilliant Restoration dramatist, finding wit as difficult to define as humor, concluded that "tho we cannot certainly tell what Wit is, or what Humour is, yet we may go near to show something which is not Wit or not Humour, and yet often mistaken for both."[6] This helplessness became a source of general mirth. In the prologue to *The Northern Lass* (1684) Joseph Haynes, who was famous on the Restoration stage for witty prologues, wrote and delivered these lines:

> Ye talk of Wits, the Devil a Wit is here.
> Wherefore to let you know
> What Wit is not, I think can't be amiss,
> For no man here, I'm sure, knows what it is.

Haynes then enumerated the current styles and the slang of would-be wits as examples of what wit was not:

> Wit is no Scarf upon Phantastick Hips
> Nor an affected Cringe, t'approach the Lips.
> 'Tis not, *I gad, O Lord,* or, *let me die.*
> Nor is it *Damme ye Son of a Whore, ye Lie.*

Finally, he listed in a rising tone of levity various professional types excluded from the category:

> 'Tis not your Scholar, Trav'ler, nor Mathematician,
> Poet, not Player, and faith 'tis no Physician.

He concluded with comic irony:

> 'Tis none of these, that, singly, Wit can be,
> But all in one man meeting's, Wit: that's Me.

The incongruity of Haynes' final assertion illustrates wit's defiance of any simple definition. The principle of exclusion was used even by those men who were positive of the true nature of wit. Richard Flecknoe, dramatist and poetaster, felt that wit had "nothing of the superfice, or dross of words, as cinches, quibbles, jingles, and such like trifles have."[7] John Dryden's letter to Sir Robert Howard, in which he defined "Wit writing," asserted that it was not the "jerk or sting of an epigram, nor the seeming contradiction of a poor antithesis . . . nor the jingle of a more poor paranomasia."[8] And so it went.

This principle of exclusion was convenient and safe. It simply listed outmoded techniques of wit, or those judged generally to be so. On the other hand, the categorical nature of positive definitions was sure to arouse criticism and argument. No one challenged Dryden's exclusion of the "jerk or sting of an epigram," but many questioned the implications of his forthright definition that wit is the "propriety of words and thoughts."

The variety and unexpectedness of its manifestations caused many contemporaries to give up altogether the possibility of

variety gave it an enigmatic quality which it had never before possessed. However, the enigma was more basic than this. Essentially, the enigma lay in wit's inexplicable effects of surprise and brilliance, which have distinguished it in all ages, whatever its name. Wit has always possessed its *je ne sais quoi.*

Summary

Although the Age of Wit could not reach an agreement upon a basic, simple meaning of wit, the term did have certain definite contexts (eight, as defined in this study) in which meanings are clearly perceptible. Each of the remaining seven contexts is separate, though sometimes related to others. The first four contexts—rhetoric, psychology, truth, and grace—were part and parcel of seventeenth- and eighteenth-century literary theory. The traditions of rhetoric (Chapter 2) and of faculty psychology (Chapter 3) assimilated wit by the time of the Renaissance and made possible the other two contexts: truth and grace. The contexts of truth (Chapter 4), founded upon decorum, and grace (Chapter 5), founded upon sublimity, were unique developments of the Age of Wit and present two new pinnacles of meaning for the word. Still another context utilized the humanistic tradition of the Republic of Letters. In this tradition and supported by the contexts of truth and grace, men dedicated their lives to the ideals which wit had come to represent, ideals which became embodied in a Republic of Wit (Chapter 6). The last two contexts developed during the age as a result more of social than of literary forces. In the caricature of wit (Chapter 7) the scribbling, foppish imitators and pretenders moved and had their being. Their wit was a rude approximation of real wit, and their popular influence debased the whole concept. The final context, the stigma of wit (Chapter 8), contains the general reactions to the excesses of wit, reactions which not only engulfed the imitators and pretenders but stained the reputations and altered the lives of true wits.

The remaining contexts are arranged in approximate chronological order, that is, in the order in which each became important during the Age of Wit, and reveal the rationale the age itself achieved to distinguish between true and false wit. They give also sharp separations to the kaleidoscopic image of this enigmatic word.

> Arte may giue out precepts and directoryes in *communi forma;* but it is superexcellent wit that is the mother pearle of precious Invention, and the goulden mine of gorgeous Eloqution. Na. It is a certaine pregnant and lively thing without name, but a queint mistery of mounting conceit, as it were a knacke of dexterity, or the nippitaty of the nappiest grape, that infinitely surpasseth all the Invention and Eloqution in the world.
>
> —GABRIEL HARVEY in *Pierce's Supererogation* (1593)

2

The Rhetoric of Wit

IN THE LATE MONTHS of 1579 and for some years thereafter, the adventures of a sophisticated young man and his modish manner of expression captivated the attention of the learned society of London, an audience which extended from the Queen herself down to the most ignoble fop. This audacious young man, "preferring fancy before friends, and this present humour before honour to come," shocked his intended readers, the "gentle women of England," with his ideas, especially his ideas of them. On the other hand, his distinctive manner of expression started a contagion of imitation. The shock came from his basic cynicism toward the fair sex: "Though the tears of the hart be salt, yet the tears of the boar be sweet, and though the tears of some women be counterfeit to deceive, yet the tears of many be current to try their love." The contagion arose out of the appeal of his highly rhetorical style of writing, which employed neatly poised parallelisms of balance and antithesis and abundant alliteration. The young man was of course Euphues, a creation of John Lyly, graduate of Oxford, noted wit, and brilliant writer. The subtitle of the book bearing his name was, very significantly, *The Anatomie of Wyt.*

Wit in its rhetorical context had many temporary fashions throughout the Age of Wit. Typical of them was euphuism, which exhibits three normal phases in the life of each fashion: innovation, imitation, and irritation. Each new fashion was initiated by a poet or group of poets as an innovation. When successful, the fashion was almost immediately imitated, becoming *de rigueur* among other literary figures and their coteries. After a relatively short popularity at this esoteric level, the fashion was dropped suddenly for a newer fashion. At this point another wave of popularity ordinarily occurred. Though now out of fashion with the literati, the mode had filtered down meanwhile to lesser poets and to the dilettantes. At this lower and degenerative level the now outmoded fashion could remain popular for many years. Thus, the popularity of euphuism as an innovation was largely over by 1590, when the new style of wit in the *Arcadia* of Sir Philip Sidney replaced it. Shakespeare ridiculed euphuism in *King Henry IV, Part I,* and possibly in *Love's Labour's Lost.* Jonson and Donne ignored it. But euphuism was aped to the point of irritation in certain Court and other social circles on into the reign of Charles I. Euphuism was the first of a number of modes of wit during the seventeenth century which comprised the more spectacular aspects of rhetorical wit.

Rhetoric as a context of wit was relatively new in the Renaissance. Historically, rhetoric has meant the art of effective oral and written communication, but it refers specifically in this context to the embellishment of thought by means of verbal ornamentation. The discipline of rhetoric always utilized the quality of intellectual wittiness, as denoted by the Greek εὐφυΐα and by the Latin *ingenium.* The ultimate association of English wit with rhetoric was therefore natural and logical. Early in the sixteenth century in England, wit became associated with the intellectual ingenuity of rhetorical devices.

The fashions of rhetorical wit continued successively from Elizabethan days through the seventeenth century, when they increased greatly, and into the eighteenth century. Each new fashion was a conscious variation of rhetorical ornamentation in new complexity and subtlety. Gabriel Harvey had this kind of ingenuity in mind when he described "superexcellent wit" as not only the "mother pearle of precious Invention" but also the "goulden mine of gorgeous Elocution." Many devices and terms of rhetoric were redefined in terms of wit. Thus, sentences were called "the pithy and sweet flowers of wit, compiled in a ready and deliberate brain, and uttered in short and elegant phrases."[1]

Wit as rhetoric presented a problem to the neoclassical mind. Rhetorical ornamentation was clearly necessary in poetic art, but at the same time the "pregnant and lively" nature of wit gave it an inherent knack for extravagance, which was unacceptable to neoclassical standards of propriety. Because of wit's dual nature—its value and its inherent excess—the neoclassical poet was obliged to criticize and distrust certain techniques which he had at the same time to use. These techniques were the verbal devices of effective writing which were his stock-in-trade. Thus, wit in this context reached a fruition in the seventeenth century, which was in a definite sense increasingly hostile to it. To understand the impact of the rhetorical tradition and the dilemma into which it forced the neoclassical poet, one must understand the developments in rhetoric before and during the Age of Wit.

The Background of Rhetoric

Classical rhetoric, the study of effective oratory or oral expression, was founded by Demosthenes and other Greek orators. Aristotle distinguished between the style of rhetoric and that of poetry. Rhetoric, most of which pertained to style, contained more verbal devices than did poetics. Herein lies the key to what happened ultimately to rhetoric: since verbal devices always tend to usurp all other means of expression and since writing techniques tend to subsume oral ones, the once dominant study of rhetoric was slowly relegated to a division of poetics under the general category of style.[2]

The actual fusion of theories of oratory and poetry is generally attributed to Cicero.[3] His aims in *De oratore,* i.e. "*docere, delectare, et movere,*" combined the qualities of poetry (to delight and to move emotionally) with the aim of oratory (to persuade). He discussed wit (*ingenium*) as a means of developing a full, ornate style through imitation of the Greek orators and pointed out parallels between *ingenium* as he used it and Plato's comments on εὐφυΐα (wit) in *The Republic* (VII, 535) and εὐφυής (witty) in *The Phaedrus* (Sections 269[d]–270[a]). He was also acquainted with Plato's idea, stated in *The Laws*, that a person who is εὐφυής (witty, i.e. having excellent natural endowments) may do more harm to the state than an ignorant citizen, if such a witty person has evil intentions.

Despite the early fusion of theories, rhetoric still retained during the Middle Ages its classical meaning of effective oral expression and was (excepting possibly grammar) the most important study in the trivium. Rhetoric consisted of five traditional parts: *inventio* (invention), *dispositio* (arrangement), *elocutio* (style), *memoria* (memory, particularly of a ready argument), and *pronunciatio* (delivery). However, as explained above, the concept of rhetoric changed slowly from the art of speaking to the art of writing, and only some of these parts continued to be emphasized.

By the Renaissance,[4] only the first three of the traditional parts retained any importance—a natural development, since *memoria* and *pronunciatio* pertained largely to oral expression and since rhetoric was by that time a part of the discipline in the writing of both prose and poetry. In practice during the Renaissance, *elocutio* became the important part of rhetoric. It included figures of both amplification and ornamentation. Understandably, William Webb in his *Discourse of English Poetry* (1586) treated rhetoric as a matter of style. He considered *Euphues* to be a work of "singular eloquence and brave composition of apt words and sentences," which exhibited "all the partes of Rethoricke, in fitte phrases, in pithy sentences, in gallant tropes, in flowing speech, in plaine sence."[5]

Another development was the gradual simplification of figurative language. Medieval treatises had gradually reduced the complex categories of rhetoric to tropes and figures. Even as early as postclassical criticism, these two categories had failed to maintain separate status and distinctions. Quintilian had noted that "many authors have considered figures identical with tropes"; furthermore, "there are some who call tropes figures." He admitted that "the resemblance between the two is so close that it is not easy to distinguish between them," and his definitions reflect this difficulty; irony, for instance, "belongs to figures of thought [*figurae sententiae*] just as much as to tropes."[6]

By the sixteenth century, Elizabethans thought of rhetorical devices mostly in terms of figures, and rhetoricians usually listed under that classification not only tropes but also schemes and repetitions. The variety of classifications of figures became confusing. George Puttenham's *Arte of English Poesie* (III, iii) divided figures into three groups: those which serve the ear, called "auricular"; those which serve the mind, called "sensable"; and those which serve both together, called "sententious." Among the chief rhetoricians of the Renaissance, three classes of figures were considered most important.[7] The first group consisted of figures of thought: definition, division, distinction, enumeration, cause, effect, antecedent, consequence, comparison, similitude, dissimilitude, example, and citation of authority (including proverbs, apothegms, and maxims). The second group consisted of various forms of exclamation, interrogation, and description—all designed to sway the emotions. The third group consisted of some 150 figures depending upon such merely mechanical devices as spelling, diction, and syntax. Because of its importance in the creation of wit, the first group received increasing attention in the seventeenth century, especially comparison, similitude, and dissimilitude.

"Figurae Verborum et Figurae Sententiae"

The subordination of rhetoric to techniques of style, together with the simultaneous simplification of rhetorical devices into classes of figures, had great bearing upon the kinds of wit, as the English Renaissance viewed them. The simplification of rhetorical devices into classes of figures was important in the discussion of one phase of the nature of wit: the distinction between wit of words and wit of thoughts. Wit of words and of thoughts became a common distinction from the seventeenth century onwards. Such distinction is implicit in John Dryden's definition: "a propriety of thoughts and words; or in other terms, thoughts and words elegantly adapted to the subject."[8] Joseph Addison's distinction between wit of ideas and wit of letters and words (*Spectator,* No. 62) continued the same dichotomy. John Oldmixon differentiated between wit of thought and wit of expression,[9] two terms used again at mid-century by Henry Home, Lord Kames.[10]

This division of wit arose from the reduction of rhetoric to tables of figures, a reduction in which the figure (Latin *figurae;* Greek *schemata*) came to predominate verbal ornamentation. Tables of figures were subdivided traditionally into *figurae verborum* (or *dictionis*) and *figurae sententiae.* The first, figures of language (also called figures of words or of speech), sought agreeable sounds either alone or in combination, as in parallelisms, antitheses, alliterations, rhymes, and assonances. The second, figures of thought (also known as figures of matter or of sense), sought effective development of the idea in the sentence or sententious statement; it made use of exclamations, rhetorical questions, and suggestions. Quintilian, surveying the theories of rhetoric in his *Institutio Oratoria,* distinguished in one instance between the thought and the word: "every speech . . . consists at once of that which is expressed and that which expresses, that is to say matter [*rebus*] and words [*verbis*]" (III, 5). More specifically, he divided figures as follows: "It is, however, to the best of my knowledge, generally agreed by the majority of authors that there are two classes of figures, namely *figures of thought,* that is of the mind [*mentis*], feeling [*sensus*], or conceptions [*sententiarum*], since all these terms are used; and *figures of speech,* that is of words [*verborum*], diction [*dictionis*], expression [*elocutionis*], language [*sermonis*], or style [*orationis*]: the name by which they are known varies, but mere terminology is a matter of indifference" (IX, 1).

The same division of figures was common through the seventeenth century. John Smith wrote of *figura dictionis* belonging "to the matter, and as it were, to the body of speech" and of *figura sententiae* belonging "to the form, and as it were, to the soul, that is, to the sentence." Smith explained the interrelationship; the "garnishing of the frame of speech, in a sentence, called *Figura Sententiae,* is a figure, which for the forcible moving of affections, doth after a sort beautifie the sense and very meaning of a sentence."[11] Late in the century, Samuel Butler wrote of "two sorts of quibbling, the one with words and the other with sense, like the rhetoricians' *figurae dictionis et figurae sententiae.*"[12] The rhetorical discrimination between wit of words and wit of thoughts became increasingly important, for as reaction against excessive ornamentation increased in the seventeenth century, wit of words was the first object of attack.

Popular Rhetorical Modes of Wit

The reduction of rhetoric to a list of figures of amplification and ornamentation shows the widespread attraction of verbal devices. This popularity was tremendous during the Age of Wit as well as during the century which preceded it. These were years uncommonly disposed toward artifice. The first half of the seventeenth century saw a rapid increase in rhetorical devices, including elementary wordplay in anagrams, acrostics, and punning.

In early seventeenth-century prose, the stylistic ideal changed from a Ciceronian floridity to other ornate styles.[13] The admonition of the sixteenth-century humanists to "write Cicero" produced a style fashioned upon the *genus grande* of antiquity. This classical style of oratorical art took its character from the *schemata verborum* in the rhetoric of Gorgias and Isocrates and made use of such structural devices as the *isocolon, paromoeon,* and *parison.* Ornamentation consisted of *similia, exempla,* and *sententiae.* Ciceronian rhetoric was found not only in student exercises but also in pulpit oratory, courtly ceremonies, moral treatises, and romances. In England this excessively formalized prose style took one name from the prose romance briefly described above, *Euphues: The Anatomie of Wyt.*

The reaction against Ciceronian rhetoric took the form of an attempt to return to the essay or "Attic" style, which had existed in classical times concurrently with the oratorical style.[14] This Attic style used the *figurae sententiae* in place of the *figurae verborum.* The new figures of thought attempted to achieve the aims of Aristotle—clarity, brevity, and propriety—but these aims were subverted. Instead of Aristotle's style, the styles of Seneca, Tacitus, Lucan, and Juvenal were used as guides. The resulting baroque style had its own floridity in metaphor, antithesis, paradox, and point. These characteristics are exemplified in the prose of Robert Burton, Sir Thomas Browne, and John Donne.

After the late Renaissance, prose style changed more slowly. Poetry, on the other hand, became the showpiece for rhetorical ingenuity, changing its modes of dress with rapidity. The reason for this difference in pace lay in the origin and function of each. Prose was thought to be the product primarily of man's reason, whereas poetry was the product of man's imagination; further, the one was the medium for logical and objective information, whereas the other was the medium for fanciful delight and entertainment. Prose under the influence of such sober forces as Puritan clergymen, the Royal Society, and rationalist philosophers, depended increasingly upon the language of direct statement. In letters, Dryden's prose style made a significant development in this direction, and Swift's plain style was a further achievement, as illustrated by the spare, limpid style of his sermons.

The continuing disposition toward artifice is everywhere evident in the great variety of seventeenth-century verse. Figures of ornamentation and amplification suited well the effects of poetry which the age understood. School instruction emphasized imitation, not originality. The discipline and training of young poets began usually with simple, classic forms of lyric and pastoral, proceeded to odes and satires, and culminated in attempts at heroic tragedy or epics. The constant drill in the discipline of rhetoric made adornment a habit of second nature, as the inspiration of the muse was reinforced by conscious design. Poetry incorporated the more flamboyant and eccentric rhetorical devices. The result was wit of words at one level and wit of thoughts at another, with varying combinations between.

Wit of words, the *figurae verborum* traditionally considered inferior to the *figurae sententiae,* was incorporated in many kinds of slight poems, from enigmas and riddles to quips and acrostics. Known variously in the Renaissance as "fancies" and "fantastics," these verses depended upon puns and tricks for their enjoyment. The artificial and ingenious arrangement of words is obvious, for instance in the following poem, which may be read two or three ways:

Your face	Your tongue	Your wit
so faire	so smooth	so sharp
first drew	then mov'd	then knit
mine eye	mine eare	my heart
Mine eye	Mine eare	My heart
thus drawn	thus mov'd	thus knit
affects	hangs on	yeelds to
Your face	Your tongue	Your wit[15]

Ingenious manipulation is also apparent in the rebus and anagram. An anagram by George Herbert is of a more than usually complex nature for it employs a witty conceit:

Ana {Mary / Army} gram

How well her name an *Army* doth present,
In whom the Lord of Hosts did pitch his tent![16]

In a society which carefully cultivated the art of conversation, the quip became exceedingly popular. Being "a short saying of a sharp wit, with a bitter sense in a sweet word,"[17] this form of repartee flourished in both oral and written forms. The disposition of the quip for the pun is clear in this example of eighteenth-century wit:

Bon-mot of a Certain Witty Lord

His Lordship being informed, that a Lady, lately divorced, would probably be married to the Earl of *upper* O——y, said it is time she was upper O——y, for she had been under O——y long enough.[18]

The turn of thought here has not only sexual but domestic implications and is superior to the dependence simply upon a similarity of sound or arrangement of letters.

The seventeenth century was often entertained by cleverness rather than by complexity. So popular was any simple pun that James Arbuckle, looking back from late in the century upon what he called the "Age of Anagrams, Puns, and Acrosticks," recalled with rhetorical aptness that "a Man had nothing to do but make one Word carry two Meanings, and then march between them into Preferment." He concluded with the further recollection:

This Eloquence became even fashionable in the Pulpit; and every Head of Discourse was thought unfinished which did not terminate in the Point of an Epigram. I have seen an admirable Instance of this in a Sermon of that Age, wherein the Preacher, after a long detail of the Vices and Corruptions of the Times, sums up the whole in the following pathetical Exclamation. '*All Houses,*' says he, 'are turned *Ale-houses;* some Mens *Paradise* is a *Pair o'Dice;* the holy State of *Matrimony* is made *Matter o'Money*. Was it thus in the Days of *NOAH? AH NO!*[19]

This kind of pun, called the *vox et praeterea nihil,* was considered particularly weak because it relied more upon coincidence of sound than upon sense and hence disappeared in translation.

Another example of *figurae verborum* was the echo verse, which apparently derived its name and technique from a character in Ben Jonson's masque, *Cynthia's Revels.* In this masque, Eccho often repeats the last sound or word spoken by the preceding character. In Act I, scene iii, she is asked not to make "so fast away," to which the answer and succeeding conversation occur:

ECCHO. Away.

MERCURIE. Stay, let me observe this portent yet.

AMORPHUS. I am neither your Minotaure, nor your Centaure, nor your Satyre, nor your Hyaena, nor your Babion, but your mere travailer, beleeve me.

ECCHO. Leave me.

MERCURIE. I guess'd it should bee some travailing motion pursued Eccho so.

AMORPHUS. Know you from whom you flie? or whence?

ECCHO. Hence.

This clever, superficial wit was used in many poems during the century. George Herbert's poem "Paradise" is a good example:

I blesse thee, Lord, because I GROW
Among thy trees, which in a ROW
To thee both fruit and order OW.

What open force, or hidden CHARM
Can blast my fruit, or bring me HARM,
While the inclosure is thine ARM?

Inclose me still for fear I START.
Be to me rather sharp and TART,
Then let me want thy hand & ART.

When thou dost greater judgements SPARE,
And with thy knife but prune and PARE,
Ev'n fruitfull trees more fruitfull ARE.

Such sharpnes shows the sweetest FREND:
Such cuttings rather heal then REND:
And such beginnings touch their END.

This was one of the least imaginative devices of wit used by the metaphysical poets and rated only slightly above the mechanics of their shaped verse.

The epigram, a recognized classical verse genre, was popular during the century, enjoying the attention of the very best poets. It was a short poem building to a surprising turn of thought or sententious statement. The epigram varied in length from two to sixteen or more lines, though the usual length was two, four, or six lines. The last line or two always contained the "sting." Epigrams might be simple or complex in rhetorical devices, even though the content was often trivial:

Nuptiae post nummos

There was a time when men for love did marry
And not for lucre sake, as now we see:
Which from that former age so much doth vary
As all's for—what you'll give? or nought must be.
So that this ancient word called *matrimony*
Is wholly made *a matter now of money*.[20]

This epigram was written solely for the elementary play upon words in the closing couplet, certainly a threadbare pun at best. In the following adaptation of a Latin epigram, both words and thought combine in a complexity clearly superior to the bare style and simple thought of the preceding example:

Of Galla's Goodly Periwigge

You see the goodly hayre that Galla weares,
'Tis certain her own hair, who would have thought it?
She sweares it is her owne: and true she sweares:
For hard by Temple-barre last day she bought it.
So faire a haire, vpon so foule a forehead
Augments disgrace, and showes the grace is borrowed.[21]

The figurative ornamentation of both words and thoughts is abundant: alliteration, balance, and antithesis. By 1625 the epigram was losing its status of respectability, but epigrammatic traits were adapted to lyrics, elegies, and other kinds of poems, becoming a part of the rhetoric of the heroic couplet.

Wit of thought achieved a new height of development in the adaptation of the epigram to the conceit, or elaborate figure. This adaptation of *figurae sententiae* provided poets with a technique which stimulated a new complexity of originality and ingenuity. One result was a kind of poetry described by Thomas Pecke as a choice of epigrams: "For if a Poem be good, it consists of nothing else, but various Epigrams; cemented by a dexterous sagacity. And not only Verse, but Prose, is dull, and languishing, unlesse the sparkling Genius of the Epigrammatist be artificially interwoven."[22] Such a poem, a succession of conceits constructed by academic contrivance, was popular on the Continent. The Italian Giovanni Battista Marini, who wrote and discussed this kind of poem, had some influence upon the later metaphysical poets.[23]

This contrivance of epigrammatic conceits was still being composed in 1690 when Sir William Temple criticized it. He wrote of the degenerate moderns, who, not worthy to sit down at the Feast," have to "content themselves with the Scraps," that is, with lesser forms of poetry; thus, they incorporate epigrams which "were all turned upon Conceit, or some sharp Hits of Fancy or Wit."[24] One of these moderns, the churchman William Dingley, wrote a perfect example in "Upon a BEE Entomb'd in Amber" (1694), four stanzas of which follow:

> Behold this happy Insect's Tomb,
> Not sweet, but precious Honey-comb:
> You'd think the Bee had brought it forth,
> Alike in Colour, and in Worth.
> Which to the view does represent,
> A Murderer, and Monument.
> I thought 'twas Niobe alone,
> Whom Moisture harden'd into Stone:
> But now the weeping Gem I see,
> Transforms at once it self and Bee:
> Since to Beholders each does seem,
> The Gem a Bee, the Bee a Gem.
> The Pyramids in Ægypt's Land,
> Astonishment from all command:
> Yet, happy Insect, happy thou,
> A lesser, but a better Show:
> The Pyramids would envy me,
> Should I be thus Entomb'd like thee.
> Thou with Medusa may'st compare,
> Whose Viperous enchanted Hair,
> Turn'd all Spectators into Stone,
> Conquest and Trophy both in one;
> But thou excellest her in this,
> Thy self at once Medusa is,
> Thy self the Metamorphosis.[25]

The influence of the epigram is evident in the popular six-line stanzaic pattern, in the stopped couplets throughout (except for the final stanza), and in the "sting" in the last couplet of each stanza.

A further development of the wit of thought was the metaphysical conceit. It most often turned on a minutely elaborated metaphor. When developed by the metaphysical poet, the meanings became quite complex through "paradoxical inquiry, imaginative and intellectual." This inquiry exhausted, by "its use of antithesis and contradiction and unusual imagery, all the possibilities of a given idea."[26] The technique was highly rhetorical. The result was mainly *figurae sententiae* in very complex form, though not to the exclusion of *figurae verborum*.

This form of wit developed in opposition to other modes. Its intellectual unconventionality, its subtlety of thought and imagery, its compressed style, and its roughness of verse—all developed in contrast to the polish and sophistication of Cavalier verse and contemporary fashions. It faced increasing opposition from the neoclassical impulse toward propriety and conventionality but nevertheless thrived into the Restoration. It provided no less a poetic genius than John Dryden with his earliest technique.

The fascination of metaphysical poetry was infectious and occasionally caught up even Cavalier poets. In 1632, Thomas Randolph, a "Son of Ben," was merrymaking with other members of the "tribe" in London, when "as it often happens that in drinking high quarrels arise, so there chanced some words to pass between Mr. Randolph and another gentleman, which grew to be so high, that the Gentleman drawing his sword, and striking at Mr. Randolph, cut off his little finger, whereupon, in an extemporary humor he instantly made these verses,"[27] entitled "Upon the Losse of His Little Finger":

> Arithmetique nine digits, and no more
> Admits of, then I still have all my store.
> For what mischance hath tane from my left hand,
> It seemes did only for a cipher stand.

But this I'le say for thee departed joynt,
Thou wert not given to steale, nor pick, nor point
At any in disgrace; but thou didst go
Untimely to thy Death only to show
The other members what they once must doe;
Oft didst thou scan my verse, where if I misse
Henceforth I will impute the cause to this:
A fingers losse (I speake it not in sport)
Will make a verse a Foot too short.
Farewell deare finger, much I grieve to see
How soone mischance hath made a Hand of thee.

The facetious tone betrays a travesty on the metaphysical method, but the poem demonstrates practically all of the metaphysical techniques. The wit is on the level both of words and of thoughts. The first line contains a pun on "digits," meaning both "fingers" and the figures one through nine, though usually including the symbol zero. The first two lines present an enigma or riddle, which is solved in lines 3 and 4. The four lines involve a paradox within a pun, for the nine remaining fingers are complete, since what has been lost is nothing (the tenth digit, or zero). The next five lines contain an apostrophe to the finger, with which Randolph ridicules his companions for jesting at his misfortune. These lines also reveal that awareness of the transcendent that was so typical of metaphysical imagery; the finger's untimely death has served as an example to the remaining fingers of the way of all flesh. The pun on "member," connoting human relationship, is crucial. Lines 10 through 13, returning to the value of the dead finger, make use of irony ("I speake it not in sport"); paradox ("a fingers losse . . . Will make a verse a Foot too short"); and representative meter of mimetic verse in line 13. Lines 14 and 15 return to the awareness of the transcendent: ironically, the finger enjoys in death that success which, being zero in life, it was not destined in life to have. Here is the epigram, the final turn in thought upon the double meaning of the expression "made a Hand"—the literal meaning and a seventeenth-century meaning "to make a success." That a finger could finally in a state of beatification become a hand is, of course, a paradoxical hyperbole, and that mischance may hasten undreamed-of success is irony. Randolph also employs an ambiguity in using English words in their Latinate sense, specifically *digit.* Here, then, one finds the intellectualized conceit, what T. S. Eliot, speaking of Donne, called a "mechanism of sensibility which could devour any kind of experience."[28] Other characteristics of metaphysical poetry are also present: the characteristic turning of the mind upon death in even so trivial a situation; the rough diction throughout; the constant play upon words and upon the immediacy of the situation; and the interlacing of irony and paradox.

The last popular mode of wit in the seventeenth century was the turn. As wit of thought during the first half of the century concentrated upon unexpected metaphors and similes, so the wit of the last half exploited the surprise of an ingenious turn. By means of a play upon a word or thought, antithetical ideas were placed in sudden and surprising opposition. The turn was not entirely new, using old verbal techniques—the pun and the metaphor, placed in parallel and antithetical constructions. Whereas the conceit had derived multiple meanings in a single image, the turn played with or "turned" a word or idea in order to set up a multiple significance of meaning. George Puttenham called the word turn the "Traductio, or the translacer." It occurs "when we turne and translace a word into many sundrie shapes as the Tailor doth his garment, and after that sort do play with him" in one's "dittie."[29]

Milton was very fond of the turn. Satan's famous retort in *Paradise Lost* (IV, 827–30) contains the multiple turning of a word: "*Know* ye not me? . . . not to *know* me argues yourselves *unknown*" (italics mine). It occurs to a greater degree in the following passage (italics mine) in the words of God the Father:

> They therefore as to right belonged,
> So were created, nor can justly accuse
> Their *maker*, or their *making*, or their fate,
> As if predestination overruled
> Their will, disposed by absolute decree
> Or high *foreknowledge;* they themselves decreed
> Their own revolt, not I: if I *foreknew,*
> *Foreknowledge* had no influence on their fault,
> Which had no less proved certain *unforeknown.*
>
> (III, 111–19)

When adapted to the neoclassical verse line, the turn became a weapon of incisive satire. The last line of the following quatrain from Dryden's *Absalom and Achitophel* is a good example:

> The Egyptian rites the Jebusites embraced,
> Where gods were recommended by their taste;
> Such savory deities must needs be good
> As serve at once for worship and for food.
>
> (ll. 118–21)

Dryden's turns were not always equally successful; in the same poem his lines on the Popish Plot of 1673 lack this smoothness and neatness:

> From hence began that plot, the nation's curse,
> Bad in itself, but represented worse,
> Raised in extremes, and in extremes decried,
> With oaths affirmed, with dying vows denied,
> Nor weighed or winnowed by the multitude,
> But swallowed in the mass, unchewed and crude.
>
> (ll. 108–13)

Pope, on the other hand, was unfailing in the successful turn in his mature poems. In *The Rape of the Lock,* he used this device to flood the serious very suddenly with the ridiculous:

> Here thou, great Anna! whom three realms obey,
> Dost sometimes counsel take—and sometimes tea.
>
> (III, 7–8)

The turn fitted admirably into the ironic inversion of values in such poems as *The Dunciad.* In Book One the chaotic realm of the Goddess of Dulness has "nameless Somethings" crawling in the darkness of stupidity. Since the Goddess rules over false wit, the demons represent the various kinds of outmoded wit: clenches, ill-paired figures, similes, metaphors. Then follow these lines:

All these, and more, the cloud-compelling Queen
Beholds through fogs, that magnify the scene.
She, tinselled o'er in robes of varying hues,
With self-applause her wild creation views;
Sees momentary monsters rise and fall,
And with her own fool's colours gilds them all.
(ll. 79–84)

The turns of thought lie in the ideas of magnifying with fog and gilding with dullness. On the other hand, Pope could use the turn on the level largely of wordplay, as in the following occasional couplet:

I am his Highness' dog at Kew;
Pray, tell me, sir, whose dog are you?

The many modes of wit, both *figurae verborum* and *figurae sententiae* amply demonstrate the atmosphere of ferment in the rhetoric of wit. The creative minds of these years became imbued with the sheer versatility of verbal and intellectual witticism. In an age moving toward more regularity and restraint, the excessive and extravagant qualities of rhetorical wit provoked heated criticism.

Criticism of Rhetorical Wit

Much of the controversy over rhetorical theory and practice during the Age of Wit centered on the relative values of the simple and the ornate. What troubled the seventeenth century was the distortion of values which resulted from elevating form at the cost of content. Verbal devices were obviously out of control in current practice. Many attempts were made to differentiate between *res et verba*. However, this particular distinction was part of the effort to re-evaluate the metaphorical language of the *figurae verborum* and the *figurae sententiae*. Various forces were at work. Prosaic, factual minds advocated no ornamentation at all, and imaginative, artistic minds suggested moderation and propriety.

An influence in this change of taste was the contemporary reputation of empirical science whose key lay in the examination of physical phenomena by a mind free from prejudice.[30] Remarkable advances were made during the hundred years before the Age of Wit: the Copernican system and Galileo's confirmation of it; Francis Bacon's support of experimental science; the mathematics and philosophy of Descartes; the invention of logarithms by John Napier; and the discovery of the circulation of the blood by William Harvey. Then, of course, there was the work of Sir Isaac Newton in mathematics and physics during the Age of Wit itself.

The argument against metaphorical language was simply that such subjective, figurative words nullified the objectivity of scientific investigation and reporting. The metaphor, work horse of verbal images, was admitted to be "the friendly and neighborly borrowing a word" which did not express "so directly and properly as the natural name of the thing meant."[31] Objectivity in examination and communication of data was impossible with metaphors, for they regularly interpreted and altered the referent. The result was, as noted in the *Spectator*, No. 595, "no apt Resemblance," but "Confusion, Obscurity, and Noise." Pleas for an approach to truth through a plain, "naked" style were made intermittently during the seventeenth century by Francis Bacon, Thomas Hobbes, John Locke, and members of the Royal Society.[32]

In addition to the scientifically oriented minds, another force was caught up in the arguments—the morally or religiously oriented minds. Largely middle-class, they expressed a point of view that emphasized simplicity rather than affectation, utility rather than aesthetics. Men with these views were mostly Protestants, particularly Puritans, Quakers, and the latitudinarians. Truth, this view insisted, needed no adornment to commend it. Grandiloquent pulpit oratory was under attack throughout the century.[33] William Pemble, a Puritan preacher, protested against "excellent discourses" which "are tortured, wrested, and pinched in, and obscured through curiosity of penning hidden allusions, forced phrases, uncouth Epithites, with other deformities of plain speaking." He would have all remember that "good speech (make the most on't) is but the garment of Truth: and she is so glorious within, she needs no outward decking."[34] A later preacher, Samuel Parker, advocated an act of Parliament "to abridge Preachers the use of fulsome and lushious Metaphors." As a result, "all the swelling Mysteries of Fanaticism" will appear as "flat and empty Nonsense," for such beliefs would be deprived of the "Varnish of fine Metaphors and glittering Allusions."[35] Many religious groups gave impetus to this moral pressure. The plain prose style used by the Quakers undoubtedly had an effect.[36] The latitudinarian movement, in its search for literal truths, also favored the simple style.

The moralist, like the scientist, was interested in truth, not beauty. Both groups had prose in mind generally, for they considered poetry an expression tied to fanciful and emotional language and hence an inadequate medium for truth. These groups often championed sense or common sense against wit, a typical middle-class opposition.

A third critical group, more discriminatory in evaluating wit, consisted of the literati—poets, playwrights, essayists, and rhetoricians—who were interested in beauty as well as in truth. These men constituted a majority of the men of letters educated in the disciplines of literature, history, and philosophy. They indulged regularly in literary criticism, to use the phrase in its nonspecialized sense. To them poetry remained a valid form of truth. Their concern was the re-evaluation of wit in its rhetorical context to distinguish between kinds and qualities of wit. They were not agreed upon the extent to which wit should include wordplay or even ornamentation. They did agree upon the artistic validity of figurative adornment but argued over the appropriate amount and kinds.

Public taste has always moved capriciously from one innovation to another, and so it was with the modes of wit. Each of the modes was effective when executed in good taste. But well done or not, most of them continued in use despite criticism. This accretive process, lasting from the Renaissance through the early eighteenth century, explains the rich rhetorical texture of Augustan writing, particularly in poetry. This texture violated neoclassical simplicity and decorum, prompting a continuing effort to distinguish between true wit and false. The rhetorical meaning of these categories is therefore important.

Rhetorical Meaning of False Wit

False wit was assiduously defined and condemned throughout the age. Those who thought of false wit in general terms identified it as any kind of ornamentation. In principle, a play on words or a figure of speech distorted its referent; whether the figure pointed out a similarity or dissimilarity, any such statement was inevitably indirect, therefore possibly untrue, certainly misleading, and hence false. The conclusion: all rhetorical wit must be false.

In isolating differing points of view, one must exercise caution, for the more general the terms, the more relative and ambiguous their meaning. Generalities could make strange bedfellows. Some literary critics would seem to agree with the scientific and moral forces. In 1707 Samuel Cobb described the style of the seventeenth-century poet John Oldham:

> His Sense undrest, like Adam, free from Blame,
> Without his Cloathing, and without his Shame.
> True Wit requires no Ornaments of skill,
> A Beauty naked, is a Beauty still.[37]

But the seeming agreement is misleading. Cobb's very style belies his thought. His lines contain balance, repetition, parallelism, a simile, and a metaphor.

This extreme view was often voiced but nowhere practiced. Robert Wolseley, a friend of the Earl of Rochester and a defender of wit, had described wit in 1685 as "a true and lively expression of nature," adding that "to draw and describe things that either are not in Nature or things that are otherwise than they are" is "the only false Wit and the vicious Poetry."[38] This condemnation of describing things "otherwise than they are" could be understood to apply to all figurative language. Such an attitude would place Wolseley in the same camp with the scientific and moral forces, but obviously the style that Wolseley had in mind was not the plainness which many of these critics urged. One must perforce conclude that discussions of false wit can be understood only in terms of special kinds of ornamentation.

During the Age of Wit one kind of ornamentation unfailingly classified as false was wordplay. This form of wit was known by many names: pun, clench, quibble, equivocation, carwhitchet, echo word. In his argument with Thomas Shadwell over the nature of Ben Jonson's merits, Dryden criticized Jonson's humor and praised contemporary wit. Although he considered wit to be the glory of his own age, he judged Jonson's wit to be the "lowest and most grovel kind . . . which we call clenches, of which *Every Man in his Humour* is infinitely full." Dryden did not blame Jonson but attributed the fault to "the mode of wit, the vice of the age."[39] Even Shakespeare was "many times flat, insipid; his comic wit degenerating into clenches, his serious swelling into bombast," although Dryden admitted that "he is always great, when some great occasion is presented to him."[40]

The most extensive discussion of wordplay as false wit was developed by Joseph Addison in Numbers 58 through 63 of the *Spectator*. In No. 62, he made the pat distinction between wit of ideas and wit of letters and words. He would not admit the propriety of word wit; wit of words was completely false. This category consisted of the "Resemblance and Congruity sometimes of single Letters, as in Anagrams, Chronograms, Lipograms, and Acrosticks: Sometimes of Syllables, as in Ecchos and Doggerel Rhymes: Sometimes of Words, as Punns and Quibbles; and sometimes of whole Sentences or Poems, cast into Figures of Eggs, Axes or Alters." The *Spectator*, No. 63, contains a dream of the "Region of False Wit," governed by the Goddess of Falsehood. Addison described several of the inhabitants: a "Set of merry People" whose diversion was "to mistake one Person for another." He explained further:

To give Occasion for these ludicrous Mistakes, they were divided into Pairs, every Pair being covered from Head to Foot with the same kind of Dress, though perhaps there was not the least Resemblance in their Faces. By this means an Old Man was sometimes mistaken for a Boy, a Woman for a Man, and a Black-a-moor for an European which very often produced great Peals of Laughter. These I guessed to be a Party of Punns.

The wasteful and fruitless activities of false wit are interrupted by the arrival of the legions of "Wit and Truth," which are a "strong and compact Body of Figures." Addison called special attention to the position of the epigram in these ranks. He had been posted in the rear "that he might not revolt to the Enemy, whom he is suspected to favour in his Heart."

The epigram also served its time as a popular mode and came under serious question. It continued in use in classroom instruction, where distinction was made between good and bad epigrams. In one of the most popular textbooks of the seventeenth century, *Epigrammatus delectus,* the selection was justified by Pierre Nicole in his accompanying essay on the following bases:

. . . epigrams whose elegance is derived from puns are held of no account. For since verses are only composed by labor and diligence he is justly considered to be a weak and narrow spirit who wastes time in fitting such trivial wit into verse. One should add, too, that there is another disadvantage in puns, that they are so imbedded in their own language that they cannot be translated into another. For these reasons we have admitted few punning epigrams into this anthology, and those only as examples of a faulty kind.[41]

By the end of the seventeenth century epigrams were relegated categorically by many critics to the heap of outmoded wit. The "sting" of the epigram relied too often on a play on words, and the age agreed generally with Edward Phillips, a hack writer of the Restoration, who called the epigram "the fag end of Poetry."[42] As will be seen, faulty epigrams were regularly called "Gothic," a term for false wit.

All strange or mixed conceits, principally the straining after images in the epigrammatic conceit and the metaphysical quibbling with sense, were also labeled false wit. Dryden condemned the excesses of the metaphysical conceit: "We cannot read a verse of Cleveland's without making a face at it, as if every word were a pill to swallow: he gives us many times a hard nut to break our teeth, without a kernel for our pains." Dryden contrasted such imagery with that of John Donne; Donne "gives us deep thoughts in common language," whereas John Cleveland "gives us common thoughts in abstruse words."[43] This kind of outmoded imagery was later described by the Earl of Shaftesbury as the "false Sublime" consisting of the "crouded Simile and mix'd Metaphor." He ridiculed the latter as "the Hobby-Horse and Rattle of the Muses."[44] This imagery Joseph Addison called "forced" conceit.[45] Samuel Johnson entitled it *discordia concors,* describing it as a kind of wit "abstracted from its effects upon the hearer"; it was "a combination of dissimilar images, or discovery of occult resemblances in things apparently unlike." Dr. Johnson criticized the ransacking of nature and art for illustrations, comparisons, and allusions which produced "something unexpected and surprising." He was of the opinion that such "writers who lay on the watch for novelty, could have little hope for greatness," for they "produced combinations, of confused magnificence, that not only could not be credited, but could not be imagined." However, although such false conceits were farfetched, they "sometimes struck out unexpected truth."[46] Many critics of the preceding years had had less patience than Johnson on this point.

Opposition developed as the turn assumed prominence in Restoration usage. An early criticism appeared in Samuel Butler's character of "A Quibbler" in 1665, in which quibbling with words and with sense was noted. He was of opinion that "the first is already cried down," and the second, which still prevailed, is "never used by any lasting wit" and "will in wiser times fall to nothing of itself."[47] This quibbling included not only the turn but also the conceit. Dryden, who in his youth had abandoned the metaphysical conceit for the turn of Edmund Waller and Sir John Denham,[48] felt in his old age that "the Epic Poem is too stately to receive those 'little ornaments,'" i.e. turns of either words or thoughts.[49] John Dennis classed the turn in 1711 with other "modern Vices" of conceit, point, and epigram, all of which had "debauch'd" the "shining Qualities" of Waller and Denham.[50]

Richard Steele considered the turn in a class with other merely verbal devices: "It is pleasant to see the Man of Judgment start at a Turn or a Metaphor; and the Men of Taste, as they call themselves, yawn at a plain and noble Description."[51]

A common term for false rhetorical wit in the age was the word Gothic. The word originally connoted the unrefined and insensitive taste of rural living, a signification illustrated in a passage from William Congreve's *The Way of the World* (IV, i); Mrs. Millamant reads aloud while Sir Wilfull listens:

MRS. MILLAMANT (*reading a poem by Sir John Suckling*).
"I swear it will not do its part,
Though thou dost thine, employest thy power and art."
Natural, easy Suckling!
SIR WILFULL. Anan? Suckling. No such suckling neither, cousin, nor stripling: I thank heaven, I'm no minor.
MRS. MILLAMANT. Ah, rustic, ruder than Gothic!

The word came to mean more, however, than simple rural uncouthness. It also meant any improper or indecorous behavior. Richard Steele, in the Preface to *The Conscious Lovers*, referred to the scene in the fourth act, "wherein Mr. Bevil evades the quarrel with his friend, and hopes it may have some effect upon the Goths and Vandals that frequent the theatres, or a more polite audience may supply their absence."

As a lack of restraint and refinement, "Gothic" meant also freedom from rules and decorum[52] to some. Sir William Temple, for instance, stigmatized the "common vein of Gothick Runes," as "of a raving or rambling sort of Wit or Invention, loose and flowing, with little Art or Confinement to any certain Measures or Rules."[53] Gothic extravagance and false wit were often associated after the turn of the century. Shaftesbury described the "Gothick Model of Poetry" as the "horrid Discord of jingling Rhyme."[54] James Arbuckle, a minor poet and essayist, writing in 1726 of the wordplay in the "Age of Anagrams, Puns, and Acrosticks," expressed himself by means of an antithetical turn of thought: "Our Language suffered extremely under these Gothick Refinements."[55] Addison made the same connection when he avowed that one of the fictional characters in the *Tatler,* No. 163, Ned Softly, being "a true English reader," was "incapable of relishing the great and masterly strokes" of poetry but was "wonderfully pleased with the little Gothic ornaments of epigrammatical conceits, turns, points, and quibbles, which are so frequent in the most admired in our English poets." Later in the *Spectator,* No. 409, Addison identified "those false Kinds" of wit discussed in No. 62 (i.e. "Epigram, turns of Wit, and forced Conceits") with all that was meant by the term "Gothic Taste." In No. 63 he had made the same identification when, in describing the "Region of False Wit," he found "in the Center of a very dark Grove a monstrous Fabrick built after the Gothick manner . . . covered with innumerable devices in that barbarous kind of Sculpture," a "kind of Heathen Temple consecrated to the God of Dullness."

By association, the taste for Gothic characterized the little wits and pretenders who could only imitate, producing an inferior wit. In a discussion of the ballad "Chevy-Chase" (*Spectator,* No. 74), Addison concluded that if it had been written in the Gothic manner, "which is the Delight of all our little Wits, whether Writers or Readers," then it would not have possessed those universal qualities which had enabled it to survive so many ages. Addison here voiced the popular belief that the productions of modern writers were inferior because of their use of false wit, whereas the timeless writings of the ancients invariably incorporated true wit. In the same vein, John Dennis identified what is "truly the most Gothick" as being "the most oppos'd to Antique,"[56] although he later made clear that false wit was older than its cant name: "the pointed conceited way of wit was in Fashion long before the Goths were either a Name or a Nation."[57]

The use of the epithet Gothic by the men of wit to describe unnatural and extravagant taste sustained one of their chief aims —the exposure of falsity and pretense. Like Dryden, the members of the Scriblerus Club (Swift, Pope, Gay, Arbuthnot, Parnell) were aggressive in this pursuit. No work was more pointed and devastating in its exposure of false rhetoric than that masterpiece of ironic invective, ΠΕΡΙ ΒΑΘΟΥΣ, *or the Art of Sinking in Poetry,* published March 8, 1728. This satire, the work mostly of Pope, identified many of the rhetorical variations in bad taste. Employing the topsy-turvy world of inverted values, Pope, as "Martinus Scriblerus," defined those means by which the moderns excelled the ancients in fine writing. The "profundity" (i.e. density) of contemporary writers was the result of the various aids to their "Prolixity." Some of these were the periphrase, described as "a diffus'd circumlocutory Manner of expressing a known idea," which will "give the Reader the Pleasure of guessing what it is that the Author can possibly mean; and a Surprise when he finds it";[58] the amplification, about which Pope stated, "There are Amplifiers who can extend half a dozen thin Thoughts over a whole Folio"; and various tropes and figures, such as catachresis, metonymy, synecdoche, aposiopesis, metaphor, etc. By these rhetorical means "Images so wonderfully low and unaccountable" are arrived at. Pope enraged his enemies by using glaring examples from their own works. His illustrations spoke clearly for themselves, as in the astounding couplet, describing a lion:

> He roar'd so loud, and look'd so wondrous grim,
> His very Shadow durst not follow him.

He illustrated the extraordinary use of mixed figures with the lines,

> The gaping Clouds pour Lakes of Sulphur down,
> Whose livid flashes sickning Sunbeams drown.

With such sarcasm, Pope ridiculed the poetic productions of his contemporaries, productions filled with outmoded and misused rhetorical wit.

Rhetorical Meaning of True Wit

The neoclassical poet was poised uncomfortably upon the horns of a dilemma: he recognized at once the artistic necessity of imaginative embellishment and also the efficacy of simple eloquence. This disparity between theory and practice remained great, despite the distinctions made between various styles—high, middle, and low.[59] Rarely was a simple, plain style achieved by the men of wit, with the notable exception of Swift's prose.

The opinions of all of the wits reflect this dilemma. A stylist like Pope could write to William Walsh in 1706, "There is a certain majesty in simplicity, which is far above all the quaintness of wit." Yet, such was the delight in ornamentation for its own sake that he admitted elsewhere privately in his letter of March, 1718, to Robert Digby, "If I knew how to entertain you through the rest of this paper, it should be spotted and diversified with conceits all over: you should be put out of breath with laughter at each sentence, and pause at each period, to look over how much wit you have passed." Pope's wit was evidently not false but true, a double talk that shows the ambivalence concerning wit in the minds of the poets of the age. As false wit was identified in terms of rhetorical devices, so also was true wit.

The new modes of wit were always new verbal devices, "new" in the sense that old techniques had been revitalized through modification and often refinement; several were renamed. The conceit, the catachresis, and the turn made use of metaphors, similes, and comparisons. All three frequently involved wordplay of the most elemental nature. The influence of the epigram continued visibly in the closed couplet; it also made use of the newer turn, which frequently involved the lowly clench.

Thomas Hobbes, the philosopher, always took into account the rhetorical implications of wit. For example, in *Humane Nature* (1650) he described the "quick ranging minde," which he opposed to a dull mind. This quick ranging is "joyned with curiosity of comparing the things that come into [a man's] minde." The resulting comparison finds "unexpected similitude of things, otherwise much unlike"; from such comparisons "proceed those grateful Similes, Metaphors, and other Tropes, by which Poets and Orators . . . please or displease, and shew well or ill to others." The same quick ranging of the mind can discern "suddenly dissimilitude in things that otherwise appear the same."[60] Of such did the language of poets and orators consist. Robert Boyle, student of Hobbes and discoverer of the law of volume of gases, agreed with him that the comparison in the art of persuasion had a value which a "naked Syllogism" did not have:

> How great, and how acceptable, a part of Wit that is, which has the advantage to be express'd by apt Similitudes, every Man's own experience, if he please to consult it, may in some measure, inform him. And certainly, there is no one part of Wit that is so generally applicable to all kind of Persons; for good Comparisons serve equally to illustrate, to persuade; the greatest Wits disdain them not, and ev'n ordinary Wits are capable to understand them, and be affected by them.[61]

Rhetoric was essential to Dryden's view of wit and hence of poetry. In his Preface to *An Evening's Love* (1671) he used the ornaments of wit as set forth by Quintilian (*Institutio Oratoria,* VI, iii) as criteria for judging style: *urbanitas,* which is the language of the city as opposed to the Gothic style of the country; *venustas,* which is that language having the grace and charm reminiscent of Venus; *salsus,* which is the language of moderation and seasoning; *facetus,* the language of polished elegance; *iocus,* the language of merriment; and *dicacitas,* the language of banter. When Dryden first defined wit as "propriety" in his "Author's Apology for Heroic Poetry and Poetic Licence" (1677), he concluded with the comment that "sublime subjects ought to be adorned with the sublimist, and consequently often with the most figurative expressions." His discussion of figurative language in connection with sublimity is not coincidental, since the rediscovery of Longinus did much to enhance the value of metaphoric language. Dryden, knowing that figurative language is one secret of the appeal of poetry, wrote that the "masterly figures, and the copiousness of imagination" contributed to the "soul" of the Horatian ode.

The fact that propriety, as Dryden used it, was based upon controlled and decorous metaphor is amply illustrated by Richard Steele's account in the *Tatler,* No. 62, of an evening spent "in discourse of propriety of words and thoughts, which is Mr. Dryden's definition of wit." During the discourse an "odd fellow" forced himself upon the group. In subsequent conversation the newcomer asserted "that Harry Jacks was the first who told him of the taking of the citadel of Tournay" and that "Harry deserves a statue more than the boy who ran to the Senate with a thorn in his foot to tell of a victory." This comparison was immediately discussed by the group as an example of Dryden's definition. Spondee, occupying the chair on the subject of propriety of words and thoughts, asked, "What affinity is there between that boy and Harry, that you say their merit resembles so much as you just now told us?" The "odd fellow" replied, "Why, Harry you know is in the French interest, and it was more pain to him to tell the story of Tournay, than to the boy to run upon a thorn to relate a victory which he was glad of." Spondee would not allow wit in such a comparison and argued that "to have anything gracefully said, it must be natural." Furthermore, "whatsoever was introduced in common discourse with so much premeditation, was insufferable." Spondee then concluded: "Had Mr. Jacks told [this odd fellow] the citadel was taken, and another had answered, 'He deserves a statue as well as the Roman boy, for he told it with as much pain'; it might have passed for a sprightly expression." Such close analysis of a figure of speech indicates the extreme care with which distinctions between true and false wit were pursued.

The neoclassical dilemma often led to a discrepancy between theory and practice. Such discrepancy is found in Dryden's work —a discrepancy between the figures of speech used in his writing and the criteria for propriety of words and thoughts expressed in his criticism. This discrepancy was reported in his own day by Gerald Langbaine, a minor drama critic, in "An Account of the English Dramatick Poets (1691). He joined the argument over the merits of Ben Jonson, siding with Shadwell in support of Jonson against Dryden. When Dryden named conceits and clenches as "the Mode of Wit, the Vice of the Age," Langbaine made his investigation and replied as follows:

> I may add that I find it [wordplay] practis'd by several Dramatick Poets who were Mr. Jonson's Contemporaries: and notwithstanding the advantage which this Age claims over the last, we find Mr.

> Dryden himself as well as Mr. Jonson, not only given to Clinches, but sometimes a Carwichet, a Quarter-quibble or a bare Pun serves his turn as well as his Friend Bur in his *Wild Gallant;* and therefore he might have spar'd this Reflection, if he had given himself the liberty of Thinking.[62]

No one knew better than Dryden the difficulty of consistency, but in his opinion it was not necessarily desirable.

Critical comments regularly included ornamentation in the style of wit. John Hughes, a fair poet and editor of the works of Edmund Spenser, wrote an essay, "Of Poetry" (1698). He considered rhetoric essential to the elegance of thought: "To the Elegance of Words, or Style, belong all the Figures of Rhetorick, and to use these to Advantage requires a Judgement well form'd by Observation." He included metaphors, tropes, hyperboles, "and all the other Figures." Addison, in discussing John Locke's views of wit, observed in the *Spectator,* No. 62, that not only similitudes but also dissimilitudes were valid: "For not only the Resemblance, but the Opposition of Ideas does very often produce Wit; as I could shew in several little Points, Turns, and Antitheses, that I may possibly enlarge upon in some future Speculation." Later in No. 303, he praised the pleasing "kind of Structure in Milton's Similitudes," a kind in marked contrast to that enjoyed by "ignorant Readers, who have formed their Taste upon the quaint Similes, and little Turns of Wit, which are so much in Vogue among modern Poets." One wonders at his ability to refer to "little Turns of Wit" in such differing contexts within a space of months. Equally amazing is the rationale which permitted an age to define both the true and the false in the same terms.

Understandably, the consideration of both true and false wit in terms of standard rhetorical techniques made consistent practice of wit impossible. Langbaine's charge of inconsistency against Dryden could be levied against any of the poets in the Age of Wit. At the beginning of the age, Henry Vaughan in his collection of poems, *Olor Iscanus* (1651), disclaimed for true wit any kind of excessiveness; he argued this in his poem "Charnel-house," a collection of the kind of forced conceits that were even then being condemned for their excess. As the ornamentation of the *figurae verborum* gave way to more subtle and refined techniques of antithesis, parallelism, and balance, the *figurae verborum* continued to enjoy a vogue. An examination of the practice of so consummate an artist as Pope reveals extremely adept use of time-worn verbal devices, including the ignoble pun. This disparity between practice and theory has led to the recent conclusion by W. K. Wimsatt, Jr., that "there is a marked correlation not between poems and contemporary poetics but actually between poems and contemporary anti-poetics."[63] But the poetics of Dryden, Pope, and others admitted rhetoric. In view of the constant interpretation of true wit as rhetorical ornamentation, the disparity was not very great after all.

"Mixt Wit"

One further classification of wit, a late category, was described by Addison as "mixt wit," that is, a mixture of true and false wit. The general agreement by 1700 of the complete falseness of word-play upset the neat balance which Dryden had posed between two kinds of wit. With the continued popularity of verbal wit, Addison defined this new classification in the *Spectator,* No. 62. He distinguished on the one hand true wit, consisting of the "Resemblance of Ideas," and on the other hand false wit, consisting of the "Resemblance of Words." Using as an illustration one of Abraham Cowley's poems, "The Mistress," Addison clarified "mixt wit":

> The Passion of Love in its Nature has been thought to resemble Fire: for which Reason the Words Fire and Flame are made use of to signifie Love. The witty Poets therefore have taken an Advantage from the doubtful Meanings of the Word Fire, to make an infinite Number of Witticisms. Cowley observing the cold Regard of his Mistress's Eyes, and at the same Time their Power of producing Love in him, considers them as Burning-Glasses made of Ice; and finding himself able to live in the greatest Extremities of Love, concludes the Torrid Zone to be habitable.

Samuel Johnson in his own consideration of Cowley's wit described this wit as "Thoughts true in one sense of the expression, and false in the other," the result of which, in its confusion of images, entertains for a moment but soon becomes "wearisome" because it is "unnatural."[64] While Addison considered this kind of wit a "Composition of Punn and true Wit," Johnson thought of it as a mixture of true and false thoughts. Both men were critical of the distortions of truth which arose from the deliberate twisting of meanings and condemned mixed wit only as a lesser evil, not different in kind from false wit.

Distinctions between true and false wit were highly relative, despite the positive tone taken by the poets and other critics. The discrepancies between theory and practice were perceived by few men. Addison was one of these. In the famous issue of the *Spectator*, No. 62, devoted to wit, he demonstrated the element of surprise in true wit with an example involving mixed wit: if one remarks, he wrote, that "the bosom of his Mistress is as white as Snow," there is no wit, "but when he adds, with a Sigh, that it is as cold too," the comment "grows to wit." In the next issue (May 12, 1711), he discussed a region, located near false wit, which was "inhabited by the Species of Mixed Wit." He described some of its inhabitants: "There were Men whose Bodies were stuck full of Darts, and Women that had Breasts of Snow." In this jesting with his own examples, Addison informed his readers that even serious distinctions could not be maintained consistently.

The subjective nature of his distinctions, true of all neoclassical generalities, is amply illustrated by the objections raised immediately to Addison's instance of surprise. The writer of *The Miscellany*, No. 6, on June 2, 1711, found the same fault in Addison's example that Addison had found in Cowley's poem, the distortion and ambiguity of meaning through play upon words as well as upon ideas. The resulting wit is deemed false:

I humbly conceive that the same Thing that is as white as Snow, ought without any doubtful meaning to be as cold too: But here the word Bosom in the first place, where its whiteness is consider'd, is taken in its Proper and Natural Sense, and signifies that part of the Body which is so call'd, but in the second place where the coldness of it is likewise compared to Snow, Bosom is taken in a Figurative Sense and signifies the Heart, Desires, or inclinations to which the Epithet of white is Impertinent: This in my Opinion makes the Example quoted false Wit, because as soon as the double meaning of Bosom is taken off it vanishes: For if throughout the Similie we let the word keep its Genuine Signification, a Man may certainly say of his Mistress that her Bosom is as white as Snow, and add either with or without a Sigh, that it is as cold too, with all the Innocence in the World as to Wit, especially if in a Frosty Morning he should meet her without any thing about her Neck.

The pun on "bosom" reduces the whole simile to false wit, unless one admits the legitimacy of the symbol in poetic language. In this manner did plain statement clash with imaginative statement.

The Rhetoric of Wit in John Dryden's Poems: "Upon the Death of the Lord Hastings" and "Mac Flecknoe"

As we have seen, the changes in the rhetorical styles in the seventeenth century were continuous and numerous. Poets could hardly escape their influence and most often did not wish to. One of the poets most conscious of wit and most susceptible to change was John Dryden, who most shaped the poetic practice during the last half of the century. In spite of his changing notions (he had to change, as his very livelihood depended upon current taste), his poetic facility improved so much that he was able to perfect the heroic couplet, his accomplishments with which prepared the way for the finished achievement of Pope.

The expanse of Dryden's poetic production provides examples of many of the modes of rhetorical wit during the century. His first published poem, "Upon the Death of the Lord Hastings," appeared in a memorial volume of poems to that worthy gentleman in 1649, when Dryden was about eighteen years old and still a student at Westminster. Many famous poets contributed to the volume, all impressed with the portentous death of Lord

Hastings, the last heir of that family, who at the age of nineteen had succumbed to the smallpox on the eve of his marriage.

Dryden's poem depends heavily upon the rhetoric of wit, reflecting the continuing manner of conceit of metaphysical poetry, an influence also evident in many other elegiac poems in the collection. Dryden's elegy begins:

Must Noble Hastings Immaturely die,
(The Honour of his ancient Family?)
Beauty and Learning thus together meet,
To bring a Winding for a Wedding-sheet?
Must Vertue prove Death's Harbinger? Must She,
With him expiring, feel Mortality?
Is Death (Sin's wages) Grace's now? shall Art
Make us more learned, onely to depart?
If Merit be Disease, if Vertue Death;
To be Good, Not to be; who'd then bequeath
Himself to Discipline? Who'd not esteem
Labour a Crime, Study Self-murther deem?

The lines contain the typical playing with enigmas which lie in apparent paradoxes: virtue preparing the way for death; death being the reward of graceful living; art dying at the moment of its fruition; merit being disease—all with an awareness of transcendent implications. There is also play upon words, as in the turn upon the word "sheet."

The following lines develop the extended metaphor, or conceit, which the metaphysical poets exploited:

His body was an Orb, his sublime Soul
Did move on Vertue's and on Learning's pole:
Whose Reg'lar Motions better to our view,
Then Archimedes Sphere, the Heavens did shew.
Graces and Vertues, Languages and Arts,
Beauty and Learning, fill'd up all the parts.
Heav'ns Gifts, which do, like falling Stars, appear
Scatter'd in Others; all, as in their Sphear,
Were fix'd and conglobate in's Soul, and thence
Shone th'row his Body with sweet Influence;
Letting their Glories so on each Limb fall,
The whole Frame render'd was Celestial.

> Come, learned Ptolemy, and tryal make,
> If thou this Hero's Altitude canst take;
> But that transcends thy skill; thrice happie all
> Could we but prove thus Astronomical.

The neatly ordered macrocosm of the Ptolemaic cosmology is mirrored in the equally orderly microcosm of Lord Hastings. As the celestial bodies have their poles, so his life had its poles of virtue and learning, the traditional ideals of civilized man. As Ptolemy had measured the circles (and heights) of celestial bodies, so could he have measured the height of the stature and learning of Lord Hastings, for such "Altitude" was truly "Astronomical."

Perhaps an even more interesting passage occurs in the lines describing the smallpox which caused the death of Hastings. Here, the impression is not a single effect but a series, a succession of images which turn on the appearance and the idea of the pocks. The final objective is to explore the ultimate meaning of the disease which took his life:

> Was there no milder way but the Small Pox,
> The very Filth'ness of Pandora's Box?
> So many Spots, like naeves, our Venus soil?
> One Jewel set off with so many a Foil?
> Blisters with pride swell'd; which th'row's flesh did sprout
> Like Rose-buds, stuck i' th' Lilly-skin about.
> Each little Pimple had a Tear in it,
> To wail the fault its rising did commit:
> Who, Rebel-like, with their own Lord at strife,
> Thus made an Insurrection 'gainst his Life.
> Or were these Gems sent to adorn his Skin,
> The Cab'net of a richer Soul within?
> No Comet need foretel his Change drew on,
> Whose Corps might seem a Constellation.

The conceits follow each other, one after the other, much in the manner of Marini, demonstrating the ingenuity of the poet. Grotesque and extravagant though they are, Dryden's metaphors are not very different from those of the more experienced poets in the collection.

The whole poem reveals various other characteristics of metaphysical poems, chiefly the customary disregard for regularity. Note the halting and irregular rhythm in the following lines:

> Transcribe th' Original in new Copies; give
> Hastings o' th' better part: so shall he live
> In 's Nobler Half; and the great Grandsire be
> Of an Heroick Divine Progenie.

The irregular run-ons, together with awkward elision and harsh sounds, contribute to the general unevenness. The metaphysical tradition continued to experiment in the face of increasing emphasis upon regularity and symmetry.

Even with the accretion of verbal devices in the seventeenth century, the general movement of poetics was toward a more regular rhythm, even lines, end stops or pauses, and natural accents—all opposed to the excesses of metaphysical wit. Edmund Waller and Sir John Denham contributed greatly to this refinement of numbers. As a result of more exact meaning, a new strength appeared in the couplet lines. Specific ideas in inversions, antitheses, similitudes, parallelisms, and balance replaced the forced imagery of the metaphoric conceit. As George Williamson has shown, the heroic couplet, when absorbed by antithetical wit, suited extremely well the needs of satire, panegyric, argument, and portraiture. Making use of an "informing force . . . a manner of saying things ultimately derived from Latin rhetoric,"[65] this new vehicle for wit proved very effective in pointed contrast, sharp definition, novel turns, and critical poise. Such versatility explains the success of the ridicule, humor, satire, and criticism which typify so many of the verse and prose masterpieces of Age of Wit.

Dryden's "Mac Flecknoe" is such a masterpiece. This personal satire, published in 1682, was a product of the verbal wars in a contentious age. It was not acknowledged by Dryden until 1693. The poem was motivated by antagonism between Dryden, a Royalist, Catholic, and poet laureate, and Shadwell, a Whig, Protestant, and dully moralistic dramatist. A later reversal in Court influences was to replace Dryden with Shadwell as laureate. Dryden sensed the antipathy early, following a period of friendship, and upon the death in 1678 of Richard Flecknoe, a mediocre versifier, he may have planned or have even begun the satire: its plan—to elect Shadwell to succeed Flecknoe as "Prince of Nonsense."

"Mac Flecknoe" begins with a technique used to great advantage in later personal satire—the verse "character," one of the most devastating forms of mockery in English. In the opening lines, Flecknoe, prince of the "Realms of Nonsense" but near death, determines to find a worthy successor:

> This aged Prince now Flourishing in Peace,
> And blest with issue of a large increase,
> Worn out with business, did at length debate
> To settle the succession of the State:
> And pond'ring which of all his Sons was fit
> To Reign, and wage immortal War with Wit.

Since the chosen one must resemble the prince himself, Flecknoe declares, in the most memorable lines of the poem,

> Sh[adwell] alone my perfect image bears,
> Mature in dullness for his tender years.
> Sh[adwell] alone, of all my Sons, is he
> Who stands confirm'd in full stupidity.
> The rest to some faint meaning make pretence,
> But Sh[adwell] never deviates into sense.
> Some Beams of Wit on other souls may fall,
> Strike through and make a lucid intervall;
> But Sh[adwell]'s genuine night admits no ray,
> His rising Fogs prevail upon the Day:
> Besides his goodly Fabrick fills the eye,
> And seems design'd for thoughtless Majesty:
> Thoughtless as Monarch Oakes, that shade the plain,
> And, spread in solemn state, supinely reign.

The satiric effectiveness lies in the ironic turns upon the maturity of dullness, the strength of stupidity, the inability to deviate into sense, and in other reversals of common-sense values. Additional force is achieved by the epigrammatic sting, usually a turn, in the second (and closing) line in the sharpest couplets.

Flecknoe, with the full majestic power of an epic hero (the example of Satan in *Paradise Lost* was recent) begins a second speech:

> Heavens bless my Son, from Ireland let him reign
> To farr Barbadoes on the Western main;
> Of his Dominion may no end be known,
> And greater than his Father's be his Throne.
> Beyond love's Kingdom let him stretch his Pen;
> He paus'd, and all the people cry'd Amen.
> Then thus, continu'd he, my Son advance
> Still in new Impudence, new Ignorance.
> Success let others teach, learn thou from me
> Pangs without birth, and fruitless Industry.
> Let Virtuoso's in five years be Writ;
> Yet not one thought accuse thy toyl of wit.

Flecknoe's panegyric contains mock-heroic imagery, by means of which vulgar men are compared with kings and, ironically, are made even more common and insignificant. The antithesis in the fourth line, turning in meaning on "greater" as applying to nonsense, is a typical reversal employed throughout the poem. The parallel ideas in lines 9 and 10, balanced two to a line, work effectively in antithesis to point up the surprising turns of thought.

The closing lines demonstrate some of the versatility of neoclassical wit in the confines of the heroic couplet. In his supreme confidence in the great abilities of Shadwell, Flecknoe begins by contrasting him with Ben Jonson, of the past age:

> Let Father Fleckno fire thy mind with praise,
> And Uncle Ogleby thy envy raise.
> Thou art my blood, where Jonson has no part;
> What share have we in Nature or in Art?
> Where did his wit on learning fix a brand,
> And rail at Arts he did not understand;
> Where made he love in Prince Nicander's vein,
> Or swept the dust in Psyche's humble strain?
> Where sold he Bargains, Whip-stitch, kiss my Arse,
> Promis'd a Play and dwindled to a Farce?

When did his Muse from Fletcher scenes purloin,
As thou whole Eth'ridg dost transfuse to thine?
. . . .
Thy inoffensive Satyrs never bite.
In thy fellonious heart, though Venom lies,
It does but touch thy Irish pen, and dyes.
Thy Genius calls thee not to purchase fame
In keen Iambicks, but mild Anagram:
Leave writing Plays, and chuse for thy command
Some peacefull Province in Acrostick Land.
There thou maist wings display and Alters raise,
And torture one poor word Ten thousand ways.
Or if thou would'st thy diff'rent talents suit,
Set thy own Songs, and sing them to thy lute.
He said, but his last words were scarcely heard,
For Bruce and Longvil had a Trap prepar'd,
And down they sent the yet declaiming Bard.
Sinking he left his Dragget robe behind,
Born upwards by a subterranean wind.
The Mantle fell to the young Prophet's part,
With double portion of his Father's Art.

Dullness, as we shall see in the next chapter, is the very antithesis of wit, and therefore Dryden can assign to the new prince of nonsense such areas of outmoded and false wit as anagrams, acrostics, shaped verse, and puns.

Summary

Wit seems to have become the signal word during the Age of Wit for extending those arguments that had beset the Renaissance rhetoricians and critics: simplicity versus ornamentation, word versus thought, reason versus imagination, delight versus instruction, and, finally, imaginative perception versus the literal statement of truth. These issues had the widest aesthetic, literary, and social implications. The value of rhetorical wit was questioned by scientific and moral forces, almost never by literary interests. However, a constant effort was made by poets to distinguish between true and false rhetoric. The changing neoclassical mood discarded in quick succession the pun, the epigram, the conceit, and the turn, but these devices continued in popularity.

This discriminating urge, which insisted upon defining true wit and then distinguishing true wit from false, created an ambivalence in the mind of poets. Typically, the ambivalence consisted of defining both in the same terms, of condemning and using the same devices. The Renaissance had been relatively free of such fine distinctions. Jonson could indulge in the rhetorical devices which suited his purpose without misgivings or concern. On the other hand, Dryden found it impossible to follow the constantly varying dictates of acceptable wit and was forever justifying his practice to square it with his theory. And as his conservatism grew, his theories changed until he finally apologized for his earlier practice, while justifying at the same time his present practice with his new theory.

In such a state of flux, the neoclassical mind found itself at times in much confusion. Wit was particularly aggravating in being at once necessary and reprehensible. One can understand the state of mind that stimulated Alexander Pope, in an exposition of wit entitled "An Essay on Criticism," to question its very nature; for he, like Dryden, was dedicated to the search of the age, the search for true wit, and aware of the dangers inherent in it:

> Some foreign writers, some our own despise;
> The ancients only, or the moderns prize.
> Thus wit, like faith, by each man is applied
> To one small sect, and all are damn'd beside.
> Meanly they seek the blessing to confine,
> And force that sun but on a part to shine,
> Which not alone the southern wit sublimes,
> But ripens spirits in cold northern climes;
> Which from the first has shone on ages past,
> Enlights the present, and shall warm the last;
> Though each may feel increases and decays,
> And see now clearer and now darker days.
> Regard not then if wit be old or new,
> And blame the false, and value still the true.
>
> (ll. 394–407)

I make, you see, a great difference between Reason, and Fancy. All the World talks of this, and would have it [fancy] in Perfection, and no Man explains what it is. For ought I know, it may be one of those Things we should make more obscure by attempting to define it.

—HENRY BARKER, *The Polite Gentleman* (1700)

3
The Psychology of Wit

IN THE SEVENTEENTH and eighteenth centuries several of the persistent arguments with respect to wit developed in debates over psychology.[1] The resulting mass of literature was subjective in nature, highly speculative and seemingly confused, but very influential in the thinking of the age. Because of the relationship of wit to various mental activities, these arguments revealed new meanings of wit. The psychological aspects of wit had been subordinate to rhetorical considerations, but as the early seventeenth century moved toward the Age of Wit, the psychological aspects of wit assumed major importance. By the end of the century, wit was identified with so many of the mental faculties as to seem hopelessly entangled. "All the world," in Henry Barker's words, "talks of this," the relationship of mental faculties.

In the shift of emphasis from the rhetoric of wit to the psychology of wit, two facts predominate. First, psychological theory was being re-evaluated. The inquiries of Thomas Hobbes and John Locke became foundations for modern psychology, and their speculations influenced new views of wit. Second, there were new psychological implications in the changing criteria of aesthetics. These new criteria, however formless in the seventeenth century, were nevertheless perceptible in the antithetical arguments which plagued the age: the mental faculty of judgment against the faculty of imagination; the ancient rules against individual taste; reason against emotion; and imitation against originality.[2] The universality of aesthetic taste as embodied in the traditional modes and forms came under serious question at the hands of contemporary English poets and critics. By the end of the Age of Wit, a basic characteristic of English temperament had become more evident: judgment by general effectiveness rather than by mechanical application of rules. As a result, experimentation replaced imitation; emotionalism replaced rationality; and indulgence in the imagination replaced reliance upon the judgment. In general, art—and particularly poetic expression—was felt to have a secret grace which, although eluding analysis, was still perceptible to the sensitive reader or listener.[3]

Wit in its psychological context was directly involved in these changes. It was a matter of conjecture whether wit was a product of the judgment or of the imagination. As a product of judgment, wit would state natural truth decorously; as a product of imagination, wit embodied fanciful delight. The fact that judgment and imagination were increasingly at odds in basic aesthetic questions forced wit into the midst of the arguments. The far-reaching implications of the psychology of wit become clear only when viewed against those theories of the mind historically called faculty psychology.

The Background of Psychology

Ancient, medieval, and Renaissance psychology explained the learning process of the mind or soul in terms of several special powers or faculties. The basic assumption was that the mind could not function without the body. Plato had proposed a dual functioning in which the mind contributed ideas and the body supplied sensations; the two faculties involved were the intellect and the senses. Aristotle recognized the same two faculties. Later, a third faculty, the memory, was added; and still later a fourth, the imagination, was described and accepted. The imagination consisted of those images called up by the sensory memory.

Classical psychology divided the mind or soul into further functions. Aristotle described five: vegetative, appetitive, sensitive, locomotive, and rational. Later, some philosophers described only four. By the time of the Renaissance, there was general agreement upon a division of three subsouls, instead of four or five: vegetative, sensitive, and rational. The last two possessed important mental functions which require brief attention.

As viewed in the Renaissance, the mental processes of the sensitive and rational subsouls are complex.[4] The sensitive soul is endowed with two faculties: sense and motion. Of the first there are two kinds: external senses (i.e. sight, hearing, smell, taste, and touch) and internal senses (i.e. common sense, imagination, and memory—all located in the brain). The common sense receives impressions from the external senses and relays them to the imagination, which stores them in the memory.

The imagination, called the eye of the mind, has the important function of conveying sensory experience from this repository to the rational soul, specifically to the intellectual division, or faculty, called the reason. The reason (or judgment) is capable of sifting sensory impressions and thereby perceiving the essence of truth. This perception is conducted by logic, which is motivated and guided by the judgment. Truth thus arrived at is communicated by the reason to another division of the rational soul, the volitional faculty, called the will. The will is free to act upon the dictates of truth. In this manner, the noblest purpose of the human being was realized under faculty psychology: the perception of moral truth as the basis for human action. This perception was recognized throughout the Age of Wit as the highest aim of man.

At no time in the long tradition of faculty psychology could any general agreement be reached on the number of mental faculties. Five are named above: common sense, imagination, memory, reason, and will. Francis Bacon accepted only three—reason, imagination, and memory. He distributed the sources of human knowledge as follows: philosophy from reason, poetry from imagination, and history from memory. Robert Burton believed the three faculties to be common sense, imagination, and memory. However, during the Age of Wit, four faculties were frequently mentioned: imagination (or fancy) and memory—the two internal senses of the sensitive soul—and judgment (or reason) and understanding (or intellect)—functions of the rational soul.

The relative importance of these faculties changed during the Age of Wit. The mid-seventeenth-century view is expressed in *Paradise Lost,* where Adam, after hearing Eve's dream, fears evil and looks for the source in the mind:

> But know that in the soul
> Are many lesser faculties that serve
> Reason as chief; among these Fancy next
> Her office holds; of all external things,
> Which the five watchful senses represent,
> She forms imaginations, airy shapes,
> Which Reason joining and disjoining, frames
> All what we affirm or what deny, and call
> Our knowledge or opinion; then retires
> Into her private cell when Nature rests.
> Oft in her absence mimic Fancy wakes
> To imitate her; but misjoining shapes,
> Wild work produces oft, and most in dreams,
> Ill matching words and deeds long past or late.
> (V, 100–113)

Faith in reason or judgment and distrust of fancy or imagination were basic to later seventeenth-century thought. The mid-eighteenth-century view is expressed in these remarks of John Brown:

> The divine Author of our Being having given us several different Powers, Sense, Imagination, Memory, and Reason, as the Inlets, Preservers, and Improvers of Knowledge; it may be proper here briefly to remark their respective Provinces. As the Senses are the Fountains whence we derive all our Ideas; so these are infinitely combined and associated by the Imagination: Memory preserves these Assemblages of Things: Reason compares, distinguishes, and separates them: By this Means determining their Differences, and pointing out which are real, and which fictitious.[5]

Here, emphasis has changed. Association has replaced rationalism, as evident in the special attention to senses, those "Fountains whence we derive all our Ideas" (showing the influence of Locke's empiricism), and to imagination, which "infinitely" combines and associates images (indicating early romantic theory). Here imagination makes a valid and positive contribution to the mental processes, whereas earlier the imagination had worked irresponsibly—especially in the absence of reason.

Wit, a curious and extraordinary manifestation of man's mind at work, was intimately related to these faculties. Often called a mental faculty, it had been associated since ancient times with several of them. In the seventeenth century, wit was identified not only with the mind itself but with its two most controversial faculties, judgment and imagination. The meaning of wit differed as its identification with these mental processes differed.

Wit as Intellect

Wit, coming from the Old English *witan* (to know), had meant "intellect" from early times, as in line 589 in *Beowulf: þeah þin wit duge* (though your mind [intelligence] be strong). As meaning mental capacity, the term was related variously during the following centuries to consciousness, sanity, intellectual ability, good judgment, and also innate wisdom. The *witenagemot* (literally, "a meeting of wise men") was the first parliamentary body in early England. Much later (about 1650) John Selden wrote, "No man is the wiser for his Learning; it may Administer matter to work in, or Objects to work upon, but Wit and Wisdom are born with a man."[6] Numerous expressions, many still in modern use, retain the implications of intellect: "to lose one's wits," or "to be at wit's end." Epithets also indicate the same meaning: "half-wit," "quarter-wit," "nitwit," and "dimwit."

In the Age of Wit, wit as intelligence can usually be distinguished from other meanings by context. When Bishop Thomas Sprat wrote, "Of all the labors of mens Wit, and Industry, I scarce know any that can be more useful to the World, than Civil History, if it were written with that sincerity, and majesty, as it ought to be, as a faithful Idea of humane Actions,"[7] he was obviously referring to intelligence. John Evelyn reported in his diary on July 6, 1679, the accomplishments of the son of the Reverend Henry Wotton, who upon examination gave evidence of a phenomenal intellect: "what was more admirable than his vast memory, was his judgment and invention." He was, "in sum, an *intellectus universalis,* beyond all that we read of Picus Mirandula, and other precocious wits, and yet withal a very humble child."[8] Daniel Defoe, in discussing before the Scandal Club happenings of a current trial, described one man who was called as a witness as very foolish, for he had "Wit enough to speak Truth, but not Sense enough to hide it."[9] John Dennis referred to such a man as a half-wit because he had "Wit without Judgement."[10] There was no substitute for native intelligence. Addison was fond of a Scotch saying: "An Ounce of Mother-Wit is worth a Pound of Clergy."[11]

Wit as Understanding

Wit meant also "understanding," for "intellect" or "intelligence" included the ability to comprehend and reason.[12] Accordingly, Robert Burton wrote in *The Anatomy of Melancholy* (1628) that "Understanding is a power of the soul, by which we perceive, know, remember, and judge, as well singulars as universals."[13] This is clearly the functioning of the intelligence. The Schoolmen had divided this faculty into the *intellectus,* or intuitive intellect, and the *ratio,* or discursive intellect.[14] In English, these divisions became understanding and reason, terms much used and abused during the Age of Wit.

In its identity with understanding, wit was often considered the source or seat of the understanding. John Bodenham's popular copybook, *Politeuphuia,* or *Wit's Common-Wealth* (1597), described wit as "the first and principal part of the Soul, wherein the Mind, the Understanding, and the Memory are contained."[15] However, wit was more often thought of as synonymous with understanding. This relationship is described at some length by a pupil of Hobbes, Walter Carleton, in his essay *A Brief Discourse Concerning the Different Wits of Men* (1664). He began typically with a discussion of the difficulty of his task. He considered wit a mental faculty but also "a thing whereof Men have formed to themselves various Conceptions, and for which they have accordingly invented various names"—all tending to confuse rather than clarify. Further, a major difficulty was the vastness and complexity of the brain, "one of those Arcana of Nature, whose knowledge the wise Creator seems to have reserved to Himself." Carleton accepted the "Natural Capacity of Understanding" as innate, but some persons "have more Wit than others." A man who cultivated his wit became learned,[16] although wit could exist without learning.

Carleton, in seeking the chief characteristics of good wit, seemed most satisfied with acumen, which he defined as "a quick or nimble apprehension of what is taught." He added two others: *animadversio,* "a Faculty whereby a man, from what he hath learned, hunts after what he hath not learned," and called by "our incomparable Mr. Hobbes . . . Ranging"; and *memoria,* which is a "Retention of what is learned." The total effect of these characteristics was an "Acuteness of Wit," which Carleton posed as the direct opposite of dullness.

Wit, the Antithesis of Dullness

The Age of Wit made a difference between "those we call Wits, and those we call Stupid."[17] Two different explanations of this opposition are to be found—one physiological, the other psychological.

Physiologically, the presence of dullness was explained by the prevalence of melancholy, one of the four humors. The melancholy, heavy and sluggish with a resulting tendency to sink, was naturally inimical to wit. Therefore, as Henry Barker believed, the usual "Vivacity of Mind" of the men of wit was marred by "unlucky Melancholy Days, when it is apparent the Sprightliness of their Wit has not its wonted Heat and Lustre."[18] Barker's reference to lack of "heat and lustre" indicates that melancholy brought on coldness and dryness. He speaks elsewhere of "the Stupid, being both Dull and Dumb," whose brain has received "the weak Impressions of the heavy and pusillanimous Animal Spirits," which, in turn, are "produc'd in little quantity from a gross thick Blood, which circulates but slowly."[19]

The seat of the melancholy was the spleen, an abdominal organ located in the left side of the body. Its function was to absorb excess black bile from the blood. A disordered spleen could either fail to absorb it or discharge too much into the veins. Any confined humor tended to produce heat, and confined melancholy particularly produced gas or windiness, called flatulent melancholy. The functioning of the spleen was necessarily an influence in the quality and amount of wit. Anne Finch, Countess of Winchilsea and a very good poet, addressed her subject in a poem "The Spleen" thus:

> The fool, to imitate the wits,
> Complains of thy pretended fits,
> And dullness, born with him, would lay
> Upon thy accidental sway;
> Because sometimes thou dost presume
> Into the ablest heads to come.
>
> (ll. 63–68)

Wit had the ability because of its properties to drive away melancholy; thus William Cowper, a pre-Romantic poet, referred in his poem "Conversation" (1781) to the friend

> Whose wit can brighten up a wintry day,
> And chase the splenetic dull hours away
>
> (ll. 581–582)

The third Earl of Shaftesbury proposed the same cure, wit, against "serious Extravagances and splenetick Humours."[20]

Psychologically, the presence of dullness was explained by a sluggish imagination. Hobbes believed that "a slow Imagination maketh that Defect, or fault of the mind, which is commonly called Dulnesse, Stupidity, and sometimes by other names that signifie slownesse of motion, or difficulty to be moved."[21] Elsewhere, he stated that both fancy and judgment were commonly grouped under the term "Wit," which appeared to be a "Tenuity and Agility of Spirits, contrary to the restiness of the Spirits supposed in those that are dull."[22] The opposition of wit and dullness appeared also in the changing emphasis from judgment to imagination throughout the age. Thus Hobbes asserted in the Preface to Homer's *Odysses* (1675), that men had come to admire fancy more than judgment, whereby they account "Reason and Judgment but for a dull entertainment."

The charge of dullness became standard invective against the enemies of the wits. Robert Wolseley censured severely those who had accused the Earl of Rochester with "failing in Wit: he whose Name was the very Mark it pass'd by." On the other hand, Wolseley charged in the Preface to *Valentinian* that such accusers were

> . . . Men who have got the Form of Poetry without the Power, and by a laborious Insipidness, a polish'd Dulness, seem not design'd to't [wit] as a Penance for some yet unexpiated Sin of their Forefathers: Men who, like old Lovers, are curst with a strong Inclination and weak Abilities, to whom nothing is more unlucky than an opportunity to satisfie their unnatural longings: . . . they do but betray the Impotence of their Wit.

As we have seen, Dryden satirized Thomas Shadwell in "Mac Flecknoe" as mature in dullness, hence lacking wit. Pope, using the same standard technique, wrote the *Dunciad* to excoriate his enemies and the would-be wits. The *exordium,* in mock-epic vein, is addressed to the patron saint and "mighty mother," the Goddess of Dullness. In her rule,

> Dullness o'er all possess'd her ancient right,
> Daughter of Chaos and eternal Night.
>
> (ll. 11–12)

As for the nature of her realm,

> Laborious, heavy, busy, bold, and blind,
> She rul'd, in native anarchy, the mind.
> Still her old empire to restore she tries,
> For, born a goddess, Dullness never dies.
>
> (ll. 15–18)

The son of the Goddess was first Lewis Theobald and later Colley Cibber—both men among those unfortunate personal enemies elevated by Pope to the high status of the ridiculous. Cibber, an actor and good dramatist, was made poet laureate in 1730, but he incurred Pope's wrath for ridiculing him in a revival of *The Rehearsal* in 1741. Pope used the same technique in *The Art of Sinking in Poetry,* which title signifies in faculty psychology "the art of being dull," for "sinking" was one effect of heavy melancholy.

Dullness as False Wit

Dullness and stupidity, the opposite of intelligence, became synonymous with false wit, as the above illustrations reveal. When Shadwell, Theobald, and Cibber were called dull, the obvious implication was that they were incapable of genuine wit. Cibber was called the "Anti-Christ of Wit" in the *Dunciad.* The landscape in Addison's "Region of False Wit" was dominated by a heathen temple to the God of Dullness. In "Martinus Scriblerus, of the Poem," introductory to the *Dunciad,* Pope describes the invention of printing, when "paper also became so cheap, and printers, so numerous, that a deluge of authors cover'd the land." As a result, "our author living in those times, did conceive it an endeavour well worthy an honest satyrist, to dissuade the dull and punish the malicious, the only way that was left."

By the same token, dullness was avoided by all men of wit as fatal to their craft. Addison promised early in the *Spectator* series (No. 10)

> . . . to give it over as soon as I grow dull. This I know will be Matter of great Raillery to the small Wits; who will frequently put me in mind of my Promise, desire me to keep my Word, assure me that it

is high Time to give over, with many other little Pleasantries of the like Nature, which Men of a little smart Genius cannot forbear throwing out against their best Friends, when they have such a Handle given them of being witty. But let them remember that I do hereby enter my Caveat against this piece of Raillery.

During the height of the Restoration, a high moral tone was felt at times to contribute to dullness. The attempts to eliminate obscenity and vice from Restoration plays were resisted because of the popularity of these elements and by the feeling that reformed plays would be devoid of wit and thereby dull. The Prologue to Edward Ravenscroft's *Dame Dobson the Cunning Woman* (1684) addressed the audience on behalf of the author:

> Gallants, I vow I am quite out of heart,
> I've not one smutty Jest in all my part.
> Here's not one Scene of tickling Rallery;
> There we quite lose the Pit and Gallery,
> His London Cuckolds did afford you sport.
> That pleas'd the Town, and did divert the Court.
> But 'cause some squeamish Females of renown
> Made visits with design to cry it down,
> He swore in's Rage he would their humours fit,
> And write the next without one word of Wit.
> No line in this will tempt your minds to Evil,
> It's true, 'tis dull, but then 'tis very civil.

The sobering influence of women upon the public excesses of wit is apparent even at this early date.

Wit in the Clash of Judgment and Imagination

Intellect, or understanding, was the result of the effective functioning of the mental processes—perceiving, knowing, remembering, and judging.[23] Therefore, wit had from time to time been related to one or all of these faculties, but in the production of thought and communication, two predominated: judgment and imagination. As an intellectual force, wit became bound up with the most persistent psychological issue of the period—the relative values of judgment and imagination. The extent to which wit was a crucial point is apparent in three dominant views. First, wit was accepted as a combination of both judgment and imagination, although the proportions of each varied infinitely. This view was a compromise in an age of balance and order, but it was nevertheless widely accepted. Second, wit was accepted as synonymous with judgment. This view, in an age of reason and propriety, culminated in the elevation of wit as the source and the test of truth. Third, wit was accepted as synonymous with imagination. In this association wit was identified with sublimity and the *je ne sais quoi* of graceful writing. Since the implications of all these views are reflected so often in the literature of the age, each view deserves a close scrutiny.

Wit as Both Judgment and Imagination

As intellect, wit was most simply explained as the functioning of two faculties—judgment and imagination. Such an analysis was presented by Thomas Hobbes in *Humane Nature* (X, 4), 1650:

> The contrary hereunto [i.e. to dullness], is that quick ranging of minde . . . which is joyned with curiosity of comparing the things that come into his minde one with another: in which comparison, a man delighted himself either with finding unexpected similitude of things, otherwise much unlike, in which men place the excellency of Fancie, and from whence proceed those grateful Similies, Metaphors, and other Tropes, by which Poets and Orators have it in their power to make things please or displease, and shew well or ill to others, as they like themselves; or else in discerning suddenly dissimilitude in things that otherwise appear the same. And this vertue of the minde is that by which men attain to exact and perfect Knowledge; and the pleasure thereof consisteth in continual instruction, and in distinction of places, persons, and seasons, and is commonly termed by the name of Judgement: for, to judge is nothing else, but to distinguish or discern; And both Fancie and Judgement are commonly comprehended under the name of Wit.

This definition not only characterizes the two faculties but also demonstrates the close relationship between faculty psychology and the creation of rhetorical effects. The fancy produced poetry and orations; the judgment produced exact knowledge.

The reason for the interdependence of judgment and imagination is obvious. Each was considered to be a vital subfaculty of the intellect or understanding; both were constantly involved in thought processes. On the subject of intellectual perception, Walter Carleton believed that "the Understanding of a Man is commonly measured either by the rectitude of his Judgment, or the celerity of his Imagination."[24] David Abercromby, a Scottish physician and metaphysician, recognized the value of both faculties in his comprehensive study, *Discourse of Wit.* Accepting, like Carleton, the view of wit as sense or intelligence, he believed that wit varied greatly among men and that each kind of wit depended upon the relative quantities of judgment and imagination. He distinguished two kinds of wit. Habitual wit arises mostly from the judgment, tends to be slow but more profound. This wit possesses a "penetrancy of understanding." Accidental wit arises mostly from the imagination and works in a singular fashion, marked by extemporaneous, superficial thought.[25]

Thus the predominance of either faculty determined the capabilities of the individual, as well as his mental production. Judgment, or reason, was necessary for the comprehension of philosophy, history, and government, whereas imagination was necessary for the understanding and production of poetry, oratory, music, and other arts.

The intelligence necessary for literary creativity consisted of both imagination and judgment. The metaphysical poet Edward Benlowes explained the "Divine Rapture" of his poetry in terms of judgment and invention: "Now't is Judgement begets the Strength, Invention the Ornaments of a Poem; both These joyn'd form Wit, which is the Agility of Spirits." He attributed invention to the faculty of the imagination, an association made clear by his assertion that "from the Excellencie of Fancie proceed graceful Similes, apt Metaphors. . . ."[26] This definition is a paraphrasing of Hobbes' view expressed two years earlier.[27]

The duality of wit was commonly accepted. John Dennis,

a dramatist and critic, reasoned that "the Fancy must run thro', and compare a great many Objects, before it can start a hint from them, which may carry with it that appearance of likeness, which may afterward by the Judgment be improved to an exact resemblance."[28] So the simile was produced. Dennis later stated that "a true description of Wit" was "a just mixture of Reason and Extravagance,"[29] which in faculty psychology meant judgment and imagination. Sir Richard Blackmore, a physician and fair poet, accepted the same combination: "Wit is a Qualification of the Mind, that raises and enlivens cold Sentiments and plain Propositions," which come from the judgment. "Wit is therefore the Accomplishment of a warm, sprightly, and fertile Imagination, enriched with great Variety of proper Ideas; . . . under the Direction of a regular Judgement, that takes care of the Choice of just and suitable Materials."[30]

Wit as Judgment

Judgment continued in an age of reason to be the faculty of sanity, source of stability and discretion. Its evidences were well known:

> They that observe . . . differences, and dissimilitudes; which is called Distinguishing, and Discerning, and Judging between thing and thing; in case, such discerning be not easie, are said to have a good Judgement; and particularly in matter of conversation and businesse; wherein, times, places, and persons, are to be discerned, this Vertue is called Discretion.[31]

Notice that judgment was considered particularly valuable in conversation and business. To Hobbes, discretion was a synonym of judgment and was the means of attaining "exact and perfect Knowledge."[32] John Locke's concept of judgment was similar—that faculty which separates "carefully, ideas wherein can be found the least difference," avoiding thereby "being misled by similitude and by affinity to take one thing for another."[33] He identified judgment with the process of discovering differences in things, as opposed to wit, which discovered similarities. Note should be taken of the fact that, whereas Hobbes had set judgment against fancy, Locke posed judgment against wit, arguing that the procedures of judgment are "quite contrary to metaphor and allusion, wherein for the most part lies that entertainment and pleasantry of wit." But the age was in general agreement on the nature of judgment:

> Judgment's the Act of Reason; that which brings
> Fit Thoughts to Thoughts, and argues Things from Things,
> True, Decent, Just, are in its Balance try'd,
> And thence we learned to Range, Compound, Divide.[34]

Because it had always meant intellect, wit had early been identified with judgment. With its particular properties, wit served to enhance the esteemed reason in a period proud of its rationalism. The rationalist Hobbes, excepting the realm of poetry, felt that "where Wit is wanting, it is not Fancy that is wanting, but Discretion. Judgement therefore without Fancy is Wit, but Fancy without Judgement not."[35]

A similar contemporary view, published fourteen years later, was expressed by the French writer of maxims, La Rochefoucauld: "It has been a mistake to believe that wit [*esprit*] and judgment are two different things. Judgment is only the greatness of the illumination of the wit, or mind [*esprit*]. This illumination penetrates the depth of things. It notices there everything that must be noticed and perceives those things which seem imperceptible. Thus it must be agreed that it is the extent of the illumination of wit which produces all the effects that are attributed to judgment."[36] La Rochefoucauld's conclusion, well known in England, was a stronger position than that taken by most rationalists, but it was an attractive point of view for the poet in an age of reason. Dominique Bouhours, a French critic popular in England, discussed the same point in 1671, arguing that wit [*bel esprit*] is inseparable from good sense, or judgment. John Dennis used Father Bouhours' views in his "Reflections on An Essay upon Criticism" (1711).[37]

Although the acceptance of wit as judgment had been debated

in earlier times, the identification became in the Age of Wit one of the most significant concepts and will be looked at more closely in connection with the truth of wit.

Wit as Imagination, including the Humor Theory of Wit

Third and finally, wit was identified with imagination. The synthesis of the traditions of wit and imagination not only influenced the meaning of wit but also affected the future speculations about imagination and helped to shape literary theory in the Age of Wit. The imagination was the faculty of ceaseless activity, continuing a stream of images even in sleep. It was the source of fanciful, allusive expression, hence of poetry itself. But those qualities which rendered it valuable in poetry seemed to render it valueless in the pursuit of "exact and perfect Knowledge," as Hobbes put it.

Imagination and fancy (the two terms had been synonymous since the sixteenth century) were not distinguishable during the Age of Wit, in fact were not clearly distinguished until William Duff's *Essay on Original Genius* in 1767. Although intimations of differences are perceptible earlier,[38] the terms were usually treated as identical. Pierre Charron, a French philosopher whose chief work was translated early in the century, saw them as one:

> The Fancy or Imaginative Faculty, first collects the several Images receiv'd by the Sences, forms Ideas out of them, and lays them up for use. This is done in so accurate and faithful a manner, that though the Objects themselves be far distant, nay, though the Man be asleep, and all his Senses lock'd up, yet this Faculty represents them to the Mind and Thoughts in Images so strong, so lively, that the Imagination does the very same to the Understanding now, which the Object it self did, by the first and freshest Impressions heretofore.[39]

Charron, the founder of modern secularism, was influenced by the theory that all individual knowledge comes through the five senses.

This view looks forward to the trustworthy imagination of the Romantic Era rather than back to the unstable imagination of the

Renaissance. The sixteenth century considered imagination as an "unformed Chaos without fashion without day,"[40] and viewed its evidences as "these slight flashes of underground fancy (ingenious Nothings & meere imbroideries upon cobwebbs) that the world swarmes with (like sophisticate alchimy gold that will not abide the first touch, yet glitters more in the eye than the sadd, weightyer, true gold)."[41]

The ancient distrust of imagination was intensified in the seventeenth century by the further charge of unreality. Sir Philip Sidney, praising the special powers of poetry, claimed that "Only the poet, . . . lifted up with the vigor of his own invention, doth grow in effect another nature, in making things either better than nature bringeth forth, or quite anew, forms such as never were in nature."[42] Thus, although Sidney would "balance the highest point of man's wit with the efficacy of nature," this invention of unnatural figures was cause for alarm among the rationalists of the years following. Bacon argued that imagination, working within poetry, "may at pleasure joyne that which Nature hath severed, & sever that which Nature hath joyned, and so make unlawfull Matches & divorses of things."[43] Distrust of such imaginative powers was strengthened considerably by Descartes' insistence in *Discours de la Methode* (1637) upon the exclusive use of reason.

This growing distrust would have relegated imagination to an inferior status had it not been for the rise of empirical psychology. The chief empiricists, Hobbes and Locke, viewed knowledge as "dealing with aggregates, as beginning with individuals and ending in universals" and thereby, perhaps inadvertently, elevating imagination to a new importance.[44] Hobbes, with the same respect that Pierre Charron had shown, described the particular contribution of imagination in handling sensory experience. Thoughts are

> . . . every one a Representation or Apparence, of some quality, or other Accident of a body without us; which is commonly called an Object. Which Object worketh on the Eyes, Eares, and other parts of mans body; and by diversity of working, produceth diversity of Apparences.

The Originall of them all, is that which we call SENSE; (For there is no conception in a mans mind, which hath not at first, totally, or by parts, been begotten upon the organs of Sense.) The rest are derived from that originall.

The "apparences," of which thoughts consist, can only exist in the mind through sensory experience and are retained in the fancy or imagination:

For after the object is removed, or the eye shut, we still retain an image of the thing seen though more obscure than when we see it. And this is it, the Latins call Imagination, from the image made in seeing; and apply the same, though improperly, to all the other senses. But the Greeks call it Fancy; which signifies apparance, and is as proper to one sense as to another. Imagination therefore is nothing but decaying sense; and is found in men, and many other living creatures, as well sleeping, as waking.[45]

Hobbes' term "decaying sense" has led some to conclude that he shared the bias of the age against the "vagaries of the imagination."[46] But granting the fact of decay, or diminution, the above passage certainly enhances its importance to the process of thought. And in the creative process, Hobbes considered imagination an equal partner with judgment.

Beyond creative expression, however, imagination did not fare well. Distrust and condemnation continued popularly for some time. An anonymous writer attributed the Earl of Rochester's fall from religious grace to his "Excess of Wit":

The Bubbling Froth that wanton Fancy rais'd
(Which for Extravagance was only Prais'd).[47]

One possible effect of such excess of fancy, such extravagance, was madness: "The more we are conducted by the heat of Phansie, the nearer we come to Extravagancy, which is a degree of Madness; such as is observed in those Rambling Wits."[48] Thus John Sheffield, the Earl of Mulgrave, could write:

As all is dullness when the Fancy's bad
So without Judgment, Fancy is but mad.[49]

This explanation of madness was well founded in classical philosophy.

In spite of traditional distrust of imagination, the faculty reached a position of greatest prestige by its association and identity with wit. The identification of wit with imagination was augmented by the changing concept of wit. In addition to its meaning as intellect and understanding, wit had acquired additional meaning through the mental adroitness exhibited in rhetorical display. Many of these acquisitions were qualities taken directly from Latin and used as synonyms for wit. One common synonym was ingenuity, that particular trait of "liveliness or Vivacity of the Mind inbred, or radicated in its Nature, which the Latines seem to insinuate by the word *Ingenium*."[50] The Italian and Spanish derivatives, *ingegno* and *ingenio* respectively, were also translated "wit"; so in this similarity, wit benefited from rhetorical dexterity.

Wit also gained richness from Latin *inventio* (invention), one of the five parts of rhetoric and closely related to ingenuity. The common relationship to rhetoric is evident here also, for invention was known as "the Mother of Poetry."[51] It was also believed that "superexcellent witt" is the "mother pearle of precious Invention, and the goulden mine of gorgeous Elocution."[52] "Wit" and "invention" were commonly interchanged in the seventeenth century.

Another characteristic, quickness of mind, became wit's most generally recognized trait. For Hobbes, this was a "Celerity of Imagining."[53] Robert Boyle referred to "a quickness, and neatness" in expressing ideas.[54] Others expressed the quality as "vivacity," and to Shakespeare's Polonius, it was "brevity," which was "the soul of wit." A correlative of quickness was its accompanying sudden illumination of thought. Sir Richard Blackmore in his listing—"Vivacity, Brightness and Celerity"[55]—included this important quality, as did Corbyn Morris, who wrote of "the Brilliancy of Wit, or . . . the sudden Light thrown upon a Subject."[56]

A logical extension of these meanings was the element of surprise expected in wit. Surprise was closely related to novelty,[57] but it had its own special significance. Both Walter Carleton and

Henry Barker recognized this element as distinctive.[58] Addison, in amending Locke's definition of wit in the *Spectator*, No. 62, added this characteristic along with delight:

> I shall only add . . . That every Resemblance of Ideas is not that which we call Wit, unless it be such an one that gives Delight and Surprize to the Reader: These two Properties seem essential to Wit, more particularly the last of them . . . it is necessary that the Ideas should not lie too near one another in the Nature of things; for where the Likeness is obvious, it gives no Surprize.

This can be best understood in the context of rhetorical similes, for good imagery must find not only what is alike in dissimilar objects or ideas but also what is distinct in similar objects or ideas. The traits of unexpectedness and surprise distinguished wit as entertainment. Barker's definition is to the point: "What we commonly call to have Wit, consists in nothing but a certain Turn of the Imagination, fantastical and singular, which the brisker and livelier it is the more it surprizes."[59]

These several characteristics, products of the capricious and spirited nature of wit, were also true of the imagination, and they alienated wit from judgment and reason, with the result that to many wit became identified with imagination. Hobbes perceived in his lifetime the trend toward more positive identification of wit and imagination in creative writing. He probably had the metaphysical conceit in mind when he wrote in 1651, "Those that observe similitudes, in case [they] be such as are but rarely observed by others, are sayd to have a Good Wit; by which, in this occasion, is meant a Good Fancy." However, Hobbes preferred his definition of the year before, which reiterated the traditional view that "NATURALL WITTE" (i.e. intelligence) consists of two elements: "Celerity of Imagining, (that is, swift succession of one thought to another); and *steddy* direction to some approved end,"[60] which implies a difference between wit used in poetry and natural wit, or intellect, that opposes dullness.

Most poets, playwrights, and other literati would not accept this distinction. The truth of poetry required intellect of its own kind, and their emphasis upon imagination affected its ascendance. Hobbes, in discussing poetics again in 1675, had to recognize the current usage, which gave to fancy "alone the name of Wit."[61]

Wit's identification with imagination served as the basis for an especially interesting concept—the humor theory of wit. The term humor was undergoing radical change during the last half of the seventeenth century, taking on new (and modern) meaning. However, the humor theory of wit arose out of the old physiological theories, involving the four ancient humors. The theory was seldom discussed in detail. Its evidence exists only implicitly in discussions of wit, no doubt because the old physiology was being discredited in the seventeenth century. The concept of the humors was retained as a semantic convenience in distinguishing personality and character types and in medical terminology, and it was only in this distinguishing of personality types that the humor theory of wit survived.

The most complete explication of this theory is found in Henry Barker's discussion of the polite gentleman. Admitting that the quality of wit is not easily defined, Barker determined to describe the evidences in "certain Characters," for he felt that all men of wit have in common "a certain Disposition of the Brain and the Animal Spirits, a sportive Imagination," which are "the secret Springs, and Wheels of the Machine."[62]

Barker felt the usual distrust of imagination, setting it apart from the complete process of reasoning: "the Mind, or rational Soul, is not concern'd in it [the sportive imagination]." He considered the imagination to be a more limited and more unreliable faculty than did Hobbes, for it had no direct contact with the external world. It is "a Perception of the Soul, not caus'd by an impression made upon the Body by the Action of exterior Objects, but by the Agitation of the interiour Fibres of the Brain, produc'd by the interiour Motion of the Animal Spirits." So, "this manner of thinking which we call Imagining, to speak properly, consists only in the interiour Application of the Mind, to the Descriptions of Images drawn or imprinted in our Brain by the Action of the Animal Spirits."

The humorous composition of the body determined each man's nature. In the case of those governed by wit (i.e. by imagination), "All the Beauty and Excellence of their Genius is only the pure effect of Chance, and of a certain Order of the Parts of the Machine," both of these being "the result of an accidental Mixture of different Humours amongst themselves, and of a sort of Animal Spirits, more or less fine or agitated." The animal spirits, incidentally, were a rarification of the vital spirits; they were processed in the brain and sent through the nerves into the organs of the body. These animal spirits acted as messengers between the brain and the organs and were hence the important link between the soul and the body.[63] The ideal man had a perfect balance and proportion of the humors: most of blood, then of phlegm, third of melancholy, and least of choler. In the infinite variety of physical consistency, Barker admitted that "some Constitutions of Body contribute equally to a sound Judgment, and ready Wit."

However, many men (Barker intimated that they are the rule rather than the exception) are subject to a prevalence of imagination and hence are "wits." The "accidental Mixture of different Humours" determines the kind of wit, and the "four sorts of Characters" which Barker described correspond in general characteristics to the four humors.

The first "Constitution" is the "Bilious." In this choleric temperament, "the Blood boils more . . . than in others, and circulates more nimbly," for it has "a very fine Blood, full of volatile Salt, from which are form'd the animal Spirits also very fine, and in continual motion." If such wits "observe a delicate Diet, breathe a sharp Air, and use a moderate Exercise, they enjoy a quickness of fancy, or an elegant wit." The bilious wit gains reputation by "sparkling and new Thoughts, tho' false, and by the lively Sentiments" that he excites in others.

The second kind of wit, not named by Barker but corresponding generally to the sanguine humor, shows "the Effect of a sulphureous inflamed Blood, whose particles are very proper to produce a great quantity of Animal Spirits," which are "not only easie and ready to take fire, but also keep it in much longer." The sanguine wit is marked first by a peculiar "sort of solid Discourse, well carried on and diversify'd, by a free and easie Pronounciation" and second by "great and wonderful Volubility and Fluentness, which seems to aim at Truth, tho' it goes astray every moment, and leads the Hearers into Error."

The third kind, "a nice and delicate Constitution," is characterized by "Fibres thin and fine, and the Animal Spirits very light," and "the Blood and Humours of an indifferent Consistence, because of the Fluidity of their Parts." This is nearest to the phlegmatic humor, the wit of which is superficial, turning on "a modish Word, and affected foppish Way of Talking that humours the Times." These wits "have not Strength enough of Mind to support them in a rational Discourse, and want both Vivacity and Penetration, but they please by I know not what kind of Air and affected Meen they use, and by a kind of unusual Language, call'd, the Language of the Beau Monde, that is to say, of certain Persons who have no other Title to be thought Delicate, Nice, and Polite, but because they are Effeminate."

The fourth kind of wit is distinguished by "a strange unevenness of Temper"; it has its "unlucky Melancholy Days," when its "Sprightliness" lacks its "wonted Heat and Lustre." In the humor theory, dullness is evidence of one kind of wit, rather than the antithesis of wit. A melancholic wit suffers from "some Moistness in the Brain which stifles and Quenches this Firestone Serosity which stops the Course of the Spirits." In addition, "the Liver, the Spleen and the other Viscera incessantly furnish Ferments which disorder the Mass of Blood a thousand different ways."

The melancholy humor, traditionally marked by greediness and obstinacy, contributed during the Renaissance to the creation of several kinds of a malcontent. Their ill nature was considered a disease caused by an excess of black bile. Melancholy was characterized physically by flatulence and mentally by misanthropy. The melancholy wit is described in the lines:

> Wit's a disease that fit employment wants;
> Therefore we see those happiest in best parts,
> And fortunes under-born unto their merits,
> Grow to a sullen envy, hate, and scorn

Of their superiors; and at last, like winds,
Break forth into rebellious civil wars
Or private treasons: none so apt for these
As melancholy wits, fetter'd with need.[64]

Both the humor and the disease enjoyed a special vogue in England during the Age of Wit. The prevalence of melancholy was explained by the special weakness which the English were thought to have: the malfunctioning of the spleen. Sir William Temple attributed this weakness to the climate, which caused a widespread malfunctioning.[65] The affinity of wit for melancholy is traceable to the belief that "in melancholy men, this faculty [of phantasy, or imagination] is most powerful and strong." Melancholy "often hurts, producing many monstrous and prodigious things, especially if it be stirred up by some terrible object, presented to it from common sense or memory."[66] Swift also makes the association in writing of the effect of strong imagination: "spleen, violent anger, fear, grief, pain, and the like."[67]

The implications of this humor theory may be found in many comments on the increasing ill humor (in the modern sense) of the Age of Wit. Archbishop Tillotson believed (Sermon XLII) that "the Wit of Man doth naturally vent itself in Satire and Censure, than to Praise and Panegyrick." Walter Carleton, in speaking of kinds of wits, mentioned especially the "Malignant" type, "this virulent Humour of disgracing the Merits of Others,"[68] for which he had his own physiological explanation:

> Wits of this evil temper may not unfitly be resembled to Chymical Spirits, which are subtle and penetrating, but they also corrode: and the Spirits by which they are actuated, seem to be extracted, not out of the purest parts of their Blood (as other Mens are) but from their Gall; as if they desired to verifie the new opinion of *Sylvius de la Boe,* that that bitter and acrimonious Excrement is the Natural Ferment of the Blood, and necessary to not only the Vital, but also the Animal actions, in all living Creatures, in which it is found.[69]

This malignancy is a "disease, therefore, of the Mind being almost Epidemick," caused by "a certain Perversity of disposition," the cure of which Carleton confesses is beyond his "Art."[70] The same type is described by Richard Flecknoe in his character writing "Of a bold abusive Wit."[71]

Opposition of Wit (Imagination) and Judgment

The identification of wit and imagination led to what has been called a "wall between wit and judgment."[72] The contention of wit and judgment was undoubtedly an old one,[73] being common in Elizabethan literature.[74] Distinctions between the two became clear-cut in the seventeenth century. Flecknoe described wit as "an exuberant thing, like Nilus, never more commendable than when it overflowes," and judgment as "a stayed and reposed thing, always containing it self within its bounds and limits."[75]

This "wall" appeared in John Locke's discussion of the faculties, but his substitution of wit for fancy (or imagination) was not without precedence. Locke's personal reasons may have stemmed from "the rather dry, rationistic temper of his mind" which led him to "disparage poetry, romances, and other works of fancy,"[76] but this was a conventional disparagement. However, his definitions were influential. It was his "common observation, that men who have a great deal of wit, and prompt memories, have not always the clearest judgment or deepest reason." The reason was that "wit lying most in the assemblage of ideas," puts those ideas "together with quickness and variety, wherein can be found any resemblance or congruity, thereby to make up pleasant pictures and agreeable visions in the fancy." On the other hand, judgment "lies quite on the other side, in separating carefully, one from another, ideas wherein can be found the least difference, thereby to avoid being misled by similitude and by affinity to take one thing for another." Judgment's way is "quite contrary to metaphor and allusion wherein for the most part lies that entertainment and pleasantry of wit, which strikes so lively on the fancy, and therefore is so acceptable to all people."[77]

Locke's definition of wit was widely debated in succeeding years. It was acceptable to some, Lewis Theobald for instance,[78] and was modified by others, notably Joseph Addison[79] and Corbyn Morris.[80] Locke transferred the traditional distrust of imagination to the new faculty of wit, placing wit in a subordinate position: "It is not in the power of the most exalted wit, or enlarged understanding, by any quickness or variety of thought, to invent or frame one new simple idea in the mind."[81] This position helped to crystalize for many the argument over the value and nature of wit.

As a faculty replacing imagination, wit had in a short time moved a long distance from meaning intellect. As the specific faculty of imagination, it was a source of creative thought to some, a recalcitrant faculty in need of discipline to others. Demands for control became more urgent as the excess of wit increased. The need for judgment was emphasized by Addison in the *Spectator,* No. 225. He speaks of "discretion," the distinctive function of judgment, as the controlling force for those natural excesses inherent in the minds of all men:

> I have often thought if the Minds of Men were laid open, we should see but little Difference between that of the Wise Man and that of the Fool. There are infinite Reveries, numberless Extravagancies, and a perpetual Train of Vanities which pass through both. The great Difference is, that, the first knows how to pick and cull his Thoughts for Conversation, by suppressing some, and communicating others; whereas the other lets them all indifferently fly out in Words. . . . There are many more shining Qualities in the Mind of Man, but there is none so useful as Discretion; it is this indeed which gives a Value to all the rest, which sets them at work in their proper Times and Places, and turns them to the Advantage of the Person who is Possessed of them. Without it Learning is Pedantry, and Wit Impertinence; Virtue it self looks like Weakness; the best Parts only qualifie a Man to be more sprightly in Errors, and active to his own Prejudice.

The attraction for "shining Qualities" which permits a man to be "more sprightly in Errors" posed a problem for most men of the age, for errors should not shine.

From the neoclassical point of view, these "shining Qualities" were products of the fancy and resulted from an irresponsible and undisciplined sense of craft. The neoclassical mind could not admit such irregularity. Bishop Sprat, in his life of Cowley, said that that poet's "Fancy flow'd with great speed, and therefore it was very fortunate to him that his Judgment was equal to manage it."[82] The third Earl of Shaftesbury was concerned in his little essay "Advice to an Author" with the problem of controlling "Fancys of all kinds," as he viewed this faculty. "They must have their Field. The Question is, Whether they shall have it wholly to themselves; or whether they shall acknowledg some Controuler or Manager." The contention with one's fancy was never-ending: "Either I work upon my Fancys, or They on Me. If I give Quarter, They won't. There can be no Truce, no suspension of Arms between us." He pointed out the dangers involved with an extravagant fancy: excess, abandon, derangement, even madness.[83]

During the seventeenth century, as the propensities of imagination were added to earlier qualities of wit—invention, quickness, and surprise—wit enjoyed a new popularity. Thomas Shadwell was disturbed particularly by the new vogue of extolling wit above all other faculties, especially judgment: "They speak as if judgment were a less thing than wit. But certainly it was meant otherwise by nature, who subjected wit to the government of judgment which is the noblest faculty of the mind. Fancy roughdraws, but judgment smooths and finishes; nay judgment does indeed comprehend wit, for no man can have that who has not wit."[84] Shadwell here found it natural to interchange the terms "wit" and "fancy." The enthusiasm for wit as a faculty bothered Blackmore, Dennis, and others.

The neoclassical principle of decorum was often proposed to placate those alarmed at the increasing importance of wit. Sir William Temple's essay on poetics, published in the same year as Locke's philosophical treatise, contains probably the best description of the balance of wit and judgment in the imaginative and creative process:

> Without the Forces of Wit all Poetry is flat and languishing; without the succors of Judgment 'tis wild and extravagant. The true

wonder of Poesy is, That such contraries must meet to compose it: A Genius both Penetrating and Solid; in Expression both Delicacy and Force; and the Frame or Fabrick of a true Poem must have something both Sublime and Just, Amazing and Agreeable. There must be a great Agitation of Mind to Invent, a great Calm to Judge and correct; there must be upon the same Tree, and at the same Time, both Flower and Fruit. To work up this Metal into exquisite Figure, there must be imploy'd the Fire, the Hammer, the Chizel, and the File.[85]

Charles Gildon, a minor critic, viewed the problem of decorum as the need for observing the rules in poetry. He stated in his *Complete Art of Poetry* (1718) that no matter how strong the imagination nor how fertile the ideas, "without the Assistance of Judgment (which can only be informed and directed by the Stated Rules) there can be nothing produc'd entirely beautiful." Otherwise, " 'tis all the rude Product of uncultivated wit."[86]

The control which judgment alone could exert over wit was described by Dr. Patrick Delany in the playful "News from Parnassus," in which Jonathan Swift is declared Apollo's vicegerent on earth. The scene is Parnassus, where all the poets are assembled,

> Conven'd by Apollo, who gave them to know
> He'd have a vicegerent in his Empire below;
> But declar'd that no Bard shou'd this honour inherit,
> 'Till the rest had agreed he surpass'd them in Merit.

Various poets then step forward each to present his qualifications, but one after another is turned down. For example, one hopeful poet,

> . . . low bending, Apollo thus greets,
> " 'Twas I taught your Subjects to walk thro' the Streets."

Apollo answers:

> You taught 'em to walk, why they knew it before,
> But give me the Bard that can teach them to soar;
> Whenever he claims his Right, I'll confess
> Who lately attempted my Style with Success;

Who writes like Apollo, has most of his Spirit,
And therefore 'tis just I distinguish his Merit;
Who makes it appear by all he has writ,
His Judgment alone can set Bounds to his Wit;

Now the one qualified poet is obvious; the final two lines:

This said, the whole Audience soon found out his Drift,
The Convention was summon'd in Favour of Sw[if]t.

Delaney, friend of Swift and Chancellor of St. Patrick's, was here complimenting a serious man of wit upon the soundness of his creativity.

This seriousness and soundness, the mark of the true wit, is reflected in the Preface to the *Tatler,* in which Richard Steele comments upon his intent in his journal:

> I really have acted in these cases with honesty, and am concerned it should be thought otherwise; for wit, if a man had it, unless it be directed to some useful end, is but a wanton frivolous quality; all that one should value himself upon in his kind is, that he had some honourable intention in it.

Another serious wit, Alexander Pope, recognized the dual functioning of wit and judgment. He assigned them their proper spheres, when in his "Essay" he designated wit as the dominant faculty in imaginative literature and judgment as the dominant faculty in critical literature: "Authors are partial to their wit, 'tis true,/ But are not critics to their judgment too?" (ll. 17–18) But this was not to dispute the proper balance between the two, for both were necessary. Wit, the driving force, must be guided and controlled by discerning judgment:

Some, to whom Heav'n in wit has been profuse,
Want as much more, to turn it to its use;
For wit and judgment often are at strife,
Though meant each other's aid, like man and wife.
'Tis more to guide, than spur the Muse's steed;
Restrain his fury, than provoke his speed;
The winged courser, like a gen'rous horse,
Shows most true mettle when you check his course.
(ll. 80–87)

Pope accepted, therefore, the prevailing opinion: the balance of wit and judgment.

THE PSYCHOLOGY OF WIT IN HENRY FIELDING'S *Tom Jones* AND IN LAURENCE STERNE'S *Tristram Shandy*

One new literary genre which appeared in England during the period of the Age of Wit was the modern novel. The space of time from its appearance in the fiction of Daniel Defoe to its masterful handling by Henry Fielding, Samuel Richardson, and Laurence Sterne was astonishingly brief. One can only conclude that the times were exactly ripe for the novel. Two of these early masters of the novel, Fielding and Sterne, theorized in their novels on the psychology of wit and related faculties, and each man's views affected the kind of novel he created.

Fielding, a versatile aristocrat and brilliant wit, actually carved out for himself three careers: his early and chosen career as a playwright ended with the Licensing Act of 1737; his second career began as he resumed his interrupted education for the bar, to become one of the best magistrates London had in the century; his third career as novelist grew quietly from the endeavors of his spare time, beginning with *Shamela* and *Joseph Andrews. The History of Tom Jones,* his masterpiece, was published in 1749.

Writing at the end of the Age of Wit, Fielding reacted against wit and fancy in his essays and asides in *Tom Jones.* He thought of fancy in its seventeenth century sense as "wanton and extravagant" (VIII, i). He referred in derogatory terms to certain young gentlemen who in the last age were called men of wit and pleasure about town (XIII, v). The introductory essay to Book IX contains a prominent discussion of genius:

> By genius I would understand that power, or rather those powers of the mind, which are capable of penetrating into all things within our reach and knowledge, and of distinguishing their essential differences. These are no other than invention and judgment; and they are both called by the collective name of genius, as they are of those gifts of nature which we bring with us into the world.
>
> (IX, i)

Invention he explains as "a creative faculty," "a quick and sagacious penetration into the true essence of all the objects of our contemplation." This process, he adds, can "rarely exist without the concomitancy of judgment." One can see by a comparison of these views with those of Thomas Hobbes (see page 88) that Fielding has replaced wit with genius and fancy with invention. He concludes the above passage by rejecting wit as an instrument for the discovery of truth. Yet he states in his dedication to George Lyttleton, "I have employed all the wit and humour of which I am master in the following history; wherein I have endeavoured to laugh mankind out of their favorite follies and vices." He continues, hereby, the objectives of the men of wit without that respect for wit which they had.

Fielding felt judgment to be the primary faculty in the creative process, and his techniques of narration reveal how carefully his judgment planned and executed the plot of *Tom Jones.* The structuring of action into three equal parts and the manipulation of characters into interrelated coincidences indicate an alert, careful, and logical judgment at work. Scrupulous attention to logical order is evident in the coincidences leading to the famous scene at the inn at Upton. After Tom's banishment from the household of Squire Allworthy, he wanders almost penniless, accompanied by Mr. Partridge, a schoolmaster who has happened onto Tom. Mr. Partridge, no more honorable than Falstaff and no braver, is the rumored father of Tom and in disgrace in Somersetshire. Tom comes upon a woman struggling with a soldier and rescues her, unaware that she is Jenny Jones of Somersetshire, rumored to be his mother. Distressed by her almost naked disarray and the signs of her desperate struggle, Tom hurries her to an inn for shelter, ignorant of the landlady's expressed zeal to run a house of exceedingly good repute and "to exclude all vulgar concubinage and to drive all whores in rags from within the walls" (IX, iii). After hurriedly securing a room, Tom asks for some clothes for Jenny Jones from the landlady, who quickly perceives that her establishment is in danger of scandal.

Jones had scarce ended his request, when she fell upon him with a certain weapon, which, though it be neither long, nor sharp, nor hard, nor indeed threatens from its appearance with either death or wound, hath been, however, held in great dread and abhorrence by many wise men—nay, by many brave ones; insomuch, that some who have not dared to look into a mouth where this weapon was brandished; and rather than run the hazard of its execution, have contented themselves with making a most pitiful and sneaking figure in the eyes of all their acquaintances.

To confess the truth, I am afraid Mr. Jones was one of these; for though he was attacked and violently belaboured with the aforesaid weapon, he could not be provoked to make any resistance; but in a most cowardly manner applied, with many entreaties, to his antagonist to desist from pursuing her blows; in plain English, he only begged her with the utmost earnestness to hear him; but before he could obtain his request, my landlord himself entered into the fray, and embraced that side of the cause which seemed to stand very little in need of assistance.

There are a sort of heroes who are supposed to be determined in their choosing or avoiding a conflict by the character and behaviour of the person whom they are to engage. These are said to know their men, and Jones, I believe, knew his woman; for though he had been so submissive to her, he was no sooner attacked by her husband, than he demonstrated an immediate spirit of resentment, and enjoined him silence under a very severe penalty; no less than that, I think, of being converted into fuel for his own fire.

The husband, with great indignation, but with a mixture of pity, answered, "You must pray first to be made able. I believe I am a better man than yourself; ay, every way, that I am"; and presently proceeded to discharge half a dozen whores at the lady abovestairs, the last of which had scarce issued from his lips when a swinging blow from the cudgel that Jones carried in his hand assaulted him over the shoulders.

It is a question whether the landlord or the landlady was the most expeditious in returning this blow. My landlord, whose hands were empty, fell to with his fist, and the good wife, uplifting her broom and aiming at the head of Jones, had probably put an immediate end to the fray, and to Jones likewise, had not the descent of this broom been prevented—not by the miraculous intervention of any heathen deity, but by a very natural though fortunate accident, viz., by the arrival of Partridge; who entered the house at that instant (for fear had caused him to run every step from the hill), and who, seeing the danger which threatened his master or companion (which you choose to call him), prevented so sad a catastrophe, by catching hold of the landlady's arm, as it was brandished aloft in the air.

The landlady soon perceived the impediment which prevented her blow; and being unable to rescue her arm from the hands of Partridge, she let fall the broom; and then leaving Jones to the discipline of her husband, she fell with the utmost fury on that poor fellow, who had already given some intimation of himself, by crying, "Zounds! do you intend to kill my friend?"

Partridge, though not much addicted to battle, would not, however, stand still when his friend was attacked; nor was he much displeased with that part of the combat which fell to his share; he therefore returned my landlady's blows as soon as he received them: and now the fight was obstinately maintained on all parts, and it seemed doubtful to which side Fortune would incline, when the naked lady, who had listened at the top of the stairs to the dialogue which preceded the engagement, descended suddenly from above, and without weighing the unfair inequality of two to one, fell upon the poor woman who was boxing with Partridge; nor did that great champion desist, but rather redoubled his fury, when he found fresh succours were arrived to his assistance.

Victory must now have fallen to the side of the travellers (for the bravest troops must yield to numbers) had not Susan the chambermaid come luckily to support her mistress. This Susan was as two-handed a wench (according to the phrase) as any in the country, and would, I believe, have beat the famed Thalestris herself, or any of her subject Amazons; for her form was robust and manlike, and every way made for such encounters. As her hands and arms were formed to give blows with great mischief to an enemy, so was her face as well contrived to receive blows without any great injury to herself, her nose being already flat to her face; her lips were so large, that no swelling could be perceived in them, and moreover they were so hard, that a fist could hardly make any impression on them. Lastly, her cheek-bones stood out, as if nature had intended them for two bastions to defend her eyes in those encounters for which she seemed so well calculated, and to which she was most wonderfully well inclined.

This fair creature entering the field of battle, immediately filed to that wing where her mistress maintained so unequal a fight with one of either sex. Here she presently challenged Partridge to single combat. He accepted the challenge, and a most desperate fight began between them.

Now the dogs of war being let loose, began to lick their bloody lips; now Victory, with golden wings, hung hovering in the air; now Fortune, taking her scales from her shelf, began to weigh the fates of Tom Jones, his female companion, and Partridge, against the landlord, his wife, and maid; all which hung in exact balance before her; when a good-natured accident put suddenly an end to the bloody fray, with which half of the combatants had already sufficiently feasted. This accident was the arrival of a coach and four; upon which my landlord and landlady immediately desisted from fighting, and at their entreaty obtained the same favour of their antagonists: but Susan was not so kind to Partridge; for that Amazonian fair having overthrown and bestrid her enemy, was now cuffing him lustily with both her hands without any regard to his request of a cessation of arms, or to those loud exclamations of murder which he roared forth.

No sooner, however, had Jones quitted the landlord, than he flew to the rescue of his defeated companion, from whom he with much difficulty drew off the enraged chambermaid: but Partridge was not immediately sensible of his deliverance, for he still lay flat on the floor, guarding his face with his hands; nor did he cease roaring till Jones had forced him to look up, and to perceive that the battle was at an end. (IX, iii).

This scene, in fact the whole interlude at Upton, coming at the exact center of the plot and serving as a comic relief in the middle third of the novel, presents tangible evidence of the balance and control characteristics of judgment. Furthermore, the complications in this one scene proceed logically as the combatants enter the fray. Action rises from the initial encounter of Tom with the incensed landlady to the participation, one by one, of all protagonists and antagonists until, at the height of battle, a neat pairing accounts for every character: Tom with the landlord, Jenny with the landlady, and Partridge with the chambermaid. Then the action falls off to the final struggles of the terrified Partridge flat on the floor beneath the overpowering Susan.

Again, Fielding relates his writing to the most respected traditional form—the epic, in itself a manifestation of the achievement of classic judgment—though like Dryden, Garth, Pope, and the rest of the wits, he plays with the tradition and satirizes the conventions. Concerning one of the conventions, he writes, "Lord Shaftesbury observes that nothing is more cold than the invocation of a Muse by a modern; he might have added, that nothing can be more absurd. A modern may with more elegance invoke . . . a mug of ale, with the author of *Hudibras*" (VIII, i).

The heroic action is enhanced by the accouterments of

epic struggle—all in satire mockery. The initial antagonist is a woman; the weapons are first a broom and then a cudgel; the fatal descent of the broom upon poor Tom is interrupted "not by the miraculous intervention of any heathen deity," but by Partridge, an unseemly substitute; Fortune delayed her decision at the height of battle in a vivid passage of epic metaphor: "Now the dogs of war being let loose, began to lick their bloody lips; now Victory, with golden wings, hung hovering in the air; now Fortune, taking her scales from her shelf, began to weigh the fates" for one side against the other. So the destiny of human kind is judged in classic fashion. The age recognized the wit in this mockery for what it was—the very skillful ordering of material by Fielding's own judgment.

Laurence Sterne, quite unlike Fielding, was in his youth one of the young men of wit and pleasure about town; and in spite of being a curate, he was a member of the rollicking group of blades known as the "Demoniacks." He took great pleasure in jesting and from this stumbled onto his true ability, satire. He attempted a satire in the manner of Jonathan Swift, which was directed at a personality in the diocese and for that reason suppressed. He rewrote a more generalized version of it for public reading and in 1759 published two volumes of *The Life and Opinions of Tristram Shandy, Gentleman.* Seven other volumes appeared before Sterne's death in 1768.

From the first moment of its appearance, *Tristram Shandy* was a controversial success, stimulating a cult of "Shandyism" on the one hand and a wave of epithets on the other. In contrast with *Tom Jones, Tristram Shandy* does not move steadily to a point of denouement; on the contrary, it gets practically nowhere very slowly—it could have gone on indefinitely. Instead of being carefully planned in coincidences, it wanders with the whimsy of thoughts. The author credits "the great Locke" with the basic principle of his illogical progression: associated sensations leading to associated ideas of sensations, ad infinitum.

Theoretically, Sterne followed the standard neoclassical position of Dryden, Pope, and Swift in supporting "the proper balance" between wit (fancy) and judgment. In the execution of his art, however, one sees the same discrepancy between theory and practice which is found in most neoclassical productions. In this instance, it is the difference between his theory of the relationship of judgment and wit and his practice in putting them to work. His fullest discussion occurs in the "Author's Preface" (which he placed in the middle of Chapter 20 of Book III). Through his fictitious narrator Tristram Shandy, he compares the two faculties with the two knobs on the back of a cane chair, "the highest and most ornamental parts of its frame—as wit and judgment are of ours; they answer one another."

However, in practice Sterne's very manner of description betrays his personal sympathy. His style in characterizing wit imitates his own style in *Tristram:*

> Bless us!—what noble work we should make!—how should I tickle it off!—and what spirits should I find myself in, to be writing away for such readers!—and you—just heaven!—with what raptures would you sit and read—but oh!—'tis too much—I am sick—I faint away deliciously at the thoughts of it—'tis more than nature can bear!—lay hold of me—I am giddy—I am stone blind—I'm dying—I am gone.—Help! Help! Help!—But hold—I grow something better again, for I am beginning to foresee, when this is over, that as we shall all of us continue to be great wits—we should never agree amongst ourselves, one day to an end:—there would be so much satire and sarcasm—scoffing and flouting, with rallying and reparteeing of it—thrusting and parrying in one corner or another—there would be nothing but mischief among us—Chaste stars! what biting and scratching, and what a racket and a clatter we should make, what with breaking of heads, rapping of knuckles, and hitting of sore places—there would be no such thing as living for us. (III, 20)

This is obviously ironic jesting at the spirit he loved most. He says elsewhere (IX, 12) that "Fancy is capricious—Wit must not be searched for." He permits his ideas to flow out of his imagination, ostensibly governed only by the logic of association. This does not mean that there is no method in his madness, however, for Sterne never completely surrenders the control of judgment. The digressive or the far-fetched tack always turns back to the central motive—the life and opinions of Tristram himself. However, this control is not readily apparent. One's first impression is of fancy run mad.

The early books of the novel develop the complications incident to the birth of the hero: the disturbance at the very moment of his conception on the first Monday of March, 1718; the arguments over the place of Mrs. Shandy's lying-in; the disagreements over whether to use a London doctor or a country male-midwife (Dr. Slop). Then there are the misfortunes incident to Tristram's birth: the bungling by Dr. Slop, the injury to the baby's nose, and the catastrophe of misnaming the new-born.

The events of the night of birth are presented largely through conversation—that of Mr. Shandy and Uncle Toby, two kind gentlemen, who discuss interminably any conceivable subject, guided by the pedantry of the former and the simple, one-track mind of the latter. When it is reported from the birth-room upstairs that during labor the forceps have smashed the baby's nose, Mr. Shandy begins looking up all references to noses in his library to judge the portent of this disastrous happening. He soon finds a brief classical treatment of noses, which he analyzes for Uncle Toby:

> "*Nihil me paenitet hujus nasi,*" quoth Pamphagus;— that is—"My nose has been the making of me."—"*Nec est cur paeniteat,*" replies Cocles; that is, "How the deuce should such a nose fail?"
>
> The doctrine, you see [the narrator interposes], was laid down by Erasmus, as my father wished it, with the utmost plainness; but my father's disappointment was, in finding nothing more from so able a pen, but the bare fact itself; without any of that speculative subtlety or ambidexterity of argumentation upon it, which Heaven had bestowed upon man on purpose to investigate truth, and fight for her on all sides.—My father pished and pughed at first most terribly —'tis worth something to have a good name. As the dialogue was of Erasmus, my father soon came to himself, and read it over and over again with great application, studying every word and every syllable of it thro' and thro' in its most strict and literal interpretation—he could still make nothing of it, that way. Mayhap there is more meant, than is said in it, quoth my father.—Learned men, brother Toby, don't write dialogues upon long noses for nothing.—I'll study the mystic and the allegoric sense—here is some room to turn a man's self in, brother.

My father read on.—

Now I find it needful to inform your reverences and worships [Sterne's readers], that besides the many nautical uses of long noses enumerated by Erasmus, the dialogist affirmeth that a long nose is not without its domestic conveniences also; for that in a case of distress—and for want of a pair of bellows, it will do excellently well, *ad excitandum focum* (to stir up the fire).

Nature had been prodigal in her gifts to my father beyond measure, and had sown the seeds of verbal criticism as deep within him as she had done the seeds of all other knowledge—so that he got out his penknife, and was trying experiments upon the sentences, to see if he could not scratch some better sense into it.—I've got within a single letter, brother Toby, cried my father, of Erasmus his mystic meaning.—You are near enough, brother, replied my uncle, in all conscience.—Pshaw! cried my father, scratching on—I might as well be seven miles off.—I've done it—said my father, snapping his fingers—See, my dear brother Toby, how I have mended the sense. —But you have marred a word, replied my uncle Toby.—My father put on his spectacles—bit his lip—and tore out the leaf in a passion.

This brief passage (III, 37) ridicules pleasantly Mr. Shandy's outmoded scholastic, authoritarian approach to truth, the import of which is so neatly punctured by Toby's simple observation.[87] The method of narration, pursing logically a conversation, together with the comments conventionally interjected by the fictitious narrator Tristram, differs very little from the technique in *Tom Jones*. But this straight line of narrative is not maintained for long.

A more extensive passage, which illustrates the indirect path determined by the association of ideas and conversation, describes Shandy's desire to name his child Trismegistus and the subsequent miscarriage of his dearest wish:

CHAPTER 11 We shall bring all things to rights, said my father, setting his foot upon the first step from the landing.—This Trismegistus, continued my father, drawing his leg back and turning to my uncle Toby—was the greatest (Toby) of all earthly beings—he was the greatest king—the greatest law-giver—the greatest philosopher—and the greatest priest—and engineer—said my uncle Toby.

—In course, said my father.

CHAPTER 12 —And how does your mistress? cried my father, taking the same step over again from the landing, and calling to Susannah, whom he saw passing by the foot of the stairs with a huge pincushion in her hand—how does your mistress? As well, said Susannah, tripping by, but without looking up, as can be expected.—What a fool am I! said my father, drawing his leg back again—let things be as they will, brother Toby, 'tis ever the precise answer—And how is the child, pray?—No answer. And where is Dr. Slop? added my father, raising his voice aloud, and looking over the ballusters—Susannah was out of hearing.

Of all the riddles of a married life, said my father, crossing the landing in order to set his back against the wall, whilst he propounded it to my uncle Toby—of all the puzzling riddles, said he, in a marriage state,—of which you may trust me, brother Toby, there are more asses' loads than all Job's stock of asses could have carried—there is not one that has more intricacies in it than this—that from the very moment the mistress of the house is brought to bed, every female in it, from my lady's gentlewoman down to the cinder-wench, becomes an inch taller for it; and give themselves more airs upon that single inch, than all the other inches put together.

I think rather, replied my uncle Toby, that 'tis we who sink an inch lower.—If I meet but a woman with child—I do it.—'Tis a heavy tax upon that half of our fellow-creatures, brother Shandy, said my uncle Toby—'Tis a piteous burden upon 'em, continued he, shaking his head—Yes, yes, 'tis a painful thing—said my father, shaking his head too—but certainly since shaking of heads came into fashion, never did two heads shake together, in concert, from two such different springs.

God bless
Deuce take } 'em all—said my uncle Toby and my father, each to himself.

CHAPTER 13 —Holla!—you, chairman!—here's sixpence—do step into that bookseller's shop, and call me a day-tall critic. I am very willing to give any one of 'em a crown to help me with his tackling, to get my father and my uncle Toby off the stairs, and to put them to bed.

—'Tis even high time; for except a short nap, which they both got whilst Trim was boring the jack-boots—and which, by the bye, did my father no sort of good, upon the score of the bad hinge—they have not else shut their eyes, since nine hours before the time that Dr. Slop was led into the back parlour in that dirty pickle by Obadiah.

Was every day of my life to be as busy a day as this—and to take up—Truce.

I will not finish that sentence till I have made an observation upon the strange state of affairs between the reader and myself, just as things stand at present—an observation never applicable before to any one biographical writer since the creation of the world, but to myself—and I believe, will never hold good to any other, until its final destruction—and therefore, for the very novelty of it alone, it must be worth your worships attending to.

I am this month one whole year older than I was this time twelvemonth; and having got, as you perceive, almost into the middle of my fourth volume—and no farther than to my first day's life—'tis demonstrative that I have three hundred and sixty-four days more life to write just now, than when I first set out; so that instead of advancing, as a common writer, in my work with what I have been doing at it—on the contrary, I am just thrown so many volumes back—was every day of my life to be as busy a day as this—And why not?—and the transactions and opinions of it to take up as much description—And for what reason should they be cut short? as at this rate I should just live 364 times faster than I should write—It must follow, an' please your worships, that the more I write, the more I shall have to write—and consequently, the more your worships will have to read.

Will this be good for your worships' eyes?

It will do well for mine; and, was it not that my Opinions will be the death of me, I perceive I shall lead a fine life of it out of this self-same life of mine; or, in other words, shall lead a couple of fine lives together.

As for the proposal of twelve volumes a year, or a volume a month, it no way alters my prospect—write as I will, and rush as I may into the middle of things, as Horace advises—I shall never overtake myself whipped and driven to the last pinch; at the worst I shall have one day the start of my pen—and one day is enough for two volumes—and two volumes will be enough for one year.—

Heaven prosper the manufacturers of paper under the propitious reign, which is now opened to us—as I trust its providence will prosper every thing else in it that is taken in hand.—

As for the propagation of Geese—I give myself no concern—Nature is all bountiful—I shall never want tools to work with.

—So then, friend! you have got my father and my uncle Toby off the stairs, and seen them to bed?—And how did you manage it?—You dropped a curtain at the stair-foot—I thought you had no other way for it—Here's a crown for your trouble.

CHAPTER 14 —Then reach me my breeches off the chair, said my father to Susannah.—There is not a moment's time to dress you, Sir, cried Susannah—the child is as black in the face as my—as your what? said my father, for like all orators, he was a dear searcher into comparisons.—Bless me, Sir, said Susannah, the child's in a fit.—And where's Mr. Yorick?—Never where he should be, said Susannah, but his curate's in the dressing-room, with the child upon his arm, waiting for the name—and my mistress bid me run as fast as I could to know, as Captain Shandy is the godfather, whether it should not be called after him.

Were one sure, said my father to himself, scratching his eyebrow, that the child was expiring, one might as well compliment my brother Toby as not—and it would be a pity, in such a case, to throw away so great a name as Trismegistus upon him—but he may recover.

No, no,—said my father to Susannah, I'll get up—There is no time, cried Susannah, the child's as black as my shoe. Trismegistus, said my father—But stay—thou are a leaky vessel, Susannah, added my father; canst thou carry Trismegistus in thy head, the length of the gallery without scattering?—Can I? cried Susannah, shutting the door in a huff.—If she can, I'll be shot, said my father, bouncing out of bed in the dark, and groping for his breeches.

Susannah ran with all speed along the gallery.

My father made all possible speed to find his breeches.

Susannah got the start, and kept it—'Tis Tris—something, cried Susannah—There is no christian-name in the world, said the curate, beginning with Tris—but Tristram. Then 'tis Tristram-gistus, quoth Susannah.

—There is no gistus to it, noddle!—'tis my own name, replied the curate, dipping his hand, as he spoke, into the bason—Tristram! said he, etc. etc. etc. etc., so Tristram was I called, and Tristram shall I be to the day of my death.

My father followed Susannah, with his night-gown across his arm, with nothing more than his breeches on, fastened through haste with but a single button, and that button through haste thrust only half into the button-hole.

—She has not forgot the name? cried my father, half opening the door.—No, no, said the curate, with a tone of intelligence.—And the child is better, cried Susannah.—And how does your mistress? As well, said Susannah, as can be expected.—Pish! said my father, the button of his breeches slipping out of the button-hole—So that whether the interjection was levelled at Susannah, or the button-hole—whether Pish was an interjection of contempt or an interjection of modesty, is a doubt, and must be a doubt till I shall have time to write the three following favourite chapters, that is, my chapter of chamber-maids, my chapter of pishes, and my chapter of button-holes.

> All the light I am able to give the reader at present is this, that the moment my father cried Pish! he whisked himself about—and with his breeches held up by one hand, and his night-gown thrown across the arm of the other, he turned along the gallery to bed, something slower than he came.

Mr. Shandy does not yet know that his son has been misnamed and does not find out for two more chapters.

Sterne did not search for his wit; it simply tumbled out of his mind as one association led to another. He states early in *Tristram* (I, 14), "Could a historiographer drive on his history, as a muleteer drives on his mule,—straight forward;—for instance, from Rome all the way to Loretto, without ever once turning his head aside either to the right hand or to the left,—he might venture to foretell you to an hour when he should get to his journey's end:—but the thing is, morally speaking, impossible." Sterne, in all honesty, was presenting life just as accurately as was Fielding. Both were basically moral and serious. To Stern life was confusing and ambiguous, as meandering as a leisurely journey through the countryside or as willy-nilly as the thoughts running through a man's head. An apparently chaotic, fanciful novel hides his gravity. He explained later in *Tristram* (VI, 17) that he wrote one-half full and one-half fasting, "so that betwixt both, I write a careless kind of a civil, nonsensical, good-humoured Shandean book, which will do all your hearts good—and your head too,—provided you understand it." In the psychology of wit, the imaginative aspects of his technique did place in question the understanding of his aim, a difficulty which Fielding's novel did not present.

Summary

Wit became the key word in psychology as well as in rhetoric. Drawing upon old conjectures in faculty psychology, in which wit had already been allied with both judgment and imagination, controversy during the seventeenth century attempted fine distinctions, especially among the creative processes of the mind.

Various combinations of the two chief faculties were debated in an effort to define the most reliable kind of intellectual activity. Three distinct views emerged: wit as intelligence consisted of a balance of judgment and imagination; wit became identified with judgment as the faculty of reasoning; and finally wit, once synonymous with imagination, replaced it as the faculty which supplied spirit to the mind, in need of control by the judgment.

In this speculation, as in the arguments over rhetorical techniques, wit took on a Januslike duality. Just as wit was argued to be both true rhetoric and false rhetoric, so wit was argued to be both reason and inspiration, control and poetic license. From this polarity arose two unique concepts in the Age of Wit. One was the concept of wit as propriety and hence truth—based upon its close association with intelligence and judgment. The other was the concept of wit as sublimity and graceful writing—based upon its identification with imagination. And these concepts led wit in opposite directions, each culminating in a new prestige.

"True wit is inseparable from good sense, and it is a mistake to confuse it with just any vivacity which has nothing solid. Judgment is, as it were, the essence of the beauty of the mind, or rather wit is of the nature of those precious stones which do not have less solidity than brilliance. There is nothing more beautiful than a well-polished and very clear diamond; it scintillates on all sides and in all its parts. . . . It is a solid substance which shines; it is a brilliant thing which has stability and body."[1]

—DOMINIQUE BOUHOURS, *Les Entretiens d'Ariste et d'Eugene* (1671)

4
The Truth of Wit

DECORUM in expression meant the appropriate wording of truth, and truth was understood to be the expression of nature. It might seem, in view of the open conflict between wit and judgment, that wit could not satisfactorily express the truth, for judgment alone was traditionally the "act of reason" and thereby the means to understanding and wisdom. Yet with few exceptions the great literary minds of the age considered wit as a medium of decorum.[2] Dryden's definition of wit as propriety was widely accepted. John Sheffield followed Dryden with the lines:

'Tis the top of wit
T' express agreeably a thing that's fit.[3]

Robert Wolseley remarked that wit is "a true and lively expression of nature," the very essence of which is propriety.[4] Pope's couplet in "An Essay on Criticism" has probably been remembered best:

True wit is nature to advantage dress'd,
What oft was thought, but n'er so well express'd.

This interpretation of wit, with its implications of the rational perception of truth, was one of the motivating ideas of the age. In such context, the word wit was also identified with nature, with the image of light as it illuminated ignorance and pretense, and with correct style. Conversely, the impropriety of unbounded wit gave additional meaning to false wit in the sense of excessive ornamentation. However, the theoretical basis for the truth of wit lay in the speculations on the relationship of wit and judgment.

The Psychology of Decorum

Decorum, the observance of neoclassical proprieties, required the use of reason. As wit became the most desirable attribute in written and spoken English, its psychological affinity elevated it to the status of a faculty of the mind. But which faculty? Various interpretations of wit which relate to decorum have been clarified in the preceding chapter: wit as intellect or understanding, wit as both judgment and imagination, wit as judgment itself. A common opinion held with wit as an essential part of judgment or with judgment as an essential part of wit, either view adhering to wit as intellect. Father Dominique Bouhours, arguing that wit and judgment were inseparable, stated this general view: wit is "a shining Solid, like a Diamond, which the more solid it is, is always the more glittering."[5]

The chief contention centered upon wit as the imaginative faculty. As such, it was acceptable to decorum only as it became a submissive partner to judgment, the rational faculty. Defenders of judgment always objected to the elevation of wit above, or even equal to, the reasoning faculty. Two famous arguments illustrate this controversy.

One argument occurred between John Dryden and Thomas Shadwell over the proportions of wit (imagination) and judgment in the comedies of Ben Jonson. Though Dryden always valued both faculties, his opinion of their relative importance changed through the years. He wrote in 1664 that "imagination in a poet is a faculty so wild and lawless, that like an high-ranging spaniel, it must have clogs tied to it, lest it out-run the judgment."[6] Nevertheless, he was intrigued, along with the rest of his age, with the qualities of the imagination—the flight of fancy, the sudden comparison, the flash of recognition—all of which delighted the reader of poetry. "Wit in the poet," he wrote in 1666, "is no other than the faculty of imagination in the writer, which, like a nimble spaniel, beats over and ranges thro' the field of memory, till it springs the quarry it hunted after."[7] The "high-ranging spaniel" of the earlier passage has now become the "nimble spaniel." The animal who needed the curb now is endowed with superior (poetic) power. Wit no longer relies on materials selected from the memory by the judgment; it makes the selection itself.

Soon after the onset of the influence of Longinus upon Dryden and his increased respect for imagination, he became involved in his notable argument with Shadwell. In his Preface to *An Evening's Love* (1671) he argued that the composition of a play turns on the use of fancy, the chief quality required of the poet. He analyzed Jonson's abilities and shortcomings as a writer of comedy: "To make men appear pleasantly ridiculous on the stage, was, as I have said, Jonson's talent; and in this he needed not the acumen of wit but that of judgment." His implied criticism of reliance primarily upon judgment became clear when he next explained: "I would have more of *urbana, venusta, salsa, faceta,* and the rest which Quintilian reckons up as the ornaments of wit; and these are extremely wanting in Ben Jonson."[8]

Shadwell answered Dryden in the same year, in the Preface to *The Humorists,* upholding Jonson's humor as a product of judgment. He felt that both humor and judgment were superior to wit in Jonson's comedy:

> Nor can I think, to the writing of his humours . . . that wit was not required, but judgment; where by the way, they speak as if judgment were a less thing than wit. But certainly it was meant otherwise by nature, who subjected wit to the government of judgment, which is the noblest faculty of the mind. Fancy rough-draws, but judgment smooths and finishes; nay judgment does indeed comprehend wit, for no man can have that who has not wit.

The last two sentences clearly paraphrase Hobbes' views.

The argument continued over a period of many months,[9] but it was some years before Dryden's elevation of wit above judgment was modified. His espousal of wit as imagination and secret grace are discussed in the next chapter. He did arrive at the neoclassical position of balance in his famous statement of 1685: "Propriety of thoughts is that fancy which arises naturally from the subject, or which the poet adapts to it. Propriety of words is the clothing of those thoughts with such expressions as are naturally proper to them; and from both these, if they are judiciously performed, the delight of poetry results."[10] The significance of these comments lies in the elevation of wit, now the product of fancy, in appropriate rhetorical expression "judiciously performed," by which Dryden meant constrained by the judgment. The definition stands as one logical balance between the forces of wit and those of reason.

Years later, John Dennis, who agreed in general with Shadwell, criticized Alexander Pope, whose position resembled Dryden's. The occasion was the publication of Pope's "An Essay on Criticism," which, in the first edition, included the couplet:

> For Wit and Judgment ever are at strife,
> Tho' meant each others, are like Man and Wife.
> (ll. 82–83)

Dennis commented, "Now cannot I for my Soul conceive the reciprocal Aid that there is between Wit and Judgment. For tho' I can easily conceive how Judgment may keep Wit in her Senses, yet cannot I possibly understand how Wit can control, or redress, or be a help to Judgment."[11] Dennis could not comprehend "how any one can have store of Wit without Judgment." He recalled Bouhours' comment on the identity of wit and judgment, concluding, "Now how any thing in the Works of the Mind can be solid without Judgment, I leave to Mr. Bays [Pope] to consider." Pope altered his wording but not his meaning in subsequent editions.

No matter how troublesome the relationship of wit and judgment, preponderant neoclassical opinion insisted upon the supremacy of a control by judgment. The majority agreed with Dryden and Pope, who viewed both faculties as separate but important elements in proper writing. Thus allied with judgment, wit qualified as a vehicle of truth and of decorum.

Wit as Decorum in Style

Wit, the facility of expressing ideas deftly and effectively, became a valuable asset in what has been called the Augustan cult of "correctness,"[12] which promoted the search for *le mot juste.* As the right word in the right place, wit functioned, as John Sheffield wrote in his "An Essay upon Poetry" (1682), "t' express agreeably a thing that's fit." Dryden's definition of propriety of words and thoughts drew upon the rhetorical distinction between *figurae verborum* and *figurae sententiae.* He attributed this definition in his Preface to *Sylvae* (1685) to his study of Virgil. However, the influence of Longinus is quite evident. Dryden explained the adornment of sublime subjects with the most sublime figurative expressions, which included the five Longinian sources of elevated language. In his Preface to *Albion and Albanius* (1685) he explained propriety of thought as "that fancy which arises naturally from the subject, or which the poet adapts to it" and propriety of words as "the clothing of those thoughts with such expressions as are naturally proper to them," both "judiciously performed."

Dryden's view expressed for many the requisites for decorum. Hobbes echoed the position.[13] Sheffield pleased Dryden by borrowing immediately the phrasing in a passage in "An Essay upon Poetry," in which he was writing of the poetry of the Earl of Rochester:

> So Songs should be to just perfection wrought;
> Yet where can we see one without a fault,
> Exact propriety of words and thought?
> Th' expression easy, and the fancy high,
> Yet that not seem to creep, nor this to fly;
> No words transpos'd, but in such just cadance,
> As, though hard wrought, may seem the effect of chance.

Pope's early definition paraphrased it: "a justness of thought, and a facility of expression." He later restated the view metaphorically: "in the midwives' phrase, a perfect conception, with an easy delivery."[14]

Dryden's definition ultimately received adverse criticism. As the Age of Wit moved into the eighteenth century, the general rejection by Augustan critics of wordplay as wit made his balance unacceptable. Addison, for example, felt that the definition was "not so properly a Definition of Wit, as of good Writing in general." He argued (*Spectator*, No. 62) that if it defined true wit, then "Euclid was the greatest Wit that ever set pen to paper." He felt that mere wit of words was not true but false wit.

Dryden's definition also held a psychological weakness. Addison charged that wit was more than decorum in style, for one essential element was surprise. Corbyn Morris agreed in general with Addison on this element, which he likened to the brilliance of "sudden Light thrown upon a Subject." Morris further pointed out that Dryden described a process of reasoning, whereas wit makes no "Pretension to Reasoning."[15] These various criticisms make it clear that no view of wit, no matter how popular, could long exist without opposition. Not only the speculative but also the subjective nature of all this critical controversy is extraordinary.

Definitive consideration of decorous, balanced writing was a hazardous task, because no style was acceptable without the proper amount of that "noblest faculty of the mind," judgment, and yet manifestations of its influence were always subtle and debatable. All writing exhibited some evidences of rhetorical wit. Some either flouted any apparent control or defied any analysis by rule. The line of balance between control and license, between judgment and wit in style, was thin indeed, granting that it actually existed. Judging from the changing views of most men of wit on the appropriate relationship of wit and judgment, one may conclude that such a line could exist only in theory and never in practice.

The metaphor of the thin line of balance indicates the cause for the various arguments and explains changes of opinion. The principles of this balance were most easily defined in abstract terms. Dryden's requirement that propriety of thoughts and words must be "judiciously performed" posed a subjective criterion. Dennis described decorous style as "a just mixture of Reason and Extravagance," again a subjective measurement fearfully difficult in distinguishing the decorous from the indecorous. Extravagance, like wit, was a chameleon, its quality changing with every new context.

The effects of this subjectivity appear in the changing relationships of wit and judgment within the arguments of one person. The shifting opinions of Hobbes have been examined.[16] Dryden described very early the nature of wit at the expense of judgment. Under the influence of Longinus, he praised the secret grace of wit as its more distinctive element. Later, checking his own extravagance, he retreated across the thin line, and elevated judgment above fancy (wit). He wrote in his Dedication to the *Aeneis* (1697), "Whereas poems which are produced by the vigour of imagination only have a gloss upon them at the first which time wears off, the works of judgment are like the diamond; the more they are polished, the more lustre they receive." Again the solid diamond of Bouhours replaces the ephemeral sublimity of Longinus.

Another effect of subjectivity was the inconsistency into which a critic fell in spontaneous polemics. John Dennis usually supported a balance between imagination and judgment in true wit —with control by judgment. However, on one occasion he quoted the 474th Maxim of La Rochefoucauld, "*Il n'y a point de Sots si Incommodes que ceux qui ont de l'Esprit,*" to the effect that no fools are as troublesome as those who have wit, admitting for the moment the quality of wit in a fool.[17]

The quality of wit was indeed elusive in its connotations of excess and surprise. No middle stand was easy when exaggerated claims were put forth for it, especially when its devotees placed it above or equal to judgment. The protectors of neoclassicism argued *ad hominem,* adopting a particular point of view to suit the moment, which either met their opposition head-on or placed it at a disadvantage. The contentious spirit of the age encouraged this wavering.

Indecorum of Excessive Ornamentation

The principle of propriety ruled out not only extravagant fancy but excessive ornamentation. There is little wonder that Richard Flecknoe shocked many of his contemporaries by audaciously defining wit as "an exuberant thing, like Nilus, never more commendable than when it over-flowes."[18] To this the majority replied that to overflow in wit is to display no wit at all. Such overflowing became a kind of false wit violating decorum.

Sheffield used a new phrase when he condemned this excessiveness:

> That silly thing men call sheer Wit avoid,
> With which our Age so nauseously is cloy'd.[19]

John Dennis clarified for his readers this "sheer Wit," using the occasion of the publication of Pope's "An Essay on Criticism" to take the author to task. He took exception to the following four lines from the "Essay":

> What is this Wit that does our Cares employ,
> The Owner's Wife that other Men enjoy?
> The More his Trouble as the more admired,
> Where wanted scorn'd, and envy'd where acquir'd.
> (ll. 500–503)

The implication of acquired wit was unacceptable. "If he means Genius," wrote Dennis, "that is certainly never to be acquir'd: and the Person who should pretend to acquire it, would be always secure from Envy. But if by Wit he means Conceit and Point, those are things that ought never to be in Poetry, unless by chance sometimes in the Epigram, or in Comedy, where it is proper to the Character and the Occasion."[20] Dennis then quoted Sheffield's lines, equating sheer wit with conceit and point, two of the outmoded types of rhetorical ornamentation.

The metaphysical poets were especially criticized for this particular violation of decorum. Abraham Cowley was often singled out. Ironically enough, his contemporaries had praised him for his restraint.[21] However, as new modes displaced the old, Cowley was accused of violating restraint, even though in his "Ode: Of Wit" he had been one of the first voices to warn against excess of wit:

> Yet 'tis not to adorn, and gild each part;
> That shows more Cost, than Art.
> Jewels at Nose and Lips but ill appear;
> Rather then all things Wit, let none be there.
> Several Lights will not be seen,
> If there be nothing else between.
> Men doubt, because they stand so thick i' th' skie,
> If those be Stars which paint the Galaxie.
> (stanza 5)

So John Sheffield also felt obliged to criticize. Having more respect for flights of fancy than did many of his contemporaries, Sheffield nevertheless insisted upon the observance of regularity. He was especially critical of the kind of ode written by Cowley, which he described as "the Muses most unruly Horse."[22] Cowley could have written better if he had combined nature with the rules. Critics blamed Cowley's excesses upon his fancy, the weakness usually attributed to metaphysical poetry; this exuberance was criticized by Addison in his "Account of the Greatest English Poets":

> Great Cowley then (a mighty genius) wrote,
> O'er run with wit, and lavish of his thought:
> His turns too closely on the reader press:
> He more had pleas'd us, had he pleas'd us less.
> (ll. 32–35)

But in the turn of the last line, Addison gently mocks his own attempts to keep distinctions clear.

Decorum of Ornamentation

While excessive ornamentation was condemned, decorum in the use of ornamentation was accepted as evidence of true wit. Hobbes's Preface to his translation of Homer's *Odysses* (1675) expressed respect for fancy, the faculty which gathers "Matter and Words." If these materials are used discreetly—a responsibility of the judgment—then "they are greater ornaments of a Poem by much than any other." Hobbes conceded that a metaphor is not unpleasant, except when it is "sharp and extraordinary." The anticipation of an apt metaphor was always attractive. Dr. Isaac Barrow defined wit, fairly early in the age, and included even the possibility of a conceit: "It is, in short, a Manner of speaking out of the simple and plain Way (such as Reason teacheth, and proveth Things by) which by a pretty, surprizing Uncouthness in Conceit or Expression, doth affect and amuse the Fancy, stirring in it some Wonder, and breeding some Delight thereto."[23] Obviously, he was not concerned here with decorum but with pleasure.

On the other hand, most critics insisted on fitting words to matter. Pierre Nicole, whose *Essay of True and Apparent Beauty* received wide acceptance in England upon publication in 1683, makes proper style its major consideration. Nicole argued "that lofty words should be fitted to lofty subjects, and lowly to lowly." Although "simplicity is essential . . . it is no less faulty to treat high and weighty subjects in a slight and unassuming style than it is to treat what is slight and unassuming in a high and weighty style." On either level one must not depart from "that agreement with nature in which, we have said, beauty resides." His concept of decorum included even figures of speech: ". . . not every piece of writing admits the rhetorical figures and ornaments, and likewise not every one excludes them. The answer lies wholly in whether there is throughout a complete harmony between diction and subject."[24] Sir William Temple likewise admitted the necessity of ornamentation in his analysis of the composition of poetry.[25]

Thus, although figurative language was generally recognized as effective expression, the stability of judgment was also demanded. John Hughes referred to wit as "Elegance of Thought," which added beauty to propriety. But he also believed that "To the Elegance of Words, or Style, belong all the Figures of Rhetorick, and to use these to Advantage requires a Judgment well form'd by Observation."[26] Hughes did not consider wit as synonymous with propriety, but rather as a companion of propriety. Wit was elegance, a quality already noted by Dryden. Elegance and wit were the same, as the age well knew. As Pope wrote in his "Essay,"

> False eloquence, like the prismatic glass,
> Its gaudy colours spreads on ev'ry place.
> (ll. 311–312)

Nevertheless,

> Expression is the dress of thought, and still
> Appears more decent, as more suitable.
> (ll. 318–319)

Wit and Nature

The neoclassical age was convinced of the need for harmony between man and nature. Nature was a term of subtle gradations, but in all its connotations was considered the embodiment of truth. Naturalness was truthfulness, and in literary expression wit was often identified with nature. This was a logical association, since in the context of decorum wit was the natural expression of truth.

The association of propriety with nature was found not only in proper style (i.e. wit of words) but also in wit of thought. The very essence of propriety was to keep within bounds of the subject. Bishop Sprat recommended Cowley's invention because it arose out of the nature of its preoccupation. Dryden's justification of propriety of thoughts was that they arise "naturally from the subject," and of propriety of words that they "are naturally proper to" the thoughts.

A stock criticism of conceits and other figurative language was that they were violations of nature. Such ornamentation could be used appropriately, as William Davenant claimed was his objective in *Gondibert* (1650). But he hesitated to call his ornaments "wit"; he simply stated that his "endeavour was, in bringing Truth, too often absent, home to mens bosoms, to lead her through unfrequented and new ways," all by means of "representing Nature, though not in an affected, yet in an unusual dress." Dryden also advocated "the strength and vehemence of figures" which were "suited to the occasion, the subject, and the persons." Furthermore, "All beyond this is monstrous . . . 'tis out of Nature, 'tis an excrescence, and not a living part of Poetry."[27] George Granville, Lord Landsdowne, a minor poet and dramatist whose chief criticism is contained in his "Essay upon Unnatural Flights in Poetry" (1701), voiced a strident objection to the poetry of unnatural figures:

> Gygantick forms and monstrous Births alone
> Produce, which Nature shockt disdains to own.
> (ll. 18–19)

It was the peculiar characteristic of this kind of imaginative poetry to soar,

> And mounting up in Figures out of Sight,
> [Leave] Truth behind in her audacious flight.
> (ll. 23–24)

He blamed such extravagance upon rhetorical distention:

> Fables and Metaphors that always lie,
> And rash Hyperboles, that soar so high,
> And every Ornament of Verse, must die.
> (ll. 25–27)

Granville was demonstrating the violation of content by its form, which characterized much neoclassical criticism of style. Naturalness was a criterion for judging "Witticisms," inferior kinds of verbal wit. Dryden considered them artificial and hence a substitute for nature,[28] and Addison agreed.[29]

Psychological theory readily supported wit as the expression of nature. Judgment, as Hobbes had said, was "the severe Sister" to fancy and busied itself with a "grave and rigid examination of all the parts of Nature."[30] Wit had an important share in this examination. Sheffield felt that in literary expression "Nature's chief Master-piece is writing well."[31] Such expression was a reflection of the master subject itself, one corollary of the Neo-Platonic line of reasoning. With the same respect for wit, Robert Wolseley explained wit as "a true and lively expression of Nature." By "Nature" he meant "not only all sorts of material Objects and every species of Substance whatsoever, but also general Notions and abstracted Truths, such as exist only in the Minds of men and in the property and relation of things one to another, —in short, whatever has a Being of any kind." Significantly, he equated his definition of wit with Dryden's; "true" expression meant "propriety," and a "lively" expression was one that was "elegantly adapted."[32]

Necessarily, it was *true* wit that was "nature to advantage dress'd." In searching for true wit, most critics were inclined to consider contemporary productions inferior to ancient ones. Current modes appeared as degenerate and vulgar, dependent merely upon fashions and popular parlance, lacking the universality achieved by the ancients. The battle of the ancients and the moderns frequently revolved about the question of the quality of the wit each produced. Majority opinion favored the wit of the ancients with its apparent timelessness and universality—qualities attested to by its survival. Current wit was too prone to topical conversation and mundane personalities.

Since harmony with nature was essential, wit deficient in harmony was untrue, false wit. Addison remarked upon receiving a letter full of jests in poor taste, "I am more pleased with a Letter that is filled with Touches of Nature than of Wit" (*Spectator*, No. 181). Pope had much the same distinction in mind when he wrote the four lines in the "Essay,"

> Oft, leaving what is natural and fit,
> The current folly proves the ready wit;
> And authors think their reputation safe,
> Which lives as long as fools are pleas'd to laugh.
> (ll. 448–451)

This was a renunciation of ready wit but not of proper wit, which Pope had upheld to William Wycherley as "a better notion of wit" than the "fancy or conceit" of former years (letter of November 29, 1707).

Wit and Truth, including the "Test of Truth"

Finally, decorum in wit insured the expression of truth. This elevation of wit was a significant development within the neoclassical frame of reference. Four distinct considerations came into play. First, the linking of wit and judgment, either as identical or as companionate faculties; second, the belief that wit was itself an expression of nature. A natural extension of these beliefs was that wit had to serve both truth and virtue. This function was inherent psychologically in the early associations of wit and judgment. Hobbes had referred to judgment as the faculty which attained "exact and perfect knowledge."[33] La Rochefoucauld, Bouhours, and Boileau supported this traditional idea. Addison summarized the views of the last two in the *Spectator*, No. 62, by way of reinforcing his own position on wit as supported by judgment: "That it is impossible for any Thought to be beautiful which is not just, and has not its Foundation in the Nature of Things: That the Basis of all Wit is Truth; and that no Thought can be valuable, of which good Sense is not the Ground-work." Dennis paraphrased Bouhours in support of his own view.[34]

The third influence in the identification of wit with truth was the coincidence of the image of light with wit and with the ability of wit to illuminate an idea quickly. La Rochefoucauld had expressed this coincidence admirably in his remark upon judgment as "only the greatness of the illumination of wit," an illumination which "penetrates the depths of things." This metaphor of the probing quality of light rests upon the ancient belief in the coincidence of light and sound. Present-day figures of speech bear out the same meaning: "bright sayings," "scintillating conversations," "brilliant wit."

Wit was commonly credited with the light which accompanies the understanding, illuminating the darkest corners of ignorance. So John Sheffield wrote in "An Essay upon Poetry" (1682):

And of all sorts of Writing none there are
That can the least with Poetry compare;
No kind of work requires so nice a touch,
And if well done, there's nothing shines so much;
But Heav'n forbid that we should so prophane,
To grace the vulgar with that sacred name;
'Tis not a Flash of Fancy which sometimes
Dasling our Minds, sets off the slightest Rimes,
Bright as a blaze, but in a moment done;
True Wit is everlasting, like the Sun,
Which though sometimes beneath a cloud retir'd,
Breaks out again, and is by all admir'd.

Implicitly, true wit is equated here with judgment, expressing the eternal verities. On the other hand, fancy is depicted as misleading, dazzling but momentary.

This image of light readily supported the concept of decorum. For example, in one passage remarkably concentrated in neoclassical meanings of wit, Dennis related wit to good sense. Accepting the dictum that gentlemen were to use good sense and judgment, he criticized the particular kind of writing which "has nothing of a Gentleman in it, little of good Sense, and consequently little of true Wit." He continued,

For tho there may be good Sense found without Wit, there can be no true Wit, where there is no good Sense. For a Thought that is really witty, must necessarily be true, and have something in it that's Solid; So that Quibbles and all Equivocals can have little or nothing of true Wit in them. Wit is a just mixture of Reason and Extravagance, and the Extravagance must be there, only in order to give the Reason the more lustre.[35]

All of the characteristics of decorum are here combined: good sense, gentlemanliness, true wit, "a just mixture of Reason and Extravagance," truth, and the light ("lustre") which accompanies the discovery of truth. Wit is thus distinguished in a significant role; whether an associate of judgment or a product of both fancy and judgment, wit gathers to itself the traditional coincidence of light and understanding.

This identity was extremely meaningful in poetic expression as well as in the search for truth and virtue. Sir William Temple discussed this synthesis of meanings at length in "Of Poetry":

> The more true and natural Source of Poetry may be discovered by observing to what God this Inspiration was ascribed by the Antients, which was Apollo, or the Sun, esteemed among them the God of Learning in general, but more particularly of Musick and of Poetry. . . . By the influence of this Sun are produced those Golden and Inexhausted Mines of Invention, which has furnished the World with Treasures so highly esteemed and so universally known and used in all the Regions that have yet been discovered.

To this "Invention" Temple would add the "liveliness of Wit," for poetry is born naked and must be clothed. However, judgment is necessary in choosing among the "infinite productions of Wit and Fancy" those "which are worth preserving and cultivating," and those "which are better stifled in the Birth, or thrown away when they are born, as not worth bringing up."

The fourth influence in identifying wit with truth (and probably the most basic) was the traditional meaning of wit as intellect. Georges de Scudery implied this intellectual function in his Preface to *Ibrahim* (1674), commenting that "when as falsehood and truth are confounded by a dexterous hand, wit hath much adoe to disintangle them, and is not easily carried to destroy that which pleaseth it." The pleasure in this instance results from the artifice of various rhetorical ornamentations, which is supplied by the "dexterous hand." In order to avoid these imaginative elements, de Scudery followed "true History" so that he might adhere to "a more true resemblance to things."

David Abercromby had intellect in mind when he defined wit as "a senseful discourse, word, or Sentence."[36] "Sense" here meant common sense, natural understanding, and intelligence, as well as practical soundness of judgment.[37] Thus, Abercromby reasoned that men without wit were "mere Fools, and senseless."[38] A unique corollary to his view was his belief in wit of action, by which he attributed a certain low kind of wit to animals, since "I never understood why we should deny some share both of Reason and Wit to several of those inferior Creatures, that do things we do neither imitate, nor account for, without granting them, in some measure, this reasoning faculty, we would feign Monopolize to our selves."[39] Abercromby also equated wit with judgment elsewhere in his discourse.[40]

The rationale of wit as truth is one of the pinnacles of the meaning of wit. Addison had as high a regard for true wit as any of his contemporaries. His purpose in writing the *Spectator* series, stated in issue Number 10, reveals his respect for genuine wit. The dream-vision of the "Region of False Wit" dramatizes the high esteem true wit had achieved by 1711. Addison's description of the Goddess of Falsehood and her cohorts of puns, anagrams, and quibbles is interrupted by a sudden invasion of the area by the army of Wit and Truth. The legions are led by Truth, "a Person of the most beautiful Aspect," accompanied by a "very shining Light." The assistant on her right hand is Wit, "a Male Deity, who bore several Quivers on his Shoulders, and grasped several Arrows in his Hand." At the approach of this formidable army, the many false wits are scattered. Addison turned his attention again to the figure of Wit and concluded with a pleasant self-effacement:

> I was very much awed and delighted with the Appearance of the God of Wit; there was something so amiable and yet so piercing in his Looks, as inspired me at once with Love and Terror. As I was gazing on him to my unspeakable Joy, he took a Quiver of Arrows from his Shoulder, in order to make me a Present of it; but as I was reaching out my Hand to receive it of him, I knocked it against a Chair, and by that means awaked.

Addison made use of the light image to reinforce Wit's position at the right hand of Truth.

The piercing quality of wit's illumination implied a certain sharpness, which by analogy was the ability to cut through irrelevancies to truth. Wolseley, describing the Earl of Rochester's efforts to improve society, spoke of his having

> . . . a Wit whose Edge cou'd ease by cutting, and whose Point cou'd tickle while it prob'd: A wit that us'd to nip in the very Bud the

growing Fopperies of the Times, and keep down those Weeds and Suckers of Humanity; nor was it an Enemy to such only as are troublesome to men of sence in Conversation, but to those also (of a far worse Nature) that are destructive of public Good and pernicious to the common Interest of Mankind.[41]

All of the great wits of the period accepted wit seriously as a weapon against all untruths. The Scriblerus Club, for example, aimed to expose the "abuses" of learning, as Bishop William Warburton later explained.[42]

This concept represents the most noble impulse in neoclassical decorum, for the pursuit of truth and virtue was the traditional aim of all men of learning. Since wit was viewed as the mode of truth, Dryden praised wit as the medium of the age and held up poetry as the equal to philosophy in presenting truth:

> Moral truth is the mistress of the poet as much as of the philosopher; Poesy must resemble natural truth, but it must be ethical. Indeed, the poet dresses truth, and adorns nature, but does not alter them:
>
> *Ficta voluptatis causa sint proxima veris.*
>
> Therefore that is not the best poesy which resembles notions of things that are not, to things that are: though the fancy may be great and the words flowing, yet the soul is but half satisfied when there is not truth in the foundation.[43]

Dryden's high concept of the poet differed only slightly from the noble concept described by Sir Philip Sidney in his *Defense of Poesy*.[44]

Many serious minds of Dryden's day agreed with him on the moral seriousness and usefulness of wit. Some of the clergy supported true wit. Joseph Glanvill, a preacher and philosopher, thinking of wit as composed of intellect and imagination, considered its possible use in sermons: "For true Wit is a perfection in our Faculties, chiefly in the Understanding, and Imagination: Wit in the Understanding is a Sagacity to find out the Nature, Relations, and Consequences of things; Wit in the Imagination, is a quickness in the phancy to give things proper Images."[45] Bishop Sprat had a more general use of wit in mind when he wrote:

The true Raillery should be a defence for Good and Virtuous Works, and should only intend the derision of extravagant, and the disgrace of vile and dishonourable things. This kind of Wit ought to have the nature of Salt, to which it is usually compar'd; which preserves and keeps sweet the good, and the sound parts of all Bodies, and only frets, dries up, and destroys those humours which putrify and corrupt.[46]

Bishop Francis Atterbury, in a sermon preached in 1694, stated that "Wit, indeed, as it implies a certain uncommon Reach and Vivacity of Thought, is an Excellent Tallent; very fit to be imploy'd in the Search of Truth, and very capable of assisting us to discern and embrace it."[47] All three men would have agreed with Archbishop John Tillotson, who felt that wit was commendable but that "a wise man should always have the keeping of it." All four men were aware of dangers inherent in wit but recognized its suitability for the "great and noble Exercises of the Mind." It was a "Faculty to dive into the depth of things, to find out their Causes and Relatives, Consonancies and Disagreements, and to make fit, useful, and unobvious Applications of their respective Relations and Dependencies."[48]

The development of wit as the expression of decorum, nature, enlightenment, and truth forms the background for the eighteenth century concern with the "Test of Truth."[49] This test was argued by Anthony Ashley Cooper, the third Earl of Shaftesbury, to whom the word ridicule was synonymous with wit. The fact that this test of truth became identified during the following century with ridicule is ironic, but it is also illustrative of the rapidly changing views of wit and related intellectual media. Shaftesbury presented this test as a function of wit, though he often used the word ridicule in referring to wit.

In "A Letter Concerning Enthusiasm," written in 1707 at the peak of wit's popularity, Shaftesbury attacked the perennial question of freedom of thought and of the security of virtue in a society in which the spirit of raillery prevailed: "Never was there in our Nation a time known, when Folly and Extravagance of every kind were more sharply inspected, or more *wittily rid-icul'd*" (sect. ii. italics mine.) In answer to the increasing cries against the prevailing spirit of satire and personal abuse, he replied that such "Liberty may seem to run too far." However, "who shall be Judge of what may be freely examin'd, and what may not? Where Liberty may be us'd; and where it may not?" Shaftesbury felt that the search for "Justness of Thought and Style, Refinement in Manners, good Breeding, and Politeness of every kind" should continue freely, for "Whatever Humour has got the start, if it be unnatural, it cannot hold; and the Ridicule, if ill plac'd at first will certainly fall at last where it deserves" (sect. ii).

In this letter Shaftesbury proposed wit as the test of truth. We have already seen that Dryden, Sprat, and Wolseley had considered true wit as the embodiment of truth. Tillotson declared that "the proper use" of wit is "to season conversation, to represent what is praise-worthy to the greatest advantage, and to expose the vices and follies of men, such things as are in themselves truly ridiculous."[50] Wit and ridicule are naturally associated here. Shaftesbury's own wording of this function of wit, shifting emphasis to ridicule, keeps entirely within the context of wit, for he often used the two words interchangeably:[51]

> I have often wonder'd to see Men of Sense so mightily alarm'd at the approach of any thing like Ridicule on certain Subjects; as if they mistrusted their own Judgment. For what Ridicule can lie against Reason? Or how can any one of the least Justness of Thought endure a Ridicule wrong plac'd? Nothing is more ridiculous than this itself. The Vulgar, indeed, may swallow any sordid Jest, any mere Drollery or Buffoonery; *but it must be a finer and truer Wit which takes with the Men of Sense and Breeding.*[52]

Basic to Shaftesbury's plan for the preservation of truth is the preservation of wit and its necessary freedom—a freedom which he considered essential in the society of his day: " 'Tis a hard matter for a Government to settle Wit. . . . I am sure the only way to save Mens Sense, or preserve Wit at all in the World, is to give Liberty to Wit. Now Wit can never have its Liberty, where the Freedom of Raillery is taken away: For against serious Extravagances and splenetick Humours there is no other Remedy than this" (sect. ii). In "An Essay on the Freedom of Wit and Humour" (1709) Shaftesbury was more concerned with the actual way an application of wit could reveal truth:

> Truth, 'tis suppos'd, may bear all Lights: and one of those principal Lights or natural Mediums, by which Things are to be view'd, in order to a thorow Recognition, is Ridicule it-self, or that Manner of Proof by which we discern whatever is liable to just Raillery in any Subject. . . . The gravest Gentlemen, even in the gravest Subjects, are suppos'd to acknowledg this: and can have no Right, 'tis thought, to deny others the Freedom of this Appeal; whilst they are free to censure like other Men, and in their gravest Arguments make no scruple to ask, *Is it not Ridiculous?* (Part I, sect. i)

Although there has been some argument over whether or not Shaftesbury explicitly proposed ridicule as a test of truth,[53] it is clear, in view of the function of wit as an expression of truth, that he was simply rephrasing this aptitude in his question, "How comes it to pass, then, that we appear such Cowards in reasoning, and are so afraid to stand the Test of Ridicule?" (sect. ii). Interpreting ridicule as a kind of reasoning, he could only be referring to wit. When he asserted that "Truth, 'tis supposed, may bear all Lights: and one of those principal Lights . . . is Ridicule it-self,"[54] specifying the light which illuminates truth, then he could only mean wit. And when he stated elsewhere that "without Wit and Humour, Reason can hardly have its proof or be distinguished,"[55] then the case for wit as a test of truth is clear. There was no such meaning for ridicule outside of its increasing identity with wit.

The same identity of wit and ridicule is found in Shaftesbury's pupil and defender, John Brown. When Brown asserted that "Truth delights in the Day; and demands no more just Light" and added that "a rigid Examination is its only Test,"[56] then "ridicule" could only mean "wit," for wit alone had had such contextual meanings. Brown also used the words interchangeably. For example, Brown defended Shaftesbury's tone of "Gaiety of Spirit" and the "Freedom of Wit and Humour" he proposed in arguments, for the reason that "to have argued seriously, would have destroyed his Argument" for the "Power of Ridicule."[57] Brown then concluded: "Here then we discover why the noble Author is *so witty in Defence of Wit,* and chuses to maintain the Cause of Raillery by Raillery itself."[58] Wit is ridicule is raillery, and vice versa.[59]

If wit, then, is an expression of truth and also a test of truth, how was truth examined by the men of wit? There were many methods, as many almost as there were different temperaments and attitudes among wits: the personal satire of Dryden's "Mac Flecknoe," the burlesque of Samuel Butler's *Hudibras,* the comedy of Congreve's *The Way of the World,* the raillery of Addison and Steele's *Spectator* papers, the moral satire in Pope's epistles, the mock heroic of Dr. Samuel Garth's *The Dispensary,* the ridicule of John Gay's *Beggar's Opera,* and the irony of Swift's *Gulliver's Travels.*

The Truth of Wit in Jonathan Swift's *Gulliver's Travels*

Jonathan Swift, English divine and man of wit, was a disillusioned idealist and a congenital misanthropist. One finds in his literary remains a great variety—sermons, political pamphlets, religious allegories, travel adventures, journalistic essays, a personal journal to a girl friend, public letters, private letters, and poems varying from odes to occasional and personal pieces to *jeux d'esprit.* This amazing display reveals a complex and very serious mind, disturbed more by the frustrations of human nature than by his own disappointments in life—a mind which hid so thoroughly its thoughts in a façade of brilliant wit that Swift became the most misinterpreted and misunderstood man of his day. Epithets from atheist to mad man were hurled at him, even though his life was marked by competence, religious devotion, and a sober adjustment to duty. His first position after education at Trinity College, Dublin, was that of secretary to Sir William Temple, in which capacity he was unusually successful. After the death of Temple in 1699, Swift spent much time in London, writing and advancing in his career as a churchman. He was a chief adviser to the Tory ministry during the years 1710 to 1714. Because of his role as a man of wit, he did not receive the bishopric he desired but was made dean of St. Patrick's Cathedral in Dublin, in which office he was eminent.

As the man of wit he always considered himself to be, Swift conducted a serious and intense search for truth. This search is obvious, once his techniques of wit are understood, in everything that he wrote, except perhaps in some of his slight epigrams and occasional verse. After his appointment to St. Patrick's, he became deeply concerned with the unfair treatment of the Irish. The result was a major body of literature which so moved the sympathies of the English public for Ireland that Parliament was influenced to enact less oppressive laws. Chief among these works was his *Drapier's Letters* (1724–1725), which drew from his good friend Alexander Pope some commendatory lines:

> Let Ireland tell, how Wit upheld her cause,
> Her Trade supported, and supply'd her Laws;
> And leave on SWIFT this grateful verse ingrav'd,
> The Rights a Court attack'd, a Poet sav'd.

But although Swift put Ireland's cause high in his interest, he placed mankind's even higher. His major works examine human nature and institutions. They expose man's vices and his follies. Swift was not just a satirist or a moralist; he was a man of wit, or, as the role found particular expression in his nature, a moral satirist. His special forte was the ironic posture of dissembling, always couched in the guise of a fictitious narrator. He took pride in developing this technique of wit in prose and wrote facetiously in his "Verses on the Death of Dr. Swift":

> Arbuthnot is no more my Friend,
> Who dares to Irony pretend;
> Which I was born to introduce,
> Refin'd it first, and shew'd its use.

And so he had, beginning with *A Tale of a Tub* and *The Battle of the Books* (1704).

Swift's mastery of ironic wit is nowhere more dazzling than in his most complex achievement, *Travels into Several Remote Parts of the World,* published in 1726 as the work of a Captain Lemuel Gulliver and now known as *Gulliver's Travels.* Drawing, as so often he did in his earlier works of wit, upon the *eiron* and the *ethopoeia* of classical rhetoric, as well as the well-established convention of the fictitious narrator, Swift so created the habits and character of the imaginary Lemuel Gulliver that a real-life adventurer emerges: gullible (as his name suggests), vain, patriotic, literal-minded, and naïve—so real that Swift's contemporaries argued publicly over his actual existence.

It is important for the reader of Swift to always keep in mind this device of the fictitious narrator or persona, in order to remember that not only does he not actually exist but he is not Swift. Swift, the master ironist, was perfectly in control of his creation; his fiction never controlled him. Gulliver, kept at an aesthetic distance, is made to serve the purposes of his creator. Swift had mastered the technique long before the writing of the *Travels* and, at the height of his powers in 1726, had no difficulty in maintaining the distance. A few examples from the first, second, and fourth voyages will make Swift's facility in wit clear.

In the first and second voyages, Swift views society and the human being from two vantages—one at a distance and one closeup—or as through both ends of a telescope—one diminishing, one magnifying. The distant, diminishing view observes man's social, political, and moral aspects; the magnifying, closeup view looks at man's physical and moral aspects. When Gulliver is cast among the Lilliputians, he is a giant among pygmies, twelve times taller than his captors; when he finds himself captured by the Brobdingnagians, his captors are twelve times larger than he. Thus, generally, in Lilliput the distant view is Gulliver's and the closeup view is the Lilliputians'; among the Brobdingnagians, the distant view is theirs and the closeup is Gulliver's.

In the voyage to Lilliput, Gulliver looks at the life of the tiny people about him. He observes their court antics, their political intrigues, and their overweening self-confidence and pride. Pride is satirized brilliantly when the emperor visits the confined Gulliver, who describes the person and attitude of the ruler with devastating irony:

> He is taller by almost the breadth of my nail than any of his court, which alone is enough to strike an awe into the beholders. His features are strong and masculine, with an Austrian lip and arched nose, his complexion olive, his countenance erect, his body and limbs well proportioned, all his motions graceful, and his deportment majestic. . . . For the better convenience of beholding him, I lay on my side, so that my face was parallel to his, and he stood three yards off: however, I have had him since many times in my hand, and therefore cannot be deceived in the description. His dress was very plain and simple, and the fashion of it between the Asiatic and the European; but he had on his head a light helmet of gold, adorned with jewels, and a plume on the crest. He held his sword drawn in his hand, to defend himself, if I should happen to break loose; it was almost three inches long, the hilt and scabbard were gold enriched with diamonds. (chap. 2)

Later, after the king's "gentleness and good behaviour" became apparent and after swearing a peace with the king, Gulliver is given his freedom and is able to watch the emperor and his court. The diversions include the game of rope dancing:

> This diversion is only practised by those persons who are candidates for great employments and high favour at court. They are trained in this art from their youth, and are not always of noble birth, or liberal education. When a great office is vacant either by death or disgrace (which often happens) five or six of these candidates petition the Emperor to entertain his Majesty and the court with a dance on a rope, and whoever jumps the highest without falling, succeeds in the office. Very often the chief ministers themselves are commanded to show their skill, and to convince the Emperor that they have not lost their faculty. Flimnap, the Treasurer, is allowed to cut a caper on the straight rope, at least an inch higher than any other lord in the whole empire. (chap. 3)

Gulliver is observing, of course, inconsequential and degrading machinations which Swift himself had had to undergo as well as observe during his months at the Court of Queen Anne. The range of laws and customs which Gulliver observes is wide, for there was much in human society for Swift to ridicule. On the burial practices of the Lilliputians, he comments:

> They bury their dead with their heads directly downwards, because they hold an opinion, that in eleven thousand moons they are all to rise again, in which period the earth (which they conceive to be flat) will turn upside down, and by this means they shall, at their resurrection, be found ready standing on their feet. The learned among them confess the absurdity of this doctrine, but the practice still continues, in compliance to the vulgar. (chap. 6)

At the same time that this distant view of human society is being presented, the reader receives inadvertently (though purposefully, we may be sure) a closeup view of the human being, as seen in the reactions of the Lilliputians to the monstrous size of Gulliver. Thus, when still confined by "ropes" and having to urinate, Gulliver's description of the consequences reflects the view by the surrounding Lilliputians:

> I was able to turn upon my right, and to ease myself with making water; which I very plentifully did, to the great astonishment of the people, who conjecturing by my motions what I was going to do, immediately opened to the right and left on that side, to avoid the torrent which fell with such noise and violence from me. (chap. 1)

Another instance of the closeup view, reflecting Swift's scatological interests, occurs in the account of Gulliver's participation in one of the diversions of the armed forces of Lilliput, that of marching under the outspread legs of the human colossus.

> His Majesty gave orders upon pain of death, that every soldier in his march should observe the strictest decency with regard to my person; which, however, could not prevent some of the younger officers from turning up their eyes as they passed under me. And, to confess the truth, my breeches were at that time in so ill a condition, that they afforded some opportunities for laughter and admiration. (chap. 3)

In the second voyage, the points of view are reversed. Now, the most constant view is the closeup: the diminutive Gulliver, as narrator, must be brought quite near by the Brobdingnagians to be seen and conversed with. When the nurse in the household where Gulliver is kept must quiet the baby and when other distractions do not work,

> . . . she was forced to apply the last remedy by giving it suck. I must confess no object ever disgusted me so much as the sight of her monstrous breast, which I cannot tell what to compare with, so as to give the curious reader an idea of its bulk, shape and colour. It stood prominent six foot, and could not be less than sixteen in circumference. The nipple was about half the bigness of my head, and the hue both of that and the dug so varified with spots, the pimples and freckles, that nothing could appear more nauseous: for I had a near sight of her, she sitting down the more conveniently to give suck, and I standing on the table. (chap. 1)

Similarly, Gulliver finds repugnant the sight of people eating, the smell of body odor and of perfumes, and the close view of a beheaded criminal.

Other effects besides the grossness and abhorrence of human features at close range include the personal indignity to which the weak may be subjected by the powerful and the thoughtless when Gulliver is displayed for public view and forced to perform such "fopperies" as drinking from the thimble of Glumdalclitch, which serves as his cup; exercising with a straw that serves as a pike; and flourishing his hanger—all of this until he is "half dead with weariness and vexation" (chap. 2). Still another effect is the indignity which one may bring upon himself through an attempt to show off. Once when Glumdalclitch has Gulliver out for a walk,

> . . . there was a cow-dung in the path, and I must needs try my activity by attempting to leap over it. I took a run, but unfortunately jumped short, and found myself just in the middle up to my knees. I waded through with some difficulty, and one of the footmen wiped me as clean as he could with his handkerchief; for I was filthily bemired, and my nurse confined me to my box till we returned home; where the Queen was soon informed of what had passed, and the footmen spread it about the court, so that all the mirth, for some days, was at my expense. (chap. 6)

An opportunity for the distant view of human society and nature occurs in Gulliver's attempts to communicate to his captors something of the splendor, spectacle, and importance of "the manners, religion, laws, government, and learning of Europe." The King of the Brobdingnagians is especially curious, and Gulliver responds with great eagerness. The more he talks, the more disturbed the King becomes:

> He was perfectly astonished with the historical account I gave him of our affairs during the last century, protesting it was only an heap of conspiracies, rebellions, murders, massacres, revolutions, banishments, the very worse effects that avarice, faction, hypocrisy, perfidiousness, cruelty, rage, madness, hatred, envy, lust, malice, or ambition could produce. (chap. 6)

And then occurs one of the most notorious pronouncements upon the human being in the *Travels:*

> It doth not appear from all you have said, how any one virtue is required towards the procurement of any one station among you; much less that men are ennobled on account of their virtue, that priests are advanced for their piety or learning, soldiers for their conduct or valour, judges for their integrity, senators for the love of their country, or counsellors for their wisdom. As for yourself (continued the King) who have spent the greatest part of your life in travelling, I am well disposed to hope you may hitherto have escaped many vices of your country. But by what I have gathered from your own relation, and the answers I have with much pains wringed and extorted from you, I cannot but conclude the bulk of your natives to be the most pernicious race of little odious vermin that nature ever suffered to crawl upon the surface of the earth. (chap. 6)

This judgment is made by a ruler whom Gulliver describes as a "prince of excellent understanding."

The fourth voyage affords a view of human society in a quite different dimension, symbolically presented by *le mythe animal.* Two animal societies depict further aspects of human nature and society. First, Gulliver finds himself among the Yahoos, their shape "very singular and deformed," their heads and breasts covered with thick hair, "beards like goats and a long ridge of hair down their backs and the fore-parts of their legs and feet." Gulliver is horrified when later placed beside one of them to discover "in this abominable animal a perfect human figure" (chap. 2).

Here is the potential human being stripped of all cultural accretions—clothing, cleanliness, manners, language, institutions—a member, in fact, of a subhuman society. The Yahoos have a further limitation; they exist upon an emotional level of fears and hates and other passions undiluted by reason. When Gulliver first encounters them, he angers one with a blow of his sword:

> When the beast felt the smart, he drew back, and roared so loud that a herd of at least forty came flocking about me from the next field, howling and making odious faces; but I ran to the body of a tree, and leaning my back against it, kept them off by waving my hanger. Several of this cursed brood getting hold of the branches behind, leapt up into the tree, from whence they began to discharge their excrements on my head; however, I escaped pretty well, by sticking close to the stem of the tree, but was almost stifled with the filth, which fell about me on every side. (chap. 1)

The brutality shows in their fighting among themselves, even male with female. Their highly emotional nature is revealed in the fancies and impulses which suddenly seize them. Gulliver is swimming naked one day, watched over by his guardian, the sorrel nag:

> It happened that a young female Yahoo, standing behind a bank, saw the whole proceeding, and inflamed by desire, . . . came running with all speed, and leaped into the water, within five yards of the place where I bathed. I was never in my life so terribly frighted; the nag was grazing at some distance, not suspecting any harm. She embraced me after a most fulsome manner; I roared as loud as I could, and the nag came galloping towards me, whereupon she quitted her grasp, with the utmost reluctancy, and leaped upon the opposite bank, where she stood gazing and howling all the time I was putting on my clothes. (chap. 8)

Gulliver refuses any association with the Yahoos, recognizing in them abhorrent qualities too near his own.

The sorrel nag is one of the community of the Houyhnhnms, horses nobly endowed by nature with a "general disposition to all virtues." They have "no conceptions or ideas of what is evil in a rational creature, so their grand maxim is to cultivate reason, and to be wholly governed by it." Further attributes are their two principal virtues—friendship and benevolence. Their society is so virtuous that Gulliver's account of his own country, given in his usually solicitous manner, requires several days because of the difficulty of explaining so many new concepts of vice and crime. For instance, a lying or false statement is equated in Houyhnhnm language as "the thing which was not."

This society of horses, far from being human, has attained an ideal culture far superior to the culture of Europe. Most important for Swift's purpose is the rationalistic basis of Houyhnhnm society. Without emotional complications, marriages are arranged for the sake of certain desirable colors in offspring, no fondness is centered in the colts, and children are exchanged when such exchange is deemed advantageous. The few emotions shown by the Houyhnhnms are mild and of no consequence to the social order. Therefore, the Houyhnhnm order is without emotional overtones, just as the Yahoo disorder is without rational overtones. Both lack the balance so necessary in neoclassical thinking—the balance (in psychological terms) between judgment, or reason, and imagination, or emotion. Gulliver quickly, even gladly, identifies himself with this dull, colorless—but still ideal—society. His naïve decision is based upon the empirical knowledge of what he can observe immediately about him. It is a ridiculous decision, as the Houyhnhnm society is ridiculous. In this manner does Swift satirize the limited approach to truth of such philosophers as Descartes and Locke.

The final chapters rise to a climax of grim playfulness. Gulliver's acceptance of a society of horses is irrational, for neither the horses nor their society offer a solution to human problems. The horses, after all, are only horses, albeit most unusual ones. Gulliver's choice becomes increasingly irrational and fatuous as his pride and self-confidence increase:

> When I thought of my family, my friends, my countrymen, or the human race in general, I considered them as they really were, Yahoos in shape and disposition, perhaps a little more civilized, and qualified with the gift of speech, but making no other use of reason than to improve and multiply those vices whereof their brethren in this country had only the share that nature allotted them. When I happened to behold the reflection of my own form in a lake or fountain,

I turned away my face in horror and detestation of myself, and could better endure the sight of a common Yahoo than of my own person. By conversing with the Houyhnhnms, and looking upon them with delight, I fell to imitate their gait and gesture, which is now grown into an habit, and my friends often tell me in a blunt way, that I trot like a horse; which, however, I take for a great compliment. Neither shall I disown that in speaking I am apt to fall into the voice and manner of the Houyhnhnms, and hear myself ridiculed on that account without the least mortification. (chap. 10)

Such logical extension of an illogical position was a real part of the fun of wit to the men of wit. One sees the humor in Gulliver's shock at the decision of the Houyhnhnms to expel him from their country, in his preparations of an escape canoe with the aid of the sorrel nag, "who performed the parts that required most labour," and in his farewell with his friends:

When all was ready, and the day came for my departure, I took leave of my master and lady and the whole family, my eyes flowing with tears, and my heart quite sunk with grief. But his Honour, out of curiosity, and perhaps (if I may speak it without vanity) partly out of kindness, was determined to see me in my canoe, and got several of his neighbouring friends to accompany him. I was forced to wait above an hour for the tide, and then observing the wind very fortunately bearing towards the island to which I intended to steer my course, I took a second leave of my master; but as I was going to prostrate myself to kiss his hoof, he did me the honour to raise it gently to my mouth. (chap. 10)

Gulliver attempts to avoid all Yahoos, especially the European variety. But unfortunately he is apprehended by some Portuguese sailors, and his progress from that moment is gradually toward England and home. Upon arrival, he admits to feelings only of hatred, disgust, and contempt for his family. The final paragraph of Chapter 11 reads:

As soon as I entered the house, my wife took me in her arms and kissed me, at which, having not been used to the touch of that odious animal for so many years, I fell in a swoon for almost an hour. At the time I am writing it is five years since my last return to England: during the first year I could not endure my wife or children in my presence, the very smell of them was intolerable, much less could I suffer them to eat in the same room. To this hour they dare not presume to touch my bread, or drink out of the same cup, neither was I ever able to let one of them take me by the hand. The first money I laid out was to buy two young stone-horses, which I keep in a good stable, and next to them the groom is my greatest favourite; for I feel my spirits revive by the smell he contracts in the stable. My horses understand me tolerably well; I converse with them at least four hours every day. They are strangers to bridle or saddle; they live in great amity with me, and friendship to each other.

This is the ultimate folly of the gullible narrator of the *Travels* and a genuine jibe at the reader who takes Gulliver's choice seriously. To identify Gulliver's final rejection of human society with Swift's personal opinion is to miss the irony, to take Part IV literally, and to overlook the playfulness of wit. Swift's fellow wits were not bitten. Pope had great fun with his own poems on the Houyhnhnms and Yahoos. Dr. Arbuthnot wrote to Swift in November, 1726, "Gulliver is a happy man that at his age can write such a merry work." There was also appreciation of the humor generally, as indicated in a letter to Swift from the Earl of Peterborough on November 29:

I am forced to write to you in the Yahoo language. The new one in fashion is much studied, and great pains taken about the pronunciation. Everybody, since a new turn, approves of it; but the women seem more satisfied, who declare for few words and horse performance. It suffices to let you know, that there is a neighing duetto appointed for the next opera.

The truth of *Gulliver's Travels* must be understood in terms of the consistent irony of its wit. What truth did Swift present in such a topsy-turvy tale? The various facets of truth are tied in too much with overlapping ironies to be given in detail. *Gulliver's Travels* is his own *Essay on Man,* full of evidences of man's failures, frustrations, and limitations. One sees even in the various ideal societies in the background, which are kinds of utopias (notably the societies of the Brodbingnags, Laputans, Luggnaggs, and Houyhnhnms), serious faults and inadequacies. Man knows not nor has ever known perfection; he must live somehow with the imperfections which are his own and his society's.

Swift opposed the prevailing philosophy of the day.[60] He, like other notable contemporaries, could never accept the optimistic dictum "whatever is, is right." There was too much selfishness, foolishness, and stupidity in the world. The wits were determined to lash at the vices and laugh at the follies. It was Swift's personal nature to lash more often than he laughed. But then, his vision of the human situation was closer to the truth of human existence than was the optimists' view.

Summary

Wit, then, reached one apogee in its association with decorum. In being closely identified with judgment, it was capable of realizing man's highest aim dating from the time of the Athenians—the perception of moral truth. Many of the great minds of the period devoted their attentions to wit. As late as mid-century, Samuel Johnson recognized this context of wit. He described that "more noble and more adequate conception" of wit as being "at once natural and new, that which, though not obvious, is upon its first production, acknowledged to be just." Johnson's objection to the kind of metaphysical conceit which he called *discordia concors* was that it was "unnatural," hence untrue.[61]

At the height of esteem for wit, Pope's "Essay on Criticism" drew attacks, not only because he elevated wit so high, but because his interpretation debased its nature. There is special irony in Johnson's criticism of Pope's view (that it depressed wit below "its natural dignity" and reduced it "from strength of thought to happiness of language"), for Pope, too, thought of wit as truth. The following lines in the "Essay" sum up the meanings of wit as decorum and truth, and Johnson might well have heeded their intent:[62]

> True wit is nature to advantage dress'd,
> What oft was thought, but ne'er so well express'd;
> Something, whose truth convinc'd at sight we find,
> That gives us back the image of our mind.
> As shades more sweetly recommend the light,
> So modest plainness sets off sprightly wit.
>
> (ll. 297–302)

Poetry's the feverish fit,
The o'erflowing of unbounded wit.
—Anne Finch, Countess of Winchilsea,
"An Enquiry After Peace" (1713)

Every Ass that's Romantick believes he's inspir'd.

—Robert Wolseley, Preface to *Valentinian* (1685)

5
The Grace of Wit

DECORUM was never questioned as a part of the neo-classical creed, but its role was somewhat shadowy. As already shown, its chief tenets were subjective and constantly under re-examination. The egocentric spirits of hedonism, scepticism, and libertinism elevated individual criteria above the *consensus gentium* and its notion of decorum. In consequent debate, inspiration opposed reason, personal taste challenged the rules, and true judgment was hard put to keep its supremacy over imagination. The antithesis between formality and freedom was apparent also in the discrepancies between expressed theories and prevalent practices.[1] But most important was the kind of wit which ran counter to decorum, wit of an unknown, irrational quality, the wit of sublimity and of secret grace, considered vital to the creation of poetic beauty. Here, again, psychological theory provided the ground for discussion.

Psychological Speculation on the Rules

To understand the disconcerting but logical path which wit took in its identity with sublimity and grace, we must again, as in the truth of wit, analyze these two psychological forces in opposition to each other. In its identification with imagination, wit was thrown into direct conflict with judgment, and in this extremity it clashed with the ideal of decorum. As pure imagination, wit was properly related to the *furor poeticus,* that legendary poetic inspiration which had from ancient times been considered the source of imaginative writing.

Wit therefore became involved in the conflict over the values of the "rules," a concept used in the Age of Wit not only for the classical unities but also for the proprieties which counseled regularity and general conformity in decorous writing. Arguments against these rules centered upon psychological speculations over the relative merits of the judgment and imagination.

The dominance of reason in the seventeenth century and part of the eighteenth century supported vehemently the search for order and truth, since reason was capable of perceiving the essence of truth. Reason was often considered as synonymous with judgment, although during the Renaissance judgment had been distinguished as the faculty of logic merely supporting reason. In the discussions of the psychological basis of the rules, reason rather than judgment was regarded as the necessary check to fancy, and observance of the rules was *ipso facto* evidence of the presence of reason.

The fashion for rules was of a much shorter duration than the championing of reason. The popularity of the rules reflected the prestige in England of certain French literary figures, particularly Corneille, Boileau, Dacier, and Rapin. Their vogue had been limited to an era between 1674 and 1692, the years which mark the ascendancy in England of Thomas Rymer as a critic.[2] Although few Englishmen advocated a mechanical application of the rules, many men gave lip service to them, not simply to support the principle of decorum, but to combat "the wantonness of an extravagant Fancy." It is not surprising, therefore, to find many statements praising the rules and admonishing against the excessive use of the imagination or fancy.

Rymer considered the rules as expression of truth. He argued that Aristotle had reduced them "to the severest Test of Nature and Reason" and had "scarcely left any thing for succeeding

Ages to do."[3] Rymer was alarmed over the persistent opinion that poetry was "the Child of Fancy, never to be school'd and disciplin'd by Reason," and abhorred the view that poetry is "blind inspiration, is pure enthusiasm, is rapture and rage all over." He saw the need for fancy, but not at the cost of order:

> Fancy, I think, in Poetry, is like Faith in Religion: it makes for discoveries, and soars above reason, but never clashes or runs against it. Fancy leaps and frisks, and away she's gone, whilst reason rattles the chains and follows after. Reason must consent and ratify whatever by Fancy is attempted in its absence, or else 'tis all null and void in law.[4]

The rules afforded balance to the play of fancy or wit. The influential Sheffield was perhaps more lenient toward fancy than other critics, but he felt that,

> Fancy is but the Feather of the Pen;
> Reason is that substantial, useful part,
> Which gains the Head, while t'other wins the Heart.

The fancy is "the Muses most unruly Horse," which ". . . bounds so fierce the Rider has no rest/ But foams at mouth, and speaks like one possest." And the poet, so possessed, must exert a similar "fury" to countermand this fancy. Sheffield concluded:

> Cowley might boast to have perform'd this part,
> Had he with Nature joyn'd the rules of Art.[5]

This conflict between the rules and the fancy continued long after the chief influence of the rules was at an end, owing to the increasing attention given to imagination and its importance in the creative process. Dennis pleaded effectively for control with compelling logic:

> In short, Poetry is either an Art, or Whimsy and Fanaticism. If it is an Art, it follows that it must propose an end to it self, and afterwards lay down proper Means for the Attaining that End: For this is undeniable, that there are proper Means in Poetry we call the

Rules. Again, if the End of Poetry be to instruct and reform the World, that is, to bring Mankind from Irregularity, Extravagance, and Confusion, to Rule and Order, how this should be done by a thing that is in it self irregular and extravagant, is difficult to be conceiv'd. Besides the Work of every reasonable Creature must derive its Beauty from Regularity; for Reason is Rule and Order, and nothing can be irregular either in our Conceptions or our Actions, any further than it swerves from *Rule, that is, from Reason.*[6]

The identity of rule and reason, a basic tenet of neoclassicism, was irrefutable to those who accepted the major premises guiding Dennis.

Arguments for the rules continued into the eighteenth century. Charles Gildon, in his *Complete Art of Poetry* (1718), equated art with the rules and nature with wit. To effect a fusion, he quoted the translation by the Earl of Roscommon of the *Ars Poetica:*

> Some think that Poets may be form'd by Art.
> Others maintain that Nature makes them so:
> I neither see what Art without a Vein,
> Nor Wit without the Help of Art can do;
> But mutually they need each others Aid.

This to Gildon was "the Opinion of Horace confirm'd by Reason and Experience." His conclusion is interesting: "A strict Attendance to the Rules of Nature and Reason, can never embarrass or clogg an Author's Fancy, but rather enlarge and extend it."[7] The same dichotomy of nature and art was maintained by an anonymous essayist in the following year: "It has been a common Question, whether a Man be born a Poet or made one? But both must concur. Nature and Art must contribute their Shares to compleat the Character. Limbs alone will not make a Dancer, or a Wrestler. Nor will Genius alone make a good Poet; nor the meer Strength of natural Abilities make a considerable Artist or any kind. Good rules, and these reduc'd to Practice, are necessary to this end."[8]

The rules, creation of that exclusive human possession—the reason, or judgment—provided the perfect harmony between the diversity of nature and the uniformity of the universal. A familiar passage in Pope's "Essay on Criticism" clarifies this:

> First follow Nature, and your judgment frame
> By her just standard, which is still the same:
> Unerring Nature, still divinely bright,
> One clear, unchang'd, and universal light,
> Life, force, and beauty, must to all impart,
> At once the source, and end, and test of Art.
>
> (ll. 68–73)

The "useful rules" of "learn'd Greece" must be observed, but there is no conflict with nature, for

> Those rules of old discover'd, not devis'd,
> Are Nature still, but Nature methodiz'd.
>
> (ll. 88–89)

And the rules did not account for the *furor poeticus*, as Pope well knew.

However, the validity of rules in the creative process was being challenged for several different psychological reasons. Much attention has been paid to the revolt against the rules in general,[9] but the importance of the imagination (fancy) in this revolt deserves particular attention. One challenge to the rules lay in the application of personal opinion. In 1702 the problem of opinion troubled the playwright George Farquhar because of the resulting diversity of whims to be faced in theater audiences: "The scholar calls upon us for Decorums and Oeconnomy; the Courtier cries for Wit and Purity of Stile; the Citizen for Humor and Ridicule; the Divines threaten us for Immodesty; and the Ladies will have an Intreague. Now there are a Multitude of Criticks, whereof the twentieth Person only has read *Quae Genus,* and yet every one is a Critick after his own way; that is, Such a Play is best, because I like it."[10] A few years later in 1706, Daniel Defoe commented upon the vagaries of opinion in aesthetic theory. In a remark on ornamentation, he avers that "Opinion is the Rate of Things, but this is a *deceptio visus* upon Reason"; for

> As Fancy is the Judge of Ornaments so then Fear is the Guide of Credit; but all this is setting the World with the bottom upward, for all Things have some Intrinsick Value, for which they really ought to be Valuable, and by which they ought to be Rated—And not by Opinion; Reason and stated Rules are and ought to be the Judges of Ornaments, not unguided Fancy.[11]

Another challenge to the rules came from the principle of beauty itself, for most poets found it impossible to explain all of the attractions of their lines by regularity and decorum. It had always been a subtle distinction whether good poetry is the work of art or the work of nature, created by man or inspired by God. Recognition of certain imaginative, irregular, but essential qualities and effects of great poetic passages led to what has been called "an awareness of the validity of the imagination."[12]

The basis for the validity of the imagination rested primarily on the ancient tradition of the poet-prophet, or *vates.* In Elizabethan times, Sir Philip Sidney had recognized the poet as seer and divine prophet in his *Defense of Poesy* and traced the tradition to the Romans. His contemporary Edmund Spenser in the October Ecologue of the *Shepherdes Calender* refers to the heavenly origin of "pierlesse Poesye." So did Lodge in his *Defence of Poetry, Music, and Stage-Plays.* Milton, of course, took most seriously his role as poet-prophet. The divinely inspired nature of poetry prompted many popular aphorisms, such as "Art is taught by art, but Poetry only is the gift of God."[13] In this way the irregularity of imaginative writing was defended. But such justification was in reality an incipient romantic thorn in the body of neoclassicism, as well as a real contradiction of the rules of the ancients.

The rules were also challenged by the argument that reason was after all limited. Thomas Rymer's defense of the rules inadvertently argued effectively against the strictures imposed by these rules, not only to those committed to the imagination, who agreed that poetry is pure, rapturous inspiration, but also to those with more moderate ideas. Rymer's advocacy of the constricting chains of reason seemed particularly inimical to the nature of poetry. Dryden stood somewhere between the conservative and the radical, between the view of Rymer and that of the Countess of Winchilsea. However, in an age of reason, he was shrewdly alive to reason's peculiar deficiencies. Reason (judgment) he defined in the *Essay of Dramatic Poesy* (1668):

> I grant, he who has judgment, that is, so profound, so strong, so infallible a judgment, that he needs no helps to keep it always poised and upright, will commit no faults either in rhyme or out of it. And on the other extreme, he who has a judgment so weak and crazed that no helps can correct or amend it, shall write scurvily out of rhyme, and worse in it. But the first of these judgments is no where to be found, and the latter is not fit to write at all.

The infinite variety of plenitude thus provides theoretically for every degree of judgment among human beings, but in practice no perfect supply exists. So, after dismissing infallible judgment as a chimera and weak judgment as negligible, Dryden turned to the "best poets." In considering "judgment as it is in the best poets," he felt that "they who have the greatest proportion of it want other helps than from it, within." A weighty judgment, Dryden sees, is insufficient for success in creative writing. "Judgment is indeed the masterworkman in a play; but he requires many subordinate hands, many tools to his assistance."[14]

Dryden's view of decorum embraced the inevitable balance between judgment and fancy. In his *Defence of the Essay of Dramatic Poesy* he wrote, "Fancy and Reason go hand in hand; the first cannot leave the last behind: and though Fancy, when it sees the wide gulf, would venture over, as the nimbler, yet it is withheld by Reason, which will refuse to take the leap, when the distance over it appears too large."[15] Nevertheless, for a number of years, when under the influence of Longinus, Dryden considered fancy the more important faculty. In his Preface to *An Evening's Love* (1671), describing the composition of poetry in the drama, he wrote of "those little critics" who "do not well consider what is the work of a poet, and what the graces of a poem."[16] He went on to point out that fancy alone accounts for the "life-touches of poetry."[17] This untimely praise of "wanton Fancy," made during Dryden's quarrel with Shadwell over

Jonson's humor, undoubtedly prompted the lines of ridicule in *The Rehearsal* the same year, written by George Villiers, Duke of Buckingham, when Bayes is made to say, "I despise your Jonson and Beaumont, that borrowed all they writ from Nature: I am for fetching it purely out of my own fancy, I" (II, i).

A final challenge to the rules was the belief that the conformity they imposed actually encourages dullness, that conformity curbs both genius and originality. At the end of the Prologue to Nathaniel Lee's *Constantine the Great* (1683) the aspiring poet is advised, satirically, to observe correctness and "get the Knack of Dullness." True poets, Lee maintained, lead an unhappy life; therefore, children should be warned against "the Sin of Rhime," for poets who follow their nature and refuse to conform (such as Spenser, Cowley, and Butler) suffer in various ways from an unappreciative public:

> And if such Warning they [the children] refuse
> to take,
> This last Experiment, O Parents, make!
> With Hands behind them see the Offender [the
> individualistic poet] ty'd,
> The Paris Whip, and Beadle by his Side.
> Then lead him [the child] to some Stall that does
> Expose
> The Authors he loves most, there rub his Nose,
> Till like a Spannel lasht, to know Command,
> He by the due Correction understand,
> To keep his Brains clean, and not foul the Land.
> Till he against his Nature learn to strive,
> And get the Knack of Dullness how to Thrive.

Anne Finch, the Countess of Winchilsea, was convinced that inspiration through the fancy is superior to that dullness achieved by mere reason. The following passage expresses Pre-Romantic feeling and rebellion against the constricting forces of uniformity, imitation, and decorum:

> How are we fallen! fallen by mistaken rules,
> And Education's, more than Nature's fools;
> Debarred from all improvements of the mind,
> And to be dull, expected and designed;

And if some one would soar above the rest,
With warmer fancy, and ambition pressed,
So strong the opposing faction still appears,
The hopes to thrive can ne'er outweigh the fears.
Be cautioned, then, my Muse, and still retire;
Nor be despised, aiming to be admired;
Conscious of wants, still with contracted wing,
To some few friends, and to thy sorrows sing.
For groves of laurel thou wert never meant:
Be dark enough thy shades, and be thou there content.

Dryden, though only at moments sensing this spirit of the Countess and the nature of her muse, did recognize the limitations of the mediocre poet who "judges to a hair of little decencies, knows better than any man what is not to be written, and never hazards himself so far as to fall, but plods on deliberately. . . ."[18] Samuel Cobb, a translator and versifier, described the same limitations:

Rules they can write, but like the College Tribe,
Take not that Physick which their Rules prescribe.
I scorn to praise a plodding, formal Fool,
Insipidly correct, and dull by Rule.[19]

Cobb was referring specifically to the men who lack the ability of poets and become critics because of good memories.

A superficial dependence upon the rules provoked the constant complaint that it excluded vision and inspiration. This mechanical application of the rules was ridiculed by Addison in the *Tatler*, No. 165, where he presents Sir Timothy Tittle, a fop of the ilk of Sir Fopling Flutter, who fancies himself a critic and insists upon absolute obedience to the rules. On one occasion Sir Timothy enters a coffeehouse in a state of exhaustion:

He immediately called for a chair, and desired leave to sit down, without any further ceremony. I asked him where he had been? whether he was out of order? He only replied, that he was quite spent, and fell acursing in soliloquy. I could hear him cry, "A wicked rogue;" "An execrable wretch;" "Was there ever such a monster?" The young ladies upon this began to be affrighted, and asked whether any one had hurt him? He answered nothing, but still talked to himself. "To lay the first scene," says he, "in St. James's Park, and the last in Northamptonshire." "Is that all?" says I. "Then I suppose you have been at the rehearsal of a play this morning?" "Been!" says he; "I have been at Northampton, in the park, in a lady's bed-chamber, in a dining-room, everywhere; the rogue has led me such a dance." Though I could scarce forbear laughing at his discourse, I told him I was glad it was no worse, and that he was only metaphorically weary. "In short, sir," says he, "the author has not observed a single unity in his whole play; the scene shifts in every dialogue; the villain has hurried me up and down at such a rate, that I am tired off my legs." I could but observe with some pleasure, that the young lady whom he made love to conceived a very just aversion to him, upon seeing him so very passionate in trifles. And as she had that natural sense which makes her a better judge than a thousand critics, she began to rally him upon this foolish humour. "For my part," says she, "I never knew a play take that was written up to your rules, as you call them. . . . I must confess," continued she (for I found she was resolved to exasperate him), "I laughed very heartily at the last new comedy which you found so much fault with." "But, madam," says he, "you ought not to have laughed; and I defy any one to show me a single rule that you could laugh by." "Ought not to laugh!" says she: "Pray, who should hinder me?" "Madam," says he, "there are such people in the world as Rapin, Dacier, and several others, that ought to have spoiled your mirth."

The young lady's rebellion against decorum lies in her "natural sense which makes her a better judge than a thousand critics" as well as in her freedom in laughing aloud.

Pope felt the same reaction to the mechanical application of the rules and wrote in "An Essay on Criticism" of several kinds of critics of the day, mentioning specifically

> Some drily plain, without invention's aid,
> Write dull receipts how poems may be made.
> (ll. 114–115)

This complaint recurs in his Preface to *The Iliad* (1715), where to other shortcomings of critics he added the inability to judge a mind greater than their own: "And perhaps the reason why most Criticks are inclin'd to prefer a judicious and methodical Genius to a great and fruitful one, is, because they find it easier for themselves to pursue their Observations through an uniform and bounded Work of Art, than to comprehend the vast and various

Extent of Nature." The contrast between the "judicious and methodical Genius" and the "great and fruitful" one indicates the continuing dichotomy between the judgment and the imagination. Pope continues:

> A cooler Judgment may committ fewer Faults, and be more approv'd in the Eyes of one Sort of Criticks: but that Warmth of Fancy will carry the loudest and most universal Applauses which held the Heart of a Reader under the strongest Enchantment. Homer not only appears the Inventor of Poetry, but excells all the Inventors of other Arts in this, that he has swallow'd up the Honour of those who succeeded him. What he has done admitted no Encrease, it only left room for Contraction or Regulation. He show'd all the Stretch of Fancy at once; and if he has failed in some of his Flights, it was but because he attempted every thing.

Here Pope has presented the essential case against the rules. He did not repudiate them, as he did not repudiate propriety, but he broadened his view to include the contradictions of both propriety and the rules. Like Dryden, he respected "Nature methodiz'd"; but there always remained for him that mysterious, inexplicable charm of great poetry, the secret grace, to which he paid homage in spite of decorum and the rules.

The psychological speculation over relative functions of the faculties became again significant for complex meaning of wit. Speculation into the nature of poetry returned to the older function of the imagination as the source of poetry. Walter Carleton, friend of Dryden, put it in this way: "Phancie ought to have the upper hand, because all Poems, of what sort soever, please chiefly by Novelty."[20] The surprising and unique effects of this fancy, though defying the neoclassical rules, were accredited with the magic quality of poetry.

Wit and Genius

An important and perhaps major reason for the identification of wit with secret grace was the close association of wit with genius.[21] That genius should be closely related to, even identified synonymously with, wit is not surprising because of the identical terms with which both were usually described. Addison might very easily be writing of wit in this passage in the *Spectator,* No. 160:

> Among great Geniuss, those few draw the Admiration of all the World upon them, and stand up as the Prodigies of Mankind, who by the meer Strength of natural Parts, and without any assistance of Art or Learning, have produced Works that were the Delight of their own Times and the Wonder of Posterity. There appears something nobly wild and extravagant in these great natural Geniuss, that is infinitely more beautiful than all the Turn and Polishing of what the French call a *Bel Esprit.*

The "something nobly wild and extravagant" seems like the claims for wit; so does the lack of "assistance of Art or Learning," a frank contradiction of the rules. Actually, here Addison was contrasting genius with wit. Nicholas Rowe, the first modern editor of Shakespeare as well as a dramatist, spoke of genius in terms usually applied to wit: "But certainly the greatness of this Author's [Shakespeare's] Genius do's no where so much appear, as where he gives his Imagination an entire Loose, and raises his Fancy to a flight above Mankind and the Limits of the visible World."[22] Rowe was not discussing wit even by inference, because he had just concluded a consideration of Shakespeare's use of wit in his comedies, but the evidence of genius in the flights of fancy is identical with more sympathetic descriptions of wit.

Wit and genius exhibited many of the same traits. Both were thought to be inborn, intrinsic to one's individual nature; they were commonly considered the product of the imagination (fancy), of an undisciplined, extravagant, and "wild" intensity. Only a few men thought genius was an evidence of judgment. Samuel Wesley, father of the founder of Methodism, wrote *Epistle to a Friend concerning Poetry* (1700) in which he considered genius and wit to be as mutually co-operative as judgment and fancy traditionally were thought to be:

> As Genius is the Strength, be Wit defin'd
> The Beauty and the Harmony of Mind:
> Beauty's Proportion, Air, each lively Grace
> The Soul diffuses round the heav'nly Face.
>
> (ll. 43–46)

However, majority opinion held otherwise and thought genius was a product of the fancy. As Charles Gildon bluntly put it, "Fancy is what we generally call Nature, or a Genius."[23]

The function of genius in poetry was another point of similarity with wit. French criticism, as has been asserted, "was generally agreed that genius was the primary qualification of a poet."[24] Certainly, many English critics and poets agreed; but they were likely to identify this "primary qualification" as wit instead of genius, or consider the two as mutually important. Sheffield, agreeing with the French, wrote of genius:

> Without a Genius too, for that's the Soul,
> A Spirit which inspires the work throughout,
> As that of Nature moves this World about:
> A heat that glows in every word that's writ,
> That's something of Divine, and more than Wit.[25]

The metaphysical quality attributed here to genius was another quality shared by wit. Temple wrote of the divinity of genius, "the pure and free Gift of Heaven."[26] Gildon defined genius as "a great Capacity of Soul."[27]

Because of these similarities, it was not uncommon for wit and genius to be actually equated. Abraham Cowley, for instance, made this very identity in 1656:[28]

> And if any ask me then,
> What thing right Wit, and height of Genius is,
> I'll only shew your lines, and say, *'Tis This.*
>
> (stanza 9)

In a significant discussion of Longinus, whom he called "after Aristotle, the greatest critic amongst the Greeks," Dryden used the words interchangeably. Longinus, he wrote,

> . . . judiciously preferred the sublime genius that sometimes errs, to the middling or indifferent one, which makes few faults, but seldom or never rises to any excellence. He compares the first to a man of large possessions, who has not leisure to consider of every slight expense, will not debase himself to the management of every trifle:

particular sums are not laid out, or spared, to the greatest advantage of his economy; but are sometimes suffered to run to waste, while he is only careful of the main. On the other side, he likens the mediocrity of wit to one of mean fortune, who manages his store with extreme frugality, or rather parsimony; but who, with fear of running into profuseness, never arrives to the magnificence of living. This kind of genius writes indeed correctly. A wary man he is in grammar, very nice as to solecism or barbarism, judges to a hair of little decencies, knows better than any man what is not to be written, and never hazards himself so far as to fall, but plods on deliberately, and, as a grave man ought, is sure to put his staff before him; in short, he sets his heart upon it, and with wonderful care makes his business sure; that is, in plain English, neither to be blamed or praised.[29]

Here is a passage reflecting the constantly recurring dilemma between control and abandonment, reason and emotion, judgment and fancy. Dryden treats wit and genius as one—a force that leads to an elevation of sublime and secret grace above control, judgment, and reason, an elevation which only for moments occurs in the works of the greatest minds.

The same identity is found elsewhere. Barker associated the terms when in the dedication of his study of wit he complimented his patron, the Earl of Dorset: "Wit is not the only shining Quality for which the World admires You: To a happy Imagination, and lively Genius You have reconciled the severity and profoundness of Judgment."[30] Blackmore in a tolerant mood admitted that "the Exercise of Wit and a pleasant Genius, excels all other Recreations."[31] He defined wit as the working of the fancy, which can "dress a common Notion in a strange, and becoming Garb." He then defined genius as resulting "from this particular happy Complexion . . . [it] is Nature's Gift, but diversify'd by various specifick Characters and Limitations."[32] Thomas Killigrew, Restoration dramatist, also identified the two when one of the characters in his *Chit-Chat* (1719) objects to the current idea that playwrights should shape their wit in regular plays; such plays are only for weak geniuses, a kind of crutch to wit.[33]

Killigrew's statement reveals that genius, like wit, clashed with the neoclassical rules. John Hughes related wit to the functioning of genius, and set it apart from the rules: "Elegance of Thought is what we commonly call Wit, which adds to Propriety, Beauty, and pleases our Fancy, while Propriety entertains our Judgment. This depends so much on Genius, that 'tis impossible to teach it by Rules."[34] Others concurred in the opinion that both genius and wit were beyond the discipline of the rules. Thomas Gordon, in his Preface to *Cato's Letters* (1724), felt that the force of genius in a man of wit worked against the self-discipline imposed necessarily in learning.[35]

Metaphysical Nature of Wit

Wit, like genius, was described as a metaphysical power, inscrutable and beautiful in its effects. "Metaphysical" is here used in the sense of possessing transcendent or supernatural attributes, not to be confused with the metaphysical wit of Donne and Cleveland. In this distinct metaphysical sense, both wit and genius had similar traditional meanings. Genius had originally meant the innate other-self or spirit—what religion called the soul. Wit, the earliest meaning of which had been intellect and mind, could not be distinguished from the soul in psychological theory. As David Abercromby saw it, "The first and chief Source in us of Wit is the Soul itself."[36] In philosophical terms, "Wit is the first and principal part of the Soul, wherein the Mind, the Understanding, and the Memory are contained, which are most necessary for the direction of all good and vertuous actions."[37]

This metaphysical wit arose in the fancy, which had the special power of soaring to heights unattainable by reason. Dryden wrote of the poet "who creeps after plain, dull, common sense" and is thereby "safe from committing absurdities; but can never reach any height, or excellence of wit."[38] Sir William Temple, also skeptical of regularity and other controls of invention, had asked in his essay *On Ancient and Modern Learning* "whether Learning may not even weaken Invention in a man that has great advantages from Nature and Birth." Or, as Leonard Welsted epitomized it, "the least grain of Wit one is born with, is worth all the Improvements one can make afterwards by Study."

Welsted also noted that, although Temple had not made this statement in his poetics, it "would be eminently true, apply'd to Poetry."[39] The same concern over learning and nature is present here that marked the wrangles over learning and genius.

Dryden posed a choice between learning and nature in his conclusions upon Jonson and Shakespeare. When it came to a choice between correctness and greatness—which, to the consistent neoclassical mind, were identical—Dryden chose greatness. So Neander speaks: "If I would compare him [Jonson] with Shakespeare, I must acknowledge him the more correct poet, but Shakespeare the greater wit. Shakespeare was the Homer, or father of our dramatic poets; Jonson was the Virgil, the pattern of elaborate writing; I admire him, but I love Shakespeare."[40] Jonson, who had relied upon his judgment and learning in following the rules, was inferior to Shakespeare, who followed his imagination as well as his judgment and relied upon his natural genius. Shakespeare, like Homer, made more mistakes but rose to greater heights.

Men attracted to the secret graces of poetry had unreserved admiration for wit's exuberance and never-failing plentitude. Flecknoe felt wit "never more commendable than when it overflowes."[41] A more moderate view was that of René Rapin, who desired in poetry (he was speaking of pastorals in particular) "all sorts of delicacies, and surprizing fancies, yet not be flowing, and luxuriant." The secret lay with wit, "whose nature it is to pour it self forth"; therefore, it "must rather be restrain'd than indulg'd."[42] This lively quality lent wit its kaleidoscopic attraction. Cowley noted in his "Ode: Of Wit":

> A thousand diff'rent Shapes it bears,
> Comely in thousand Shapes appears;
> Yonder we saw it plain, and here 'tis now
> Like Spirits in a Place, we know not how.
>
> (stanza 1)

Margaret Cavendish, the Duchess of Newcastle, defined wit in terms supporting her poetry as "the purest Element, and swiftest Motion of the Brain: it is the Essence of Thoughts; it incircles all things: and a true Wit is like the Elixir, that keeps Nature always fresh and young."[43]

As a metaphysical manifestation, wit exhibited divine power. William Davenant, having certain reservations about wit, nevertheless described it as

> . . . the Souls Powder, which when supprest, as forbidden from flying upward, blows up the restraint, and loseth all force in a farther ascension towards Hell, the Cell of the Devill; But breaks through all about it as farr as the utmost it can reach, removes, uncovers, makes way for Light where darkness was inclos'd, till great bodies are more examinable by being scatter'd into parcels, and till all that find its strength (but most of mankind are strangers to wit, as Indians are to Powder) worship it for the effects as deriv'd from the Deity.[44]

Flecknoe wrote of the "somewhat in it of Divine." His exposition contains many metaphysical qualities:

> It is the spirit and quintessence of speech, extracted out of the substance of things; and a spiritual fire that rarefies and renders every thing spiritual like it self; it is a soaring quality, that just as Dedalus wings, elevates those who have it above other men; and is the same in the brain, as Nobility is in the blood. In fine, it is somewhat above expression; and easier to admire, then tell you what it is: not acquir'd by Art and Study, but Nature and Conversation . . . rendring those who have it, good and vertuous, as well as witty men; and whosoever is otherwise, as may well conclude, wants as much of wit, as they do of being such.[45]

To define this most nebulous view of wit was to define the indefinable.

This metaphysical concept was popular enough to receive much direct criticism from opponents and enthusiastic support from advocates. When Sir Richard Blackmore's tirade against the disease of wit was published in 1700, scores of panegyrics answered him. One, appearing in the same year, proclaimed:

> Wit is a Radiant Spark of Heav'nly Fire,
> Full of Delight, and worthy of Desire;
> Bright as the Ruler of the Realms of Day,
> Sun of the Soul, with in-born Beauties gay.[46]

Another appeared in *The British Apollo* in September, 1708. The author rejected the many traits attributed to wit: exotic language, satire, floridity, quibbles or trifles, banter, or smart repartees. Instead,

> . . . 'tis a Thought sprung from a Ray Divine,
> Which will through Clouds of low'ring Criticks shine:
> When in a Clear, Innubilous Serene,
> The Soul's Abstracted, Purg'd from Dross and Spleen.

The use of the light image in such passages reveals the fact that, in this metaphysical meaning, wit embodied truth just as absolutely as did decorum. With its appeal to personal feeling and mysticism, this view of wit stood in opposition to decorum and rationalism. At the same time, it was adjoined to the important tradition of the sublime.

Wit and Sublimity

The metaphysical nature of wit made logical and convenient its alliance with the Longinian theory of the sublime. Their similarities were striking: both arose in the fancy, both relied upon heightened expression, and both were related to the *furor poeticus.* Surprisingly, the more liberal neoclassical mind could include the sublime as a kind of ultimate achievement of esteemed wit, because the sublime required an essential amount of discipline. Longinus had written:

> A lofty tone . . . is innate, and does not come by teaching; nature is the only art that can compass it. Works of nature are, they think, made worse and altogether feebler when wizened by the rules of art. But I maintain that this will be found to be otherwise if it is observed that, while nature as a rule is free and independent in matters of passion and elevation, yet is she wont not to act at random and utterly without system. Further, nature is the original and vital underlying principle in all cases, but system can define limits and fitting seasons, and can also contribute the safest rules for use and practice.[47]

This system, which would "contribute the safest rules," naturally appealed to the age, although such a vague kind of discipline did not displace the rules.

Psychologically, the age had been prepared for the association of wit and sublimity. Poetry had long been assigned to the imagination, which was also the center of the emotions. Hobbes noted in his Preface to Homer's *Odysses* (1675) that "men more generally affect and admire Fancie than they do either Judgment, or Reason, or Memory, or any other intellectual Vertue; and for the pleasantness of it, give to it alone the name of Wit, accounting Reason and Judgment but for a dull entertainment." Hobbes then made a surprising comment, considering his earlier reference to imagination as a decaying sense: "For in Fancie consisteth the Sublimity of a Poet, which is that Poetical Fury which the Readers for the most part call for." This statement, made concurrently with Dryden's praises of sublimity and the secret graces, shows the particular stimulation which Longinus afforded the period.

Wit, already noted for its rhetorical extravagance, gathered additional height of expression in this metaphysical context. Such phrases as "the spirit and quintessence of speech," "a Radiant Spark of Heav'nly Fire," "a Thought sprung from a Ray Divine" abound. All indicate the propensity wit possessed for the sublime.

Perhaps the first poet to relate wit and the sublime was Cowley. Certain parallels have been perceived between Cowley's attitude toward wit in his ode and the definition by Longinus of the sublime in *Peri Hupsous.*[48] For example, Longinus defined the sublime in terms of negatives. Cowley asked:

> What is it then, which like the Power Devine
> We only can by Negatives define?
>
> (stanza 7)

Longinus limited the sublime to propriety; he made it obedient to rules. Again, he said that its excellence is due to its "soul": it transports, it is found in flashes only, and it is possible only where all things agree. All of these interpretations are applied to wit in Cowley's ode.

The influence of Longinus upon Dryden may have begun as early as 1667, as indicated in Dryden's letter to Howard, "An Account of the Ensuing Poem *Annus Mirabilis*"; in it he defined wit "or wit writing (if you will give me leave to use a School distinction)" as "no other than the faculty of imagination in the writer, which, like a nimble spaniel, beats over and ranges thro' the field of memory, till it springs the quarry it hunted after; or, without metaphor, which searches over all the memory for the species or ideas of those things which it designs to represent. Wit written is that which is well defined, the happy result of thought, or product of imagination." Certainly the influence of Longinus is clear in the *Apology for Heroic Poetry and Poetic Licence,* written in 1677, in which Dryden equates sublimity with the most figurative expression. But admiration of sublimity was natural. His interest in heightened expression had appeared in his support of the "height, or excellence of wit" at the expense of "plain, dull, common sense" in 1670 and in his attention to the "secret graces" in 1671.

Dryden's intellectual milieu was comprehensive enough to include the extremes of propriety and sublimity. He discussed them simultaneously in the essay just mentioned. His definition of wit as propriety was followed by a statement on sublimity: all men admit the necessity of a dignified style in heroic poetry, but also, "all reasonable men will conclude it necessary, that sublime subjects ought to be adorned with the sublimest, and consequently often with the most figurative expressions." This point of view enjoyed wide support. Pierre Nicole, a distinguished French Jansenist, rephrased it in his exposition of the decorum necessary in style.[49] Hobbes accepted Dryden's idea of propriety. In his Preface to the *Odysses* (1675) he described fancy as gathering "Matter and Words" and discretion as distinguishing their fitness, without which distinction "their delight and grace is lost."

Sublimity always required the craftsmanship and imagination of a great poet. The popularity of sublimity at the height of the Age of Wit resulted increasingly in mediocre efforts. The attempts at the sublime by the many pretenders and false wits were the favorite targets of Swift and Pope. Both enjoyed describing graphically the new depths to which the would-be wits could sink. The narrator of *A Tale of a Tub* is "extremely solicitous" that every reader "who has got into the Taste of Wit" shall appreciate the subtleties of the *Tale* and "descend to the very bottom of all the Sublime."[50] The wittiness here consists not only in the ironic inversion of values but also in the cleverness of the narrator—from a false point of view, of course. Later in the *Tale*, Swift satirized the obscurities of what was passing for wit and sublimity when he pleaded for "certain common Privileges of a Writer, the Benefit whereof, I hope, there will be no Reason to doubt." He meant those privileges in particular by which the reader should conclude in those passages where Swift is not understandable "something very useful and profound . . . coucht underneath." Furthermore, "whatever word or Sentence is Printed in a different Character, shall be judged to contain something extraordinary either in Wit or Sublime."[51] So Swift ridiculed the cult of unintelligibility in a facetious allusion to the obscure heights claimed by the enthusiasts of witty sublimity.

To attribute bathetic depths to the height aspired to in the sublime or in wit was a frequent ploy of ironic satire, as in "Mac Flecknoe" and the *Dunciad*. *The Art of Sinking in Poetry* is a masterpiece in this kind—at once a travesty of Longinian ornamentation and a ridicule of false wits. The mediocrity of the moderns received Pope's barbs in the introduction:

> The Latins, as they came between the Greeks and us, make use of the word *altitudo*, which implies equally height and depth. Wherefore considering with no small grief, how many promising genius's of this age are wandering (as I may say) in the dark without a guide, I have undertaken this arduous but necessary task, to lead them as it were by the hand, and step by step, the gentle down-hill way to the bathos; the bottom, the end, the central point, the *non plus ultra*, of true modern poesy![52]

Although Pope's object was to satirize so-called profundity and the depths of ineptness to which the false poets of his day had fallen, he also sought to contrast this sinking of modern poetry with those sublime heights to which only great poetry can rise. Thus, he stated that "those who have a Taste of the Sublime" are "very few, but the Profund strikes universally, and is adapted to every Capacity."[53] He also contrasted the "profund," or bathos, with wit: "If a Man who is violently fond of Wit, will sacrifice to that Passion his Friend or his God; would it not be a shame, if he who is smit with the Love of the Bathos should not sacrifice to it all other transitory Regards?"[54] In the contrast neither emerges unscathed.

Wit remained identified with the sublime as long as sublimity was considered attainable through stylistic devices and means. However, this identity became increasingly difficult as the concept of the sublime changed during the first half of the eighteenth century. John Baillie, physician and minor critic, sought new criteria in *An Essay on the Sublime* (1747) and disapproved of those presented by Longinus. He consciously departed from the concept of "the Pathetic," or "Figurative Manner" of writing. In fact, only "some part" of Longinus's treatise treated what Baillie regarded as "properly called the sublime." He did promise "as the Sublime in Writing is no more than a Description of the Sublime in Nature, and as it were painting to the Imagination what Nature herself offers to the Senses, I shall begin with an Inquiry into the Sublime of Natural Objects, which I shall afterwards apply to Writing."[55] Toward the end of the Age of Wit, wit became divorced from the sublime as the sublime came to be identified with "Natural Objects" rather than with style, as the sublime became linked to the visible and external and not to the intellectual and imaginary.

Wit as the "Grace Beyond the Reach of Art"

The development of wit as the secret grace or *je ne sais quoi*, elevated by its alliance with genius and sublimity, represents a major advance in aesthetics: the shift in emphasis from regularity to effectiveness. The new emphasis approached an organic concept of creativity, soon to flourish with Romanticism. There was a "growing belief that literature was the product of historical and economic factors and that the rules themselves were susceptible to change along with the times." Moreover, the enjoyment of the freedom represented by the metaphor of the ever-ranging spaniel was supported by the notion that literature can have a "charm incapable of being analyzed or explained but which was recognized by the reader's or spectator's sensibility."[56]

A major contribution to this individualism was the popularity of gracefulness. The concept of grace was ancient,[57] having appeared early in the criticism of Horace and Longinus. It was an aesthetic quality familiar to the Latin rhetoricians Cicero and Quintilian. Castiglionie had noted in *Il Cortegiano* (1528) the platitude that grace cannot be taught, since it is a gift of nature and of heaven. He also believed that the great enemy of grace was affectation. Views of grace had only recently been discussed by Nicolas Boileau and René Rapin. Various characteristics of grace were identical with those of wit—its innateness, its tendency toward affectation, its dependence upon metaphysical resources, and its unexplainable powers that defied the rules. All of these made the association of secret grace with wit not only logical but, under the circumstances, irresistible.

This rapport was another major achievement for wit. To the great minds of the age, wit was, when properly or elegantly phrased, "the spirit and quintessence of speech," a *je ne sais quoi.* Hobbes recognized the grace that fancy (to which alone men attribute wit) can insure when properly used.[58] Dryden, in discussing the composition of a play, felt that the plot is the foundation but is less important than the grace with which it is presented. After the plot is written,

> . . . the forming it into acts and scenes, disposing of actions and passions into their proper places, and beautifying both with descriptions, similitudes, and propriety of languages, is the principal employment of the poet; as being *the largest field of fancy, which is the principal quality required in him: For* so much the word ποιητς implies. *Judgment, indeed, is necessary in him: but 'tis fancy that gives the life-touches and the secret graces to it.*[59]

Abel Boyer had much the same quality in mind when he wrote, "It often happens, that some things offer themselves to our Wit, which are naturally finer and better, than is possible for a Man to make them by the Additions of Art and Study."[60]

Sir William Temple also expressed preference for the secret graces of the fancy. He considered the inexplicable quality in the "Genius of Poetry" as "too Libertine to be confined to so many Rules." Also, "whoever goes about to subject it to such Constraints loses both its Spirit and Grace, which are ever Native, and never learnt even of the best Masters."[61] The gracefulness of decorum was explainable by the rules, but the secret grace and genius of poetry alluded to by Dryden and Temple were inexplicable. They provided the "life-touches," for which the phrase *je ne sais quoi* was at best only adequate.

This French phrase referred in aesthetics to the grace beyond the confines of the rules, a grace perceptible not only in the writing of men of taste but also in the men of taste themselves. Robert Wolseley preferred this mysterious source of power: "The loosest Negligence of a great Genius is infinitely preferable to that *obscura diligentia* of which Terence speaks, the obscure diligence and labour'd ornaments of little Pretenders." It was such power which inspired "those nicer Beauties, those Grace strokes and finishing Touches."[62]

Logically, the concurrent beliefs of wit as secret grace and as truth should have created an insurmountable conflict within the word itself. Yet, so great was the power of rationalization that most of the great men of wit accepted both meanings under the one general word.

The Earl of Shaftesbury, while advancing his "test," also recognized the importance of grace in the arts, including poetry. In a discussion of grace, or beauty, found in his *Essay on the Freedom of Wit and Humour,* he reasoned that lovers are naturally susceptible to physical beauty, but not even the men of "cooler Passions" can "withstand the Force of Beauty, in other Subjects," in art primarily. "Every-one," he maintained, "pursues a grace, and courts a Venus of one kind or another. The *Venustum,* the *Honestum,* the Decorum of Things, will force its way." Later in the same essay he elaborated: ". . . after all, the most natural Beauty in the World is Honesty, and moral Truth. For all Beauty is Truth. True features make the Beauty of a Face; and true Proportions the Beauty of Architecture; as true Measures that of Harmony and Musick. In Poetry, which is all Fable, Truth still is the Perfection." Therefore, if grace is beauty and beauty is truth, where is the antithesis? To the Platonist no disunity can exist. Indeed, there can be no basic conflict between the revelations of the judgment and those of the fancy; both must support moral truth.

Shaftesbury differentiated throughout his discussion between beauty of mind and beauty of body but insisted that each has "a moral Part." Even the "Admirers of Beauty in the Fair Sex" voice "praises of a Humour, a Sense, a *je-ne-scai-quoi* of Wit, and all those Graces of the Mind which these Virtuoso-Lovers delight to celebrate!"[63]

THE GRACE OF WIT IN ALEXANDER POPE'S *The Rape of the Lock*

Alexander Pope accepted these conflicting meanings of wit. He recognized art with its rules, but he also recognized the beauty beyond judgment and refinement. His invocation to the "bards triumphant" of the past, which ends Part One of the "Essay on Criticism," requests "some spark" of their "celestial fire" (l. 195). Just as there is a time for discipline, so there is a time for license:

> Hear how learn'd Greece her useful rules indites,
> When to repress, and when indulge our flights.
>
> (ll. 92–93)

One should have a "just esteem" for those rules, because "to copy nature is to copy them." Nevertheless,

> Some beauties yet no precepts can declare,
> For there's a happiness as well as care.
> Music resembles poetry; in each

> Are nameless graces which no methods teach,
> And which a master-hand alone can reach.
>
> (ll. 139–143)

This "happiness as well as care" recalls the ancient critical term *curiosa felicitas,* which only the great poets possessed. Pope elaborated:

> Great wits sometimes may gloriously offend,
> And rise to faults true critics dare not mend;
> From vulgar bounds with brave disorder part,
> And snatch a grace beyond the reach of art,
> Which, without passing through the judgment, gains
> The heart, and all its end at once attains.
>
> (ll. 152–157)

It is worth pointing out that the "brave disorder" of inspired writing bypasses the judgment and relies only upon the imagination: such inspiration rises paradoxically to "faults." These faults are only so ironically (except in terms of rules, i.e., the "vulgar bounds"), for they are those secret graces beyond the reach of regular art. The final line expresses the surprise which accompanied the penetration of wit.

Of all poets of the Age of Wit, Pope most often snatched "a grace beyond the reach of art" and rose "to faults true critics dare not mend." His genius, with its delicately attuned balance of a steady, perceptive judgment and a facile, fertile fancy, produced the most graceful wit of the time. In the words of Voltaire, he was "the most elegant, the most correct, and, what is much more, the most harmonious poet that England has had. He has reduced the harsh blare of the English trumpet to the sweet sound of the flute." By common acclaim his finest poem, most fanciful and graceful, is *The Rape of the Lock.*

Motivation to write the poem arose out of a quarrel among some Catholic friends. A young man of twenty, Lord Petre, in an impetuous moment cut a lock of hair from the head of Arabella Fermor. Both Arabella and her parents were angered, and a quarrel with the Petre family ensued. John Caryll, a cousin and neighbor of the Petres, took a personal interest. To keep peace among prominent Catholics during those difficult times for Catholics, Caryll suggested to his friend Pope that he help soothe tempers with a *jeu d'esprit,* laughing the estranged parties out of their pique.

Pope was inspired by the occasion and wrote a first version of two cantos, which was published in Lintot's *Miscellany* in 1712. Contrary to expectations, Pope succeeded mainly in further angering some of the principal parties, even the young lady herself, who resented the publicity. Moreover, and most upsetting to Pope, the public was not impressed by the poem. Pope next fell upon the idea of adding to it some supernatural elements from the Rosicrucian mysteries. Encouraged by Dr. Garth (author of *The Dispensary*) and discouraged by Joseph Addison, Pope altered the poem, lengthening it to five cantos, which he published in 1714. Three thousand copies were sold in four days, a generous reward for his ingenuity.

The poem exhibits a prodigious variety of wit. It blends perfectly the factual with the fanciful—in terms of psychology, a decorous balance of judgment and imagination, though Pope perhaps favored in his later years the former of the two faculties. He commented to his friend Joseph Spence, "The making that [adding the supernatural elements], and what was published before, hit so well together, is [sic], I think, one of the greatest proofs of judgment of anything I ever did."[64] The rhetorical display consists of puns, turns, parallelisms, antitheses, extended metaphors, ironies, and paradoxes. The whole effect of this wit is burlesque of the classical heroic epic and its various conventions: the proposition, the invocation, the arming of the hero, the epic speeches, the charges and countercharges in epic battle, the descent into the lower regions, the hero's lament for the heroic dead, and others. The satiric effect results from a reversal of values, which elevates the insignificant to epic proportions, deflating the epical to the insignificant in the process.

Pope describes the goddess Belinda [Arabella] at her dressing table before the theft, being prepared by her nymph to give battle in the love game. The details of toilet trivia parody the traditional process of arming the epic hero:

> And now, unveil'd, the toilet stands display'd,
> Each silver vase in mystic order laid.
> First, rob'd in white, the nymph intent adores,
> With head uncover'd, the cosmetic pow'rs.
> A heav'nly image in the glass appears,
> To that she bends, to that her eyes she rears;
> Th' inferior priestess, at her altar's side,
> Trembling begins the sacred rites of Pride.
> Unnumber'd treasures ope at once, and here
> The various off'rings of the world appear;
> From each she nicely culls with curious toil,
> And decks the goddess with the glitt'ring spoil.
> This casket India's glowing gems unlocks,
> And all Arabia breathes from yonder box.
> The tortoise here and elephant unite,
> Transform'd to combs, the speckled, and the white.
> Here files of pins extend their shining rows,
> Puffs, powders, patches, bibles, billet-doux.
> Now awful beauty puts on all its arms;
> The fair each moment rises in her charms,
> Repairs her smiles, awakens ev'ry grace,
> And calls forth all the wonders of her face;
> Sees by degrees a purer blush arise,
> And keener lightnings quicken in her eyes.
> The busy sylphs surround their darling care,
> These set the head, and those divide the hair,
> Some fold the sleeve, whilst others plait the gown;
> And Betty's prais'd for labours not her own.
>
> (I, 121–148)

Hazlitt called this burlesque of petty details the "triumph of the insignificant." The same diminution in elevation occurs in the charges given to the sylphs to protect Belinda; the sylphs in this instance are the gods and goddesses of this tempest in a teapot and the instruments of their punishment are the articles of Belinda's toilet:

Whatever spirit, careless of his charge,
His post neglects, or leaves the fair at large,
Shall feel sharp vengeance soon o'ertake his sins,
Be stopp'd in vials, or transfix'd with pins;
Or plung'd in lakes of bitter washes lie,
Or wedg'd whole ages in a bodkin's eye:
Gums and pomatums shall his flight restrain,
While clogg'd he beats his silken wings in vain;
Or alum styptics with contracting pow'r
Shrink his thin essence like a rivell'd flow'r:
Or, as Ixion fix'd, the wretch shall feel
The giddy motion of the whirling mill,
In fumes of burning chocolate shall glow,
And tremble at the sea that froths below!

(II, 123–136)

The heroic couplet is admirably suited to the concise, neat juxtaposing of ideas in parallel, antithetic, or paradoxical relationships. In this jesting at the heroic epic, the coupling of the great and the little is particularly effective. Thus, disaster is foreseen in fanciful extremes, ranging from harm to Belinda's virtue to danger to Shock, her dog:

This day, black omens threat the brightest fair,
That e'er deserv'd a watchful spirit's care;
Some dire disaster, or by force, or slight;
But what, or where, the Fates have wrapp'd in night.
Whether the nymph shall break Diana's law,
Or some frail china jar receive a flaw;
Or stain her honour, or her new brocade;
Forget her pray'rs, or miss a masquerade;
Or lose her heart, or necklace, at a ball;
Or whether Heav'n has doom'd that Shock must fall.

(II, 101–110)

The delightful surprises in the pairing of such incongruities as Diana's law and a china jar, honor and brocade, prayer and a masquerade, heart and necklace—all poised on the decision of the Fates—rest on the choices of secret fancy. Similar antitheses point up the comic-epic elements in the climactic scene. As the chief guardian sylph Ariel, observing Belinda's momentary wavering from her chaste position by thoughts of an earthly lover, relaxes his vigil, the Baron seizes his scissors in his fourth and final effort to cut the doomed lock of hair.

> The peer now spreads the glitt'ring forfex wide,
> T' enclose the lock; now joins it, to divide.
> E'ven then, before the fatal engine clos'd,
> A wretched sylph too fondly interpos'd;
> Fate urg'd the shears, and cut the sylph in twain,
> (But airy substance soon unites again)
> The meeting points the sacred hair dissever
> From the fair head, forever, and forever!
> Then flash'd the living lightning from her eyes,
> And screams of horror rend th' affrighted skies.
> Not louder shrieks to pitying Heav'n are cast,
> When husbands, or when lapdogs breathe their last;
> Or when rich china vessels fall'n from high,
> In glitt'ring dust and painted fragments lie!
>
> (III, 147–160)

Belinda is inconsolable in her anger and she desires revenge.

> "To arms, to arms!" the fierce virago cries,
> And swift as lightning to the combat flies.
> All side in parties, and begin th' attack;
> Fans clap, silks rustle, and tough whalebones crack;
> Heroes' and heroines' shouts confus'dly rise,
> And bass and treble voices strike the skies.
>
> (V, 37–42)

And in the press of the contending forces,

> A beau and witling perish'd in the throng,
> One died in metaphor, and one in song.
> "O cruel nymph! a living death I bear,"
> Cried Dapperwit, and sunk beside his chair.
> A mournful glance Sir Fopling upwards cast,
> "Those eyes are made so killing"—was his last.
>
> (V, 59–64)

In the brilliant polish of these couplets gleam "the nicer beauties, those grace strokes and finishing touches" which Robert

Wolseley praised. The tone rises occasionally above the ridicule and burlesque to sheer enchantment of imagery and music:

> But now secure the painted vessel glides,
> And sunbeams trembling on the floating tides:
> While melting music steals upon the sky,
> And soften'd sounds along the waters die;
> Smooth flow the waves, the zephyrs gently play,
> Belinda smil'd, and all the world was gay.
>
> (II, 47–52)

Summary

Wit as secret grace was a second pinnacle of meaning, as important as the truth of wit. Wit, under suspicion of favoring the enemy, imagination, actually deserted to it in this metaphysical context; for it used various traditions contrary to the strictures of judgment and neoclassical rules: irrational and extravagant fancy, the native strength and individuality of genius, the Platonic concept of the *furor poeticus,* and the elevated style of Longinian sublimity. The result was an Augustan approximation of the creative power used traditionally by the poet-prophet, a power arming the man of wit in his search for truth.

This metaphysical interpretation influenced the future eminence of the imagination and fancy. The romantic view of inspired writing was largely defined by this context, incorporating the organic theory of poetic creation and the intuitive discovery of truth. The word "romantic" itself, destined to designate the next cultural synthesis, had already acquired another basic affinity with that next synthesis (Romanticism): romantic writing was recognized as imaginative writing. Henry More referred in 1659 to "that imagination which is most free," the kind of imagination "such as we use in Romantick Inventions."[65] The origin of romantic writing, for instance in the medieval romances, was popularly attributed to the Arabs. Thomas Rymer considered this product of the Arabs to be the antithesis of proper writing: "Fancy with them is predominant, is wild, vast, and unbridled, o'er which their judgment has little command or authority: hence their conceptions are monstrous, and have nothing of exactness, nothing of resemblance or proportion."[66]

Thus Wolseley's sneer at such lack of discipline and balance: "Every Ass that's Romantick believes he's inspir'd." Only a fool would so enthuse and elevate his senses. Had not Plato said, "He who in his sober senses seeks to endite the muse of poetry finds that his best efforts are beaten all hollow by the poetry of mad men"? The Earl of Shaftesbury has Philocles, in *The Moralists* (1709), indulge, after an enjoyment of a sublime mood, in a romantic description: "rude Rocks, the mossy Caverns, the irregular unwrought Grotto's, the broken Falls of Waters, with all the horrid Graces of the Wilderness itself." Yet writers "deep in this romantick way" can only be "People either plainly out of their wits, or over-run with Melancholy and Enthusiasm."[67]

But the seventeenth-century view did not long prevail. Joseph Wharton, under the attractions of imaginative powers, felt that Shakespeare, in *The Tempest,* had "there given reign to his boundless imagination" and had "carried the romantic, the wonderful and the wild, to the most pleasing extravagance" (*Adventurer,* September 25, 1753).[68] The sublimity of divine "madness" was upon the Western mind.

Logically, wit in this context of secret grace and sublimity should have continued on through the eighteenth century into the nineteenth century with full-blown Romanticism. However, because of certain changes in status and reactions in concepts (as described in Chapters VII and VIII), wit was not destined to share later in the pleasures of the imagination.

I take upon me absolutely to condemn the fashionable and prevailing Custom of inveighing against Critics as the Common Enemys, the Pests and Incendiarys of the Commonwealth of Wit and Letters. I assert, on the contrary, that they are the Props and Pillars of this Building; and that without the Encouragement and Propagation of such a Race, we should remain as Gothic Architects as ever.

—ASHLEY COOPER, Earl of Shaftesbury, *Characteristicks* (1711)

6

The Republic of Wit

THE YEARS 1650 to 1750 fostered a gradual change in man's concept of his relationship to his environment. The new scientific methods that explored the possibilities of observation and experimentation, the new geographical discoveries that revealed radically different social systems and the possibilities for reshaping and improving old systems, the empirical approach to knowledge advanced by Bacon, Descartes, Locke, Mandeville, and others—all tended to turn man's mind from a strict orientation in the past to both a close examination of the present and an anticipation of the future.

The future assumed ever greater importance, for the forces of nature and society were perceived more and more to rest in man's own hands. The basic construct of man's view of the world was changing from that of a static mechanism to that of a dynamic organicism.[1] One immediate result was the rapid growth of modern liberalism—the recognition of more than one valid point of view on any experience or issue.

The new construct struggled within the framework of the old climate of opinion, and the age was beset by stubborn resistance to the implications of the new views. One immediate solution was compromise, and various compromises were attempted in the seventeenth century. Deism attempted to restore the ancient theophany harmoniously within the new science. The means was the application of rational thinking to theology, based upon the premise that the dictates of man's reason and the will of God were identical. Neoclassicism attempted to re-establish the *status quo* of the ancient critical theory within the framework of current aesthetic practice. The means was the rational application of classical rules to modern forms, based upon the premise that universal forms of beauty never change. This reaching backward for eternal verities attempted to restore order to a disordered century and to provide an answer to John Donne's desolate cry of "all coherence gone!"[2] But the ancient theophany and the new science, the classical rules and current aesthetic practice would not cohere. The rationale failed, not because of false logic, but because of its false premises.[3]

One important evidence of this affirmation of the past was the temporary revitalization of the tradition of the republic of letters. This idealized republic was envisioned as a timeless community of cultivated minds.[4] It had been created by Italian humanists, mainly Petrarch, to replace the ecclesiastical community of the Middle Ages when the spiritual reality of that association diminished with the onset of the Renaissance. Thus, the republic of letters was an attempt to establish a metaphysical relationship with the literary communities of Greece and Rome and to found a spiritual commonwealth of the intellect.

It is clear that such a republic depended for its existence upon a state of mind, a kind of intellectual communion of men of letters from all ages. The humanists felt particularly close to the ancients.[5] They embodied in their republic of letters the idealism of classical republicanism, which they interpreted as a society dominated by a cultivated aristocracy.

The humanists were convinced of the importance of the pursuit of knowledge and of learning, centered in the cultivation of letters, specifically belles-lettres, by which was then meant the encouragement and study of literature, philosophy, and history. A lettered man was one who consciously disciplined his mind through the study and mastery of belles-lettres. Through this discipline, he became learned and virtuous, a *homo sapiens* or man of strong moral and intellectual sense, to be distinguished from the *homo faber,* the trained craftsman or artisan. The man of letters was pre-eminent for his seriousness, high purpose, detachment from mundane matters, and search for universal truths. Altogether, the humanist's vision was of an ideal man functioning at his best in an ideal environment in pursuit of truth and virtue. Such was the adaptation of Plato's concept of the republic to the literary community of the Renaissance.

Evidences of such a republic in the Age of Wit are plentiful and varied. The metaphor of the republic gave meaning to the man of wit in his own pursuit of truth. The prevailing seriousness of the Republic is evident in such remarks as those of the Earl of Shaftesbury, which argue for a continuing freedom of the spirit of wit and learning to attack the opposing Gothic forces in society. This basic seriousness is easily overlooked in an age renowned for levity. The citizens in this republic were not only men of letters and men of learning but also men of wit. The intellectual power of their wit was their effective force against the evils of the day.

In this literary context of wit, two features of the age facilitated the functioning of the republic and determined its peculiarities. In the first place, the social surroundings of wit, flouting in their gaiety and hedonism the very essence of the republic, gave a social, contemporary cast to the Republic of Wit. And wit itself, with its intellectual vigor and variety, gave a distinctly contentious quality to the pursuit of truth.

The Social Nature of Wit

The great literary artist is most likely to appear in centers of culture and learning. Artists act and react in a social and intellectual ferment; and the social institutions of that ferment are always indigenous to the age: taverns in Elizabethan London, salons in royal Paris, transcendentalists' homes in the neighborhood of Boston. Augustan London had its coffeehouses and produced a new form of communication, the literary journal. All of these social developments enhanced the popularity of wit and the prestige of the men of wit. The urbane quality of wit was assured by the upper-class domination of society. Brilliant conversation and polished manners were aped by London middle classes.

Several conflicting tempers existed side by side in Augustan society: rationalism, skepticism, puritanism, hedonism. But probably the most obvious temper was merriment, active on many levels. Samuel Pepys enjoyed its social, even its hedonistic possibilities, concluding a description of an afternoon and evening of March 26, 1668, at the theater, with some friends: "And mighty merry we were till about eleven or twelve at night, with mighty great content in all my company, and I did, as I love to do, enjoy myself in my pleasure as being the height of what we take pains for and can hope for in this world." Steele referred appropriately to London in 1709 as "this laughing town" (*Tatler,* No. 58).

Lord Allen Bathurst expressed the more intellectual approach to merriment in the letters to Swift on April 19, 1731:

> This I send you from my closet at Ritchings, where I am at leisure to attend serious affairs; but when one is in town, there are so many things to laugh at, that it is very difficult to compose one's thoughts, even long enough to write a letter of advice to a friend. If I see any man serious in that crowd, I look upon him for a very dull or designing fellow. By the by, I am of opinion, that folly and cunning are nearer allied than people are aware of. If a fool runs out his fortune, and is undone, we say the poor man has been outwitted. Is it not as reasonable to say of a cunning rascal, who has lived miserably, and died hated and despised, to leave a great fortune behind him, that he has outwitted himself? In short, to be serious about those trifles, which the majority of mankind think of consequence, seems to me to denote folly, and to trifle with those things which they generally treat ludicrously may denote knavery. I have observed that in comedy, the best actor plays the part of the droll, while some scrub rogue is made the hero, or fine gentleman. So in this farce of life, wise men pass their time in mirth, while fools only are serious.

The struggle to keep not only from being outwitted by others but also from outwitting oneself occupied the attentions of many men of wit.

The intellectual acceptance of the comic aspects of life has appeared in all ages, though its prevalence varies greatly. Horace Walpole stated the view most concisely for the Age of Wit: "The world is a comedy to those who think, a tragedy to those who feel."[6] The temper, the whole intellectual framework did change perceptibly. As the eighteenth century moved from thinking to feeling, the spirit of wit grew dimmer, and poetry of wit was discarded for poetry of emotion. But the wit did think, and life was a comedy.

Nevertheless, the men of wit were very serious-minded, not in spite of their wit but because of it. True wits were not serious about trifles, as Lord Bathurst had written Swift, but were seriously witty about life itself. In "this farce of life," wit was salt, the preservative of values. The anonymous but worldly-wise author of the letter *Bart'lemy Fair: or, Enquiry After Wit* (1709) wrote, "To be Witty, if a Man knows how, is the only way to please. Wit is the Salt that gives a gout to any Carrion; Nothing so Profane, or Lewd, but shall be relish'd if it pass for Wit."[7] Bishop Sprat had also noted the similar functions of wit and salt.[8] A couplet on the function of wit, appearing late in the age, ran:

> But while we're on this subject, 'tis worth thinking,
> How little salt has kept this world from stinking.[9]

In this sense, the Age of Wit was the saltiest of ages.

But even with the basic seriousness of the Republic of Wit, the other tempers were evident, and the hedonistic and libertine aspects of the age had their effects. Much of the cultivated life in London, dominated by Court influences, was superficial. Richard Steele was very sensitive about this superficiality. In a tone of gentle raillery at the town's air of superiority, he wrote in the *Tatler*, No. 57, of receiving a letter from "Emilia," who was visiting in the country:

> She says, her neighbors there have so little sense of what a refined lady of the town is, that she, who was a celebrated wit in London, is in that dull part of the world in so little esteem, that they call her in their base style a tongue pad. Old Truepenny bid me advise her to keep her wit till she comes to town again, and admonish her, that both wit and breeding are local; for a fine Court lady is as awkward among country housewives, as one of them would appear in a drawing-room.

In a more severely ironic tone on the same theme, Pope wrote to John Caryll (December 28, 1717) of "certain antique charities and obsolete devotions" still being practiced at Grinstead, such as Christmas pies and plum-broth. In seemingly complete incredulity, he marveled that "a thing called christian cheerfulness . . . is really kept alive and in practice" just forty miles from London, "that feeding the hungry, and giving alms to the poor, do yet make a part of housekeeping," and concluded with feigned amazement "that prayers and roast beef do actually make some folks as happy as a whore and a bottle." The true man of wit found himself always at odds with the superficialities, the vices, and the foibles of the age. These evils did, in fact, define the area which seemed most needful of illumination by the light of wit.

The tone of merriment, then, with its superfice of pleasure and laughter, must not obscure the intellectual activities of the men of wit and learning. If life is a comedy to him who thinks, what better time for the comic aspects to be ascendant than in an age dominated by reason. Wit required an intellectual atmosphere, and the age is distinguished by its spirit of free inquiry. Called a "dissecting and most curious Age,"[10] it carried on the classical search for truth and virtue. In theology, the Arianism of Socinius and Servetus arose once again to challenge the traditional trinitarianism of orthodoxy and fundamentalism. In psychology, Locke's empiricism struck at the supposed inherent evil of man's nature. In morals, the increasing moral pressure of the increasing middle classes met head-on the licentiousness sparked by a frivolous court. In aesthetics, men of wit insisted, on the one hand, upon the regularity and universality of creativity through decorum and, on the other hand, upon the uniqueness and individuality of creativity through secret grace. The citizens of the Republic of Wit used the intellectual play of wit, both as decorum and as secret grace, in the quest for truth and virtue.

In the urbane, sophisticated London society, no matter what the nature of the inquiry, the intellectual men of wit demanded freedom—the freedom to expose pretension to learning, to satirize the superficiality of the dilettante, to ridicule dullness and ineptness, and to belabor the current addictions to vice. The real "Pests and Incendiaries of the Commonwealth of Wit and Letters" were everywhere abounding and, as enemies to truth and virtue, must be pursued and pinioned in their corners. Of such a nature was the struggle in this age to uphold the eternal verities of classical antiquity.

The Weapons of Wit

In the time-honored search for truth and virtue, many intellectual devices afforded the men of wit the incisive power they needed. Oldmixon declared, "Every thing that pleases in Writing is with us . . . resolved into Wit, whether it be in the Thought or the Expression,"[11] and any convenient means were taken in the resolution. These means—the weapons of wit—were the intellectual media; the nature of the search is revealed in the kinds of weapons used. The important ones were criticism, satire, ridicule, raillery, and humor. Coming from different sources, they were all closely identified with wit in ways that changed their meanings thereafter. The semantic identification of each can be readily demonstrated.

Criticism as Wit

The new emphasis upon individual judgment in the changing aesthetics appears to have been chiefly responsible for the increase of criticism early in the Age of Wit. But the increase was due also to wit, which thrived on its intellectual advantage over its opposition. The practice of criticizing had become so widespread that in 1750 the word critic was glossed: "Like *homo,* a name given to all the human race."[12]

If every play-goer and conversationalist considered himself a critic, then obviously the word must not be understood in any technical sense. In fact, the term critic described an attitude, not a profession. It did not in most instances even apply to the "men who followed the example of Aristotle and Horace in discussing the rules or laws of poetry instead of examining specific modern works."[13] When Shadwell addressed those "Piccaroons of Wit" in his audience who dictated public opinion,[14] he did not have only the Earl of Roscommon and John Sheffield, Dryden and Thomas Rymer in mind. His tone alone, not to mention his language and the whole occasion, indicates a much wider audience. The principal objects of his attention were the social wits, the gallants and fops, the various aesthetes and their followers, who proclaimed with such force and insistence "I like it" or "I don't like it" that they dictated popular taste. They were more likely than not to be inspired by envy and ill will than by insight and understanding, considering another man's successes their own failures. This is the attitude inferred by Sedley in the Prologue to *The Mulberry Garden* (1668):

> Our Author, seeing here the Fate of Plays,
> The dangerous Rocks upon the Coast of Praise,
> The cruel Critick and malicious Wit,
> Who think themselves undone if a Play hit.

Dryden, who thought too highly of criticism and wit to honor the hoards of little pretenders with the status of critic, nevertheless had his explanation for the increase of these so-called critics: "every one who believes himself a wit, that is, every man, will pretend at the same time to a right of judging."[15] Every little wit assumed as his prerogative the privilege of personal judgment. As Abel Boyer quipped, "After all, a Critick is the last Refuge of a pretender to Wit."[16] Swift's explanation of these small minds is found in "To Mr. Delany on the Libels Written Against

Him" (1730). He granted them very little wit—just enough to make them obnoxious:

> When Jove was, from his teeming Head,
> Of Wit's fair Goddess brought to Bed,
> There follow'd at his lying-in
> For after-birth a Sooterkin;
> Which, as the Nurse pursued to kill,
> Attain'd by Flight the Muses' Hill;
> There in the Soil began to root,
> And litter'd at Parnassus' Foot.
> From hence the Critic Vermin sprung,
> With Harpy claws and Poisonous Tongue;
> Who fatten on poetic Scraps
> Too cunning to be caught in Trapps.
>
> (ll. 115–126)

These were the nuisances who carped away at each new work by Swift and his friends, stealing their ammunition in the attack.

There was a widespread idea that these critics were, for the most part, thwarted poets. As the age was beset with would-be poets, many of them turned their limited knowledge and weak wit to criticizing. So Dryden wrote in the Dedication of *Examen Poeticum* (1693):

> Ill writers are usually the sharpest censors; for they, as the best poet and the best patron said,
>
> > When in the full perfection of decay,
> > Turn vinegar, and come again in play.
>
> Thus the corruption of a poet is the generation of a critic; I mean of a critic in the general acceptation of this age; for formerly they were quite another species of men.

St. Evremond had already expressed the same opinion. Samuel Cobb in 1707 recalled in his "Discourse on Criticism" the observation of St. Evremond, "Some Persons, who would be Poets, which they cannot be, become Criticks which they can be."[17] Pope adapted the view for his own purposes in his "Essay" (ll. 36-37). This important poem was especially directed to those "who seek to give and merit fame,/and justly bear a critic's noble name" (ll. 46–47). However, he was also mindful of the little pretenders and "Critic Vermin,"

> Those half-learn'd witlings, num'rous in our isle,
> As half-form'd insects on the banks of Nile;
> Unfinish'd things, one knows not what to call,
> Their generation's so equivocal.
>
> (ll. 40–43)

Criticism became a chief medium for wit, and as the wits exercised their critical faculties freely, the two words came to be used synonymously.

Satire as Wit

Satire was allied with wit early in the age.[18] The special value of satire as the "fearsome Nemesis of vice" was justified, as Mary C. Randolph has shown, only in proportion to the effectiveness of its violence and incisiveness.[19] Its historic role of scourging vice into reformation, as Dryden put it,[20] was a function newly attributed to wit. Thus, an epitaph on the Earl of Rochester, included in a broadside ballad of 1680, reads,

> Under this Tomb we do Interr
> The Ashes of Great Rochester;
> Whose pointed Wit (his worst of Crimes)
> So fully lasht our Foppish Times.[21]

So pervasive was the influence of wit that changes in the nature of satire were soon observed. Wolseley defended Rochester's use of wit, "for Satyre, that most needful part of our Poetry, it has of late been more abus'd, and is grown more degenerate than any other; most commonly, like a Sword in the hands of a Mad-man, it runs a Tilt at all manner of Persons without any sort of distinction or reason." For those "modern Sparks," he continued, who would as soon "libel a Woman of honour, as to kill a Constable who is doing his duty," it is obvious that "Slander therefore is their Wit, and dresse is their Learning; Pleasure their Principle, and Interest their God."[22]

Satire was losing its subtlety and decorum. Defoe, writing of the characteristics of the Pasquinade as a form of personal satire, believed that "the Sting should be so very sharp, that it should kill even all the Resentment of the Persons Satyriz'd; so that the Person pointed at should be asham'd to be Angry." Though he considered satire as a kind of wit, he was nonetheless apprehensive of the vicious satiric tendencies:

> But when Dirt throws Dirt, when great Men are made the Scorn and Contempt of Parties, and in ribaldry that has nothing but Rage in it; no Fancy, no Brightness; there's nothing to keep the stench out of our Noses; a Man cannot say it is done clean; and therefore I have long wonder'd to see how our People on both sides hug, and hand about such weak and empty Pieces, as their Fathers would not have vouchsafed to look at: But it is an Evidence of the Ascendant Rage has got over our Senses, which has debauch'd the taste of Wit.[23]

Defoe's concept of proper satire is quite similar to Dryden's. Years earlier, in *A Discourse concerning the Original and Progress of Satire* (1693), Dryden has described the most effective satire:

> How easy is it to call rogue and villain and that wittily! But how hard to make a man appear a fool, a blockhead, or a knave, without using any of those opprobrious terms! To spare the grossness of the names, and to do the thing yet more severely, is to draw a full face, and to make the nose and cheeks stand out, and yet not to employ any depth of shadowing. . . . A witty man is tickled while he is hurt in this manner, and a fool feels it not.

Both Defoe and Dryden noted the difference between the bludgeoning of the club and the neat thrust of the rapier, the "difference betwixt the slovenly butchering of a man, and the fineness of a stroke that separates the head from the body, and leaves it standing in its place."[24] Wit could easily use either technique.

Robert Wolseley, like Dryden and Defoe, connected satire

with wit, setting up his own categories. The more direct kind of satire "has much of the Nature and more of the Wit of Jack-Pudding's Buffoon'ry, for as he, tho' he flings Dirt at every body, is angry with no body, so do these Bully Writers perpetually assault People from whom they never receiv'd the least Provocation, and murder their good Names in cold Blood." The subtler, more vicious satire was "of a more serious Cast, but withal 'tis more malicious; and falling in with the baseness of a corrupt Age, does infinitely more mischief; this is made to wound where it ought to defend and cover where it shou'd expose, to contradict the very first Elements of Morality, and bid defiance to the unalterable Essence of things, by calling Good Evil and Evil Good."[25] Wolseley was describing the techniques of satiric irony used so effectively by great wits of the age—the techniques of the topsy-turvy world of inverted values.

Blackmore was vitriolic in his condemnations of wit in satire. In his "Satyr against Wit" (1700) he condemned all such forms of wit. Satire, ancient in tradition, should not be debased:

> Those who by Satyr would reform the Town
> Should have some little Merit of their own,
> And not be Rakes themselves below Lampoon.

The only way to control satire, Blackmore thought, was through the application of judgment by men of recognized judgment:

> Therefore let Satyr-Writers be supprest,
> Or be reform'd by cautious Dorset's Test.
> 'Tis only Dorset's Judgment can command
> Wit, the worst Weapon in a Madman's Hand.

Satire, subject to decorum, should observe propriety. Similarly, Defoe felt that men should "go about" satire "like poets: that is, like Men of Sense and Men of Wit." This meant that the satire would be "sharp and clever, suitable to the Quality of the Persons, and the Dignity of Satyr."[26] In 1726 James Arbuckle classified satire with ridicule as "the main Provocatives to Laughter"; the two were "reckoned the chief embellishments of Discourse by all who Aim at the Character of Wits."[27] Satire continued to be an expression of wit, and in 1744 Morris defined satire as "a witty and severe Attack of mischievous Habits or Vices."[28] Thus, satire was recognized as another medium of wit, and the two terms were commonly used interchangeably.

Ridicule as Wit

Ridicule also had its own tradition and resisted identification with wit. Dryden seems to have separated them when he maintained that the poet's primary aim is to provoke laughter. "When he writes humour, he makes folly ridiculous; when wit, he moves you, if not always to laughter, yet to a pleasure that is more noble."[29] Nevertheless, ridicule was drawn irresistibly into wit's orbit. Temple in 1690 was interested in one new development, the "Vein" of ridicule which "has entered and helpt to Corrupt our modern Poesy." His explanation was that "such modern Poets as found no better way of pleasing" had resorted to using ridicule. "This was Encouraged by finding Conversation run so much into the same Vein, and the Wits in Vogue to take up with that Part of it which was formerly left to those that were called Fools, and were used in great families only to make the Company Laugh."[30] Obviously, Temple was unimpressed with either ridicule or wit as popularly used, but he did think of the two as closely associated. In his second essay of 1690, he mentioned the satiric impact of *Don Quixote,* in which "Wit and Humour turned all this Romantick Honour and Love into Ridicule." He followed this with a discussion of the popularity of ridicule. He had, he asserted, known "more than one or two Ministers of State that would rather have said a Witty thing than done a Wise one, and made the Company Laugh rather than the Kingdom Rejoyce."[31]

Both Addison and Steele, in the *Spectator,* No. 249, showed concern over "the talent of turning Men into Ridicule, and exposing to Laughter those one converses with." The disturbing effect of such ridicule was to reverse the values respectively of vice and virtue, a technique that ridicule shared with criticism, satire, and other intellectual media. The confusion of values in this reversal received constant criticism to the end of the eighteenth century.[32] To the moralist the effect of ridicule upon society bordered upon ethical and moral anarchy; its source was wit. To this effect Steele wrote in the *Tatler,* No. 159:

> The wits of this island, for above fifty years past, instead of correcting the vices of the age, have done all they could to inflame them. Marriage has been one of the common topics of ridicule that every stage scribbler has found his account in; for whenever there is an occasion for a clap, an impertinent jest upon matrimony is sure to raise it. This has been attended with very pernicious consequences. Many a country squire, upon his setting up for a man of the town, has gone home in the gaiety of his heart and beat his wife. A kind husband has been looked upon as a clown, and a good wife as a domestic animal, unfit for the company or conversation of the *beau monde.* In short, separate beds, silent tables, and solitary homes have been introduced by your men of wit and pleasure of the age.

In an early issue of the *Tatler,* No. 63, a "Mr. Dactile" defined ridicule as a talent "to be used as a man does his sword, not to be drawn but in his own defence, or to bring pretenders and imposters in society to a true light." But, Steele continued in comment upon this view, "We have seen this faculty so mistaken, that the burlesque of Virgil himself has passed, among men of little taste, for wit; and the noblest thoughts that enter into the heart of man levelled with ribaldry and baseness."

Ridicule had the same general purpose as had satire, the exposure of the foibles of mankind, but its method was different; it aimed at highlighting the comic aspects of the foibles. This use of ridicule received much attention in the early eighteenth century, when the distinction was made between mirth (an exercise of gentlemen) and laughter (an exercise of the commoner). Addison wrote at length in the *Spectator,* No. 291, on the emotion aroused by ridicule:

> A little Wit is equally capable of exposing a Beauty, and of aggravating a Fault; and though such a Treatment of an Author naturally produces Indignation in the Mind of an understanding Reader, it has however its Effect among the Generality of those whose Hands

it falls into, the Rabble of Mankind being very apt to think that every Thing which is laughed at with any Mixture of Wit, is ridiculous in it self.

Blackmore, too, became alarmed at the subversive effects of witty ridicule upon the character of men and morals. In *An Essay upon Wit* (1716) he devoted much space to the abuses of wit, especially by those who "cannot equal the bright Example of Vertue in others" and who therefore "strive to sully or efface it" and "make it seem rather the Dishonour and Deformity, than the Beauty and Perfection of the Mind." He added in the next paragraph, "Wit is likewise misapply'd, when exercis'd to ridicule any unavoidable Defects and Deformities of Body or Mind." The new sensibility is evident here in the avoidance of personal injury.[33]

Ridicule, then, was understood as a tool of wit. The outstanding instance was the proposal by Shaftesbury and others to use ridicule as the mode of wit which could effectively put truth to the test of close scrutiny. How natural this proposal was is made clear in Morris' exposition of these various intellectual attitudes. He thought of wit as "the lustre which is thrown upon one Subject, by the sudden Introduction of another Subject." He then concluded, "Thus if any Foible of a Character in real Life is directly attacked, by pointing out the unexpected and ridiculous Affinity it bears to some inanimate Circumstances, this Foible is then ridiculed with Wit, from the Comparison which is made."[34] Wit is here thought of as basically rhetorical in nature, the ridicule existing in the risible surprise which the unexpected comparison reveals. Wit had not changed fundamentally from its use in the conceit; it had simply become more versatile.

Raillery as Wit

Raillery was associated with wit at an early date. It had always been a light and pleasant form of satire which usually appeared in the form of banter, jest, or good humor and was directed most often at individuals. As Addison defined it (*Tatler*, No. 59), "the true art of raillery" exists "when a man turns another into ridicule, and shows at the same time he is in good humour, and not urged by malice against the person he rallies." The use of raillery was one of the more innocuous kinds of wit.

Dryden attested to the use of raillery as wit in his "Defence of the Epilogue" (1672), for "by the knowledge and pattern of their wit who write before us, and by the advantage of our own conversation, the discourse and raillery of our comedies excel what has been written by them." The popularity of raillery upon the stage is evidenced by numerous prologues and epilogues of the period. A typical acknowledgment is found in the Epilogue to *The Fatal Jealousie* (1673), written by Henry N. Payne:

> Then since to rail o' th' Stage and in the Pit,
> Must in this sickly Age be counted Wit;
> And that th' Infection cannot be subdu'd,
> We Actors for our own sakes do conclude,
> The Itch to write and rail will ne'er be cur'd,
> And therefore faith let 'em be both Endur'd.

Raillery was considered a proper, mild form of entertainment. Bishop Sprat commended Cowley for his "proper measure of Wit" and his "inoffensive Raillery."[35] John Evelyn made the identification when, in writing of the death of his daughter Mary, he remarked that "though she had abundance of wit, the raillery was so innocent and ingenius that it was most agreeable."[36] It was described in much the same way a hundred years later (1753) when it was called "a delicate exertion of pleasantry upon the foibles, the slight indiscretions, the mistaken opinions, or even the virtues of men, when carried to some degree of excess." However, this media, under the impact of contention, became more biting, as reflected in Evelyn's comment which followed his statement above: "No tincture of ill-nature must be suffered to mingle in the composition of raillery. Good manners must always be the predominant quality."[37] Good-mannered raillery was swept into the general contagion of wit.

Complaints followed the debasement of raillery. An observation was made—again by Evelyn—when in 1669 he attended exercises at Oxford and observed the *Terrae Filius,* or university buffoon, entertaining "the auditory with a tedious, abusive, sarcastical rhapsody, most unbecoming the gravity of the University." It seems that a new kind of raillery had appeared: "The old facetious way of rallying upon the questions was left off, falling wholly upon persons, so that it was rather licentious lying and railing than genuine and noble wit."[38] The "genuine and noble wit" referred to here was the formal, impersonal kind of rhetorical oratory.

One new, irritating form of raillery relied upon name-calling, a hurling of epithets. Defoe resolved never to publish letters addressed to the *Review* containing "malicious Railings" (III, No. 59), a resolve he found difficult at times to keep. He gave much attention to this form of wit, which he called "Billingsgate Storms" (I, No. 100). It was his belief that attacks of raillery were too often not aimed at discovering truth but at clouding it; people too frequently "rail without Ground" and use "ill language for Argument" (III, No. 59). Once he wrote sarcastically, "How pleasant it is to see Men rail, instead of answering, and call Rogue and Rascal to defend themselves from Matter of Fact" (IV, No. 166).

Raillery was regularly referred to as one form of wit. Swift wrote slyly of "our good brethren of the Surly Sect" who made "Railing a Rule of Wit."[39] Shaftesbury used the term synonymously with wit and ridicule in his test of truth. Nothing, he believed, was "Proof against Raillery, except what is handsome and just."[40] The anonymous writer of *An Essay on Wit* (1748) agreed: "For a subject which will not bear Raillery, is suspicious; and a Jest which will not bear a serious Examination, is certain false Wit."[41]

Humor as Wit

The relationship of humor to wit differs from the relationship of wit to other intellectual weapons in two ways: first, in the strong opposition of the two before their identity; and, second, in the drastic changes in meaning that occurred in both terms—greater in humor—as a result of their association. Humor, as understood by Shadwell, remained the personality type developed by George

Chapman and Ben Jonson—a character dominated by a strong trait or combination of humors. Some earlier association of the two terms has already been discussed above—that is, in physiological theory, in which each of the four humors determined one kind of a wit, and in psychological theory, in which both humor and wit arose from the faculty of imagination. An early clash of the two terms, centering largely on psychological theory,[42] occurred in the Dryden-Shadwell argument. Shadwell argued that humor was above wit, which was a product of the fancy only, while Dryden upheld the supremacy of wit, a product of fancy but guided by sufficient judgment.

The disturbing truth was that both wit and humor contained obvious similarities which tended to confuse them. Dryden approved "the mixed way of Comedy; that which is neither all wit, nor all humour, but the result of both."[43] Both Dryden and Shadwell agreed that the two shared a similar purpose or function in exposing vice and folly.[44] Confusing similarities were noted by Congreve in his famous letter to Dennis "Concerning Humour in Comedy": "To Define Humour perhaps were as difficult as to Define Wit; for like that it is of infinite variety . . . tho we cannot certainly tell what Wit is, or what Humour is, yet we may go near to show something which is not Wit or not Humour, and yet often mistaken for both." This definition by negatives in the manner of Cowley was noted by Addison in the *Spectator*, No. 35.

Another point of relationship between the two media was the appropriateness of wit to humorous characters. Congreve agreed with Shadwell that humorous characters should speak wit—appropriate wit, of course: "Tho I make a Difference betwixt Wit and Humour, yet I do not think that Humorous Characters exclude Wit: No, but the Manner of Wit should be adapted to the Humour."[45] Swift felt that either enhanced the other. In the Apology to *A Tale of a Tub,* he stated that "as wit is the noblest and most useful Gift of humane Nature, so Humour is the most agreeable, and where these two enter far into the Composition of any Work, they will render it always acceptable to the World." He stated later in "A Vindication of Mr. Gay and The Beggar's

Opera" that humor "in its Perfection is allowed to be much preferable to Wit, if it be not rather the most useful, and agreeable Species of it."[46]

Furthermore, the characteristics of wit and humor were so coincident that descriptions of one word might easily be taken as describing the other. So Addison's description of humor in the *Spectator,* No. 35, used terms and concepts usually reserved for wit:

> If we look into the Productions of several Writers, who set up for Men of Humour, what wild Irregular Fancies, what unnatural Distortions of Thought, do we meet with? If they speak Nonsense, they believe they are talking Humour; and when they have drawn together a Scheme of absurd inconsistent Ideas, they are not able to read it over to themselves without laughing. These poor Gentlemen endeavour to gain themselves the Reputation of Wits and Humorists, by such monstrous Conceits as almost qualifie them for Bedlam; not considering that Humour should always lye under the Check of Reason, and that it requires the Direction of the nicest Judgment, by so much the more as it indulges it self in the most boundless Freedoms.

Addison virtually identifies wit with humor. Certainly, his discussion demonstrates how inevitable this association was in view of their common characteristics: wild and irregular fancy, unnatural distortion of thought, the expression of nonsense, the stimulation to laughter, the use of monstrous conceits, the need for check by reason and judgment, and the indulgence in boundless freedom. In the same number of the *Spectator* Addison also presented one of his characteristic genealogies, relating wit to humor through union with mirth:

> Truth was the founder of the family, and the father of Good Sense. Good Sense was the father of Wit, who married a lady of a collateral line called Mirth, by whom he had issue Humour. Humour therefore being the youngest of this illustrious family, and descended from parents of such different dispositions, is very various and unequal in his temper; sometimes you see him putting on grave looks and a solemn habit, sometimes airy in his behaviour and fantastic in his dress.

The time or occasion of the actual identification of wit and humor remains unknown. Congreve noted in his letter to Dennis in 1695 "Concerning Humour in Comedy" that "Wit is often mistaken for Humour." The beginnings of this fusion are evident in these lines from J. Lacy's *Sir Hercules Buffoon* (1684): "I was told you were in a gay humour last night, good company, and very witty."[47] However, as early as 1667, Bishop Sprat, in discussing the "Wits and Railleurs," wrote of their advantages over the Royal Society because of their use of "humorous" and "merry" methods instead of "the pale, or the melancholy."[48]

Simultaneously with the popular identification of wit and humor, there occurred the change in meaning of humor from the Jonsonian "humorous" quality of character to the characteristic "mirthful" and "comical," as in Bishop Sprat's remark. Congreve complained in 1695, "When a few things have been Wittily and Pleasantly spoken by a Character in a Comedy, it has been very usual for those who make their Remarks on a Play while it is acting to say, *Such a thing is very Humorously spoken: There is a great Deal of Humour in that Part.*"

It is noteworthy that the changes of meaning in humor resulted largely, though not entirely,[49] from its increasing affinity with certain traits of wit. The peculiar nature of humor allowed it to assume permanently the more pleasant aspects of wit. It is true also that as humor was competing with wit it did assume the popular meanings of wit, which it never relinquished. It remains to this day quite estranged from its Jonsonian meanings.

The changing of humor from its Jacobean context to its modern meaning illustrates the semantic dynamics constantly at work, more obvious at some times than at others. The traditional meanings of wit and its intellectual weapons intermingled, and all meanings changed—some more than others. Wit became the generic term, the chief "tag" name, the work à la mode, and hence a slang word for all the intellectual devices. Each media for wit—criticism, satire, ridicule, raillery, and humor—lost something of its former distinction as it took on its own shade of the meaning common to all—wittiness. Shaftesbury, in speaking of the freedom of raillery, wrote, "But let who will condemn the Humour thus described; for my part, I am in no such apprehension from this sceptical kind of Wit . . . I can very well suppose Men may be frighted out of their Wits: But I have no apprehension they shou'd be laugh'd out of 'em."[50] Here wit is used in two senses: as intelligence and as an intellectual attitude synonymous with humor and with raillery. The same diffuseness in distinction exists in *An Essay on Wit* (1748), anonymously written, in which occurs the following: "Humour is the only Test of Gravity; and Gravity of Humour. For a subject which will not bear Raillery is suspicious; and a Jest which will not bear a serious Examination, is certainly false Wit." Both writers were interested in the serious application of wit.

The intellectual weapons of wit[51] are not exhausted with this limited consideration of criticism, satire, ridicule, raillery, and humor, though these were the media most often named and defined. There were other attitudes and approaches, such as burlesque, caricature, mockery, mirth, and merriment; the list might well prove to be endless and involve murky areas too ambiguous and complex for meaningful examination.

One additional medium is noteworthy: irony. Swift's special love of this approach to truth has already been considered in the discussion of *Gulliver's Travels*. Irony is also implicit in the mockery or ridicule of the heroic epic, scholastic thinking, and chivalric honor so often found during the Age of Wit, both in England and on the Continent. Irony was also enjoyed privately among the wits. Lord Bathurst once wrote Swift (September, 1730) concerning the quality and effects of Swift's political tracts. His indirect approach is unmistakable:

> There is no wit in any of them: I have read them all over, and do not remember any of those pretty flowers, those just antitheses, with which one meets with so frequently in the French writers; none of those clever turns upon words, nor those apt quotations out of Latin authors, which the writers of the last age among us abounded in; none of those pretty similes, which some of our modern authors adorn their works with, that are not only a little like the thing they would illustrate, but are also like twenty other things. In short as often as I have read any of your tracts, I have been so tired with them, that I have never been easy till I got to the end of them. I have found my brain heated, my imagination fired, just as if I was drunk. A

pretty thing, indeed, for one of your gown to value himself upon, that with sitting still an hour in his study, he has often made three kingdoms drunk at once.

Here is one technique of irony—the praising with faint damning. Such high compliments in apparent criticism were twice the pleasure of a plain statement of admiration. Swift, who loved the ironic technique pleasantly used, answered the following month:

> I would give the best thing I ever was supposed to publish, in exchange to be author of your letters. I pretend to be an improver of irony on the subject of satire and praise, but I will surrender up my title to your lordship.

Swift's beloved ironic way pervades all his masterful satires. Regardless of the intellectual media, the point is, as Oldmixon stated, that everything which pleased the age was resolved into wit, for wit made use of any means to find expression and to attain the aims of the Republic of Wit.

Literary Significance of Wit

The Republic of Wit was a concept of the mind, but it did not function purely as an intellectual abstraction. The men of wit came to terms with reality, faced their social and intellectual environment, and selected their best weapons with care. In the broadest sense, wit influenced almost every part of English life. It was not only a major topic of conversation, but it set the very tone of conversation. Its social repercussions resounded as the popular man of wit made his presence felt everywhere: on the streets, at the theaters, in the coffeehouses. The most important influence, however, was literary. The Age of Wit produced masterpieces of wit written by dedicated men of wit. Just who these men were and why they wrote should be made clear, but clarification is complicated by certain ambiguities inherent in the very phrase "man of wit."

This particular republic, in the spirit of the humanistic and idealistic vision of an eternal community of men of letters, or simply cultivated gentlemen, included only the men of true wit. It had no place for mediocrity or meanness of mind. Therefore, the discriminating taste of the age set itself the task of distinguishing the true from the false wits. The two chief criteria were the quality of a man's wit and its use. As the quality of wit revealed the difference between the false wit and the *bel esprit,* so the use of the wit distinguished the little wit, or witling, from the man of taste and good sense. Addison, in the *Spectator,* No. 249, stated that ridicule should be "employed to laugh Men out of Vice and Folly" so that "it might be of some Use to the World" instead of being generally "made use of to laugh Men out of Virtue and good Sense, by attacking every thing that is Solemn and Serious, Decent and Praise-worthy in human Life." It is clear that Addison is concerned with virtue and good sense and with every thing that is solemn, decent, and praiseworthy in human life. What he also implies is that those who abuse ridicule are the "unlucky little Wits" and that those who use ridicule justly are the true wits.

This much is clear in Addison's exposition of the abuse of wit. However, in the same *Spectator,* No. 249, Addison followed this discussion with the opinion that "If *Hudibras* had been set out with as much Wit and Humour in Heroic Verse as he is in Doggerel, he [Samuel 'Hudibras' Butler] would have made a much more agreeable Figure than he does." In relegating doggerel to a class with other "trival Arts of Ridicule," Addison was suggesting that Butler was one of the little wits who practiced these arts. This kind of personal opinion or judgment presents a problem of perspective in the definition of the true wit.

Who and What Is a Wit?

The "dissecting" age showed great interest in classifying the kinds of wits. Categories are to be found in Congreve's *The Way of the World,* Wycherley's *Love in a Wood* (II, i), and in the epilogues of numerous plays.[52] Steele provided a list in the *Spectator*, No. 442, when he invited "all manner of Persons" to submit essays for publication,

> . . . whether Scholars, Citizens, Courtiers, Gentlemen, of the Town or Country, and all Beaux, Rakes, Smarts, Prudes, Coquets, Housewives, and all Sorts of Wits, whether Male or Female, and however distinguished, whether they be True-Wits, Whole, or Half-Wits, or whether Arch, Dry, Natural, Acquired, Genuine, or Deprav'd Wits; and Persons of all Sorts of Tempers and Complexions, whether the Severe, the Delightful, the Impertinent, the Agreeable, the Thoughtful, Busie, or Careless; the Serene or Cloudy, Jovial or Melancholly, Untowardly or Easie; the Cold, Temperate, or Sanguine; and of what Manners or Dispositions soever.

The variety of categories indicates the difficulty and confusion in defining all of the wits the age recognized.

Technically, anyone who used wit in writing and speaking was a man of wit. Practically, no unanimity of opinion developed on the precise nature of true wit. Since no criteria were evolved, the determination of who were wits and who were not remained a matter of personal opinion or of traditional categories. In the traditional category was Barker's classification, which followed the rhetorical classification of expression. He stated that "all Witty Compositions may be reduc'd to the three following Heads, viz. Poetry, Oratory, or History." From this he deduced that "a Man of Wit designs to pass either for a Poet, an Orator, or an Historian."[53] This category would have satisfied Plato, perhaps, but in the seventeenth century it was too restricted, for it left out philosophers, theologians, playwrights, Court gentlemen, and others.

This classification was certainly more objective, however, than the psychological one, based upon the relationship between the judgment and the imagination. A psychological classification was made by Dennis when he called Wycherley "A Man of Wit" because in him "Fancy and Judgment are like a well-match'd Pair; the first like an extraordinary Wife, that appears always Beautiful, and always Charming, yet is at all times Decent, and at all times Chast; the Second like a Prudent and well-bred

Husband, whose very Sway shows his Complaisance, and whose very Indulgence shows his Authority."[54] This criterion, although quite witty in itself with its parallel similes, is entirely subjective.

The results of varying and subjective criteria are what one would expect—inconsistency and relativity. Thus any wit, no matter what his stature or facility, was likely to be considered both true and false, depending upon the critic. Dryden was honored generally as a true wit, but not by Shadwell, the Earl of Rochester, and Blackmore. Rochester wrote of Dryden in *An Allusion to Horace* (1679):

> And may not I have leave impartially
> To search and censure Dryden's Works, and try
> If those gross faults his choice Pen does commit
> Proceed from want of Judgment or of Wit;
> Or if his lumpish fancy does refuse
> Spirit and Grace to his loose slattern Muse?
> Five hundred Verses ev'ry Morning writ,
> Proves you no more a Poet than a Wit.

Pope was considered one of the great wits at the time that Theobald called him a scribbler;[55] and Theobald, one of the more competent literary scholars, was to Pope a dullard.

Under the spirit of intense rivalry and jealousy, objective judgments were seldom desired, much less attempted. The difference between wit and dullness often turned upon the point of view. With this in mind, Sir Robert Howard wrote in his preface "To the Reader" to *Four New Plays* (1665) that those who "expose their private Wit to a publique Judgment" cannot be fairly evaluated since that "Phansie from whence the Thoughts proceed" is too sympathetic. This fact "renders Men no perfecter Judges of their own Writings than Fathers are of their own Children, who find out that Wit in them which another discerns not, and see not those Errors which are evident to the unconcern'd."

If the writer of wit himself lacked the perspective to judge his own production, the critic of wit was no less limited. Defoe condemned in the *Review* (VIII, No. 63) the "reading Wits" who "can write nothing themselves, take upon themselves Judges of

Wit, condemning not according to the Dullness of the Writers Judgment, but the Dullness of their own." He related an amusing incident to illustrate his point:

> It was but a few Days ago I came into a Coffee House, and I saw a Gentleman nodding over the *Spectator;* What have you got there said I to him, after I had wak'd him; the *Spectator,* says he, he's Damnable Dull to Day; I went on to talk of other Business to him, and by and by I was for taking the *Spectator* out of his Hand to read it—Hold, says he, I han't read it myself—Yet he could tell it was very Dull—That is to say he was very sleepy, and could not relish what he read—Well, having had his nap out, he read it over, and I perceiv'd him laughing to himself—What tickles you now, says I, D[am]n him, says he, this *Spectator* would make a Body laugh, he is a very witty Fellow—Now the Case is plain, the Man was awake; before, when his Head was Dull, the *Spectator* was damnable Dull; but when his own Wits were in Action, then the *Spectator* had a great deal of Wit.

So did a man's critical opinion change with his attitude.

Swift's changing attitude—toward the function of criticism, in this instance—illustrates this subjectivity. His attitude depended upon whether he was giving or receiving criticism. As a critic, he naturally felt the seriousness of the function to the literary community. In "Of Poetry: A Rhapsody" Swift gave advice to a young poet, whose work had been poorly received:

> But first with Care imploy your Thoughts,
> Where Criticks mark'd your former Faults.
> The trivial Turns, the borrow'd Wit,
> The similes that nothing fit;
> The cant which ev'ry Fool repeats,
> Town-Jests, and Coffee-house Conceits;
> Descriptions tedious, flat and dry,
> And introduc'd the Lord knows why.
>
> (ll. 143–156)

The tone here is respectful of the value of criticism in exposing false wit. But it is in a different tone that Swift speaks to him as an incipient critic:

But if you think this Trade [poetry] too base,
Put on the Critick's Brow, and sit
At Wills the puny Judge of Wit.
A Nod, a Shrug, a scornful Smile,
With Caution us'd, may serve a-while.
Proceed no further in your Part,
Before you learn the Terms of Art.
(Which seldom is the Dunce's Case)

(ll. 233–240)

The former would-be poet is now a would-be critic. Being as yet unlearned, as Pope put it, he cannot start out as a wit, but must slide down the hierarchy to poet to critic and may prove a plain fool at last.[56] Swift places him low in the scale of critics, those who heed the rules:

Then talk with more authentick Face,
Of Unities, in Time and Place.
Get Scraps of Horace from your Friends,
And have them at your Fingers Ends.

(ll. 243–246)

Swift even anticipates misquotations:

A forward Critick often dupes us
With sham Quotations *Peri Hupsous:*
And if we have not read Longinus,
Will magisterially out-shine us.

(ll. 255–258)

This poem, entitled "A Rapsody," is ironic and direct by turns, but such changing perspective is everywhere apparent in Swift's writings.

The evidence of total subjectivity in judging true and false wits abounds. In the letter to Charles Wogan on August 2, 1732, Swift wrote proudly of "Pope, Gay, and I," who concentrated all endeavours "to make folks merry and wise" and "to laugh the follies of mankind out of countenance, and as often to lash the vices out of practice"; he spoke also of the "taste of England" being "infamously corrupted by shoals of wretches who write for their bread." These wretches were just as positive in their own opinions. Sir Richard Blackmore was such a "wretch"—though he did not write for bread. In his *Essay upon Wit* (1716) Blackmore set out to review the present conditions of wit. At one point he wrote:

> Another pernicious Abuse of Wit is that which appears in the Writings of some ingenious Men, who are so hardy as to expose from the Press the most venerable Subjects, and treat Vertue and Sobriety of Manners with Raillery and Ridicule. Several, in their Books, have many sarcastical and spiteful Strokes at Religion in general, while others make themselves pleasant with the Principles of the Christian. Of the last kind this Age has seen a most audacious Example in the Book intitul'd, *A Tale of a Tub.*

Both Swift and Blackmore considered themselves qualified to criticize, and both thought of themselves as using wit. The instances of subjective judgment could be extended indefinitely. The point is simply that for clarity men of true wit must be described in terms other than the personal and subjective ones used during the Age of Wit.

The True Man of Wit

Regardless of the subjective nature of the phrase "man of wit," it epitomized the ideal man of letters and learning. In keeping with the aristocracy of learning, the true wit assumed a certain aristocratic condescension toward lesser wits. So Pope commented to Swift in a letter on January 6, 1734, upon a mutual acquaintance who paid Swift "no sort of civility" while visiting in Ireland: "He is too much a Half-wit to love a true wit, and too much half-honest to esteem any entire merit." The same *esprit de corps* prompted Swift's proud comments upon the activities of his friends. Certain characteristics mark these wits from the masses of pretenders about them.

In the first place, they were *les hommes d'esprit* in English society, the men of parts and of sense. They were learned in the sense of being not only well educated but cultured—in other words, true men of letters. To them the inferior minds were "unlearn'd witlings." John Gay condemned Defoe to an inferior place, because, in spite of his "excellent Natural Parts," he lacked even a "small Foundation of Learning."[57] The Earl of Rochester, in his "great Mastery of Satyre," felt it his duty to expose the "Purloiners of Wit" and the "Quacks and Mountebanks in Poetry"[58] as the pretenders and dilettanti that they were.

Second, the true wits moved in a small circle of kindred spirits—personal friends, congenial contemporaries, and the great minds of the past. Pope disciplined his spirit with all three. Of the last he wrote to Caryll on June 25, 1711: "I know too well the vast difference between those who truly deserve the name of poets and men of wit, and one who sees nothing but what he owes them; and I keep pictures of Dryden, Milton, Shakespeare, &c., in my chamber, round about us, that the constant remembrance of them may keep me always humble." The wits of the past, both recent and remote, served for study and elucidation, for too few great wits were recognizable in the present. As Pope grew older, the few "modern" wits—limited to his own friends—decreased. Late in life, on March 3, 1736/7, he wrote to Swift,

> Would to God you would come over with Lord Orrery, whose care of you in the voyage I could so certainly depend on, and bring with you your old housekeeper, and two or three servants! I have room for all, a heart for all, and, think what you will, a fortune for all. We could, were we together, contrive to make our last days easy, and leave some sort of monument, what friends two wits could be in spite of all the fools in the world.

Swift expressed the rapport between the great wits of all ages in his *Battle of the Books,* in which the ancients, few in number, rout the modern wits, characterized by their spiderlike tendency "to spit wholly out of themselves." However, a few of the greater among the moderns (Sir William Temple, Robert Boyle, and others—all friendly to Swift) are won over to the side of the ancients. In this way, Swift vindicated the ancients' principles.

A sense of dedication was a third great mark of a true wit. The role of the man of wit incorporated the ideal man of sense and learning.[59] This was Dryden's concept. Wolseley considered Rochester a dedicated man who had in his keeping the "Privy-Seal of Sense." Pope felt the seriousness of the role of wit. In his early enthusiasm for wit, he often placed it above all other literary offices. As late as February 16, 1732/3, he still had a notion "to show the silly world that men of wit, or even poets, may be the most moral of mankind." The phrase "even poets" recalls the supreme standing of the wit in the Republic of Wit, to which poets stood second, as in the couplet in the "Essay on Criticism":

> Some have at first for wits, then poets past,
> Turn'd critics next, and prov'd plain fools at last
> (ll. 36–37)

Although placed in a slightly facetious context, these lines have serious implications. A poet could only rise to the grace beyond the reach of art if he employed the *je ne sais quoi* of true wit. But despite this respect for wit, Pope, like others, wavered from complete dedication to the role.

Swift was unwavering in his devotion to wit. His early dedication is clearly presented in the "Ode to the Athenian Society" (1691), in which he stated that he belonged to the "Good-natur'd" sect of wits as opposed to the "Ill-natur'd." His comments to Charles Wogan on the objectives of Pope, Gay, and himself conclude with the following:

> I confess myself to be exempted from them in one article, which was engaging with a Ministry to prevent, if possible, the evils that have overrun the nation, and my foolish zeal in endeavouring absolutely in one important article, yet even there I lost all hope of favour from those in power here, and disobliged the Court of England, and have in twenty years drawn above one thousand scurrilous libels on myself, without any other recompense than the love of the Irish vulgar, and two or three dozens signposts of the Drapier in this city, beside those that are scattered in country towns, and even these are half worn out. So that, whatever little genius God has given me, I may justly pretend to have been the worst manager of it to my own advantage of any man upon earth.

His tenacious loyalty to the spirit of wit stands out in his words to Ford the next year, 1733: "I envy Mr. Pope for his being raild at. I think all men of wit should employ it in Satyr, if it will onely serve to vex Rogues, though it will not amend them. If my Talent that was were equal to the sourness of my temper, I would write nothing else."

Fourth and finally, true wits were distinguished by a persisting, serious purpose: the search for truth. The age relied ostensibly upon reason, since reason and judgment were considered functions of the brain-centered rational soul. These faculties could distinguish not only between pleasure and pain but also between good and evil. Man alone possessed such mental powers and alone could perceive moral and ethical truth. The men of wit accepted this highest functioning of the mind. They felt especially qualified in this search since they combined the truth of wit with its grace.

The Search for Truth

The true wits directed their search for truth in the manner of Plato and Aristotle. They accepted man as the crown of creation and hence the only worthy study by man. The proper study of mankind was man. The men of wit pursued their duty, as they saw it, of correcting man and his society. They would hold man to the divine design, as it were. Their means of correction was wit, the test of truth.

This singleness of purpose and method was not understood, much less accepted, by the age as a whole. Far from it. The very nature of truth, as well as the means of determining truth, was being re-examined. The man of scientific orientation, the collector of facts, was challenging the traditional custodian of truth, the man of letters. Specifically, the humanists, seeking always the moral and ethical nature of man through ratiocination, were having to compete for authority with the modern natural philosophers like Bacon and Spinoza, such observers as Copernicus, Galileo, Gassendi, Kepler, and Newton. Truth to these latter men was objective, and physical, the result not of rationalization but of sensory experience and investigation.

Not only truth but its very communication was under close examination, as all the arguments over rhetorical language revealed.

The seventeenth-century discussions of the relative importance of thoughts and expression often questioned the validity of poetic language. Hobbes, Locke, and others attacked the use of imaginative expression, supporting the old view that it was treacherous and misleading outside its use in poetry and other art forms. Bishop Sprat, representing the scientific view, noted among members of the Royal Society

> . . . a constant Resolution, to reject all the amplifications, digressions, and swellings of style: to return back to the primitive purity, and shortness, when men deliver'd so many things, almost in an equal number of words . . . a close, naked, natural way of speaking; positive expressions; clear senses; a native easiness: bringing all things as near the Mathematical plainness as they can; and preferring the language of Artizens, Countrymen, and Merchants, before that of Wits, and Scholars.[60]

The phrase "Mathematical plainness" leaves little doubt as to how simple such a style would have to be to please these critics.

The pursuit of truth by the men of wit was not easy. Inimical to the direct approach and often to a direct statement of truth were the techniques of wit, such as the surprise of the sudden comparison, the irony of the fictitious narrator,[61] the seeming misdirection of satire and ridicule, the constant examination of the standards of criticism. Numerous contemporaries of Blackmore agreed with his charge that wit was misused in its "Opposition to Religion, and to the Destruction of Virtue and good Manners in the World." He concluded ironically, "our Poets seem engag'd in a general Confederacy to ruin the End of their own Art, to expose Religion and Virtue, and bring Vice and Corruption of Manners into Esteem and Reputation."[62]

Many answers arose to meet these charges. Perhaps the most common, certainly a logical, answer was that vice in order to be exposed must be depicted effectively and appropriately. A fine statement of this view was made by Wolseley, who defined propriety as "the very Essence of Wit"; furthermore, it was the "only possible way to win the Understanding and engage the Affections of a rational Creature." He deplored the unnecessary use of obscenity, which was used "with as little pertinence as some of our modern Enthusiasts use godly Phrases and Scripture Expressions," which in excess will "nauseate" instead of affect the public. Appropriateness and effectiveness are the secrets to good writing. "The short and true state of the Case is this: all depends upon the Genius and Art of the Writer, for as an obscene Thought, if it be not livelily painted, will have but a small or perhaps no effect upon the Mind of the Reader, according to the proportion of flatness in the Expression, so a chast or a pious Meditation, if it has the same disadvantage, will work as little."

In most answers, the men of wit defended ultimately the validity of the imagination or fancy. Again, Wolseley, after consideration of Horace's *Ars Poetica,* concluded:

> Poets and Painters have an equal right to design and draw what they please, provided their Draughts and their Models be fram'd and govern'd by the nature of things; they must not joyn Serpents with Doves, nor Tygers with Lambs; that is, they must not couple Contraries, and show impossible Chimaeras. This is all the caution Horace gives either to Poets or Painters; he exempts nothing that is natural from the imitation of Art, *nor does he set any thing out of the reach of Fancy that is within the bounds of Truth.*[63]

Dryden, Shaftesbury, Pope, Addison, and Swift were in general agreement on this. Inasmuch as this point of view argued for secret grace, it hailed the *je ne sais quoi;* and thus men of wit opposed the objective, descriptive mind's empirical approach to truth.

The high seriousness and purpose of the arts, especially of poetry, were consistently maintained. Dryden held poetry as the equal of philosophy: "Moral truth is the mistress of the poet as much as of the philosopher; Poesy must resemble natural truth, but it must be ethical. Indeed the poet dresses truth, and adorns nature, but does not alter them."[64] The Earl of Shaftesbury, in his arguments for the freedom of wit and humor, equated beauty with truth: "And thus, after all, the most natural Beauty in the World is Honesty, and moral Truth. For all Beauty is Truth. True features make the Beauty of a Face; and true Proportions the Beauty of Architecture; as true Measures that of Harmony and Musick. In Poetry, which is all Fable, Truth still is the Perfection."[65] His test of truth was based upon the hypothesis that "truth, 'tis suppos'd, may bear all Lights,"[66] and the most penetrating light that he knew was wit. Each of the great wits applied this test in his own way. Addison and Steele reinforced morality with wit and wit with morality. The Scriblerus group were motivated in their works by a zeal to expose vice and falsehood through satire, irony, and ridicule.

The dedication of the men of wit to this search for truth was enhanced by the traditional allegiance of the poet to Apollo, the Greek god of light and prophecy, as well as music. He symbolized in the broader sense both truth and poetry. During the years under study, his domain was extended to wit. The Earl of Rochester, because of "his great Mastery in Satyre" was "particularly trusted with the Justice of Apollo,"[67] which office obliged him to pursue the "Purloiners of Wit."[68] Dr. Patrick Delany, friend of Swift, presented in "News from Parnassus" an assembly of poets who had been convened by Apollo to find a "Vicegerent in his Empire below." The spirit of raillery which marks this poem does not obscure the significance of this "Empire," over which men of wit presided under the direction of Apollo.

The Literary Community as a Republic of Wit

The Age of Wit continued the tradition of the republic of letters. Its neoclassical union with the ancients, though lacking something of the mysticism, included the revival of classical rules and the defense of the ancients against attacks by the moderns. Imitation of the ancients was never slavish, for English temperament resists all those attempts at uniformity and regularity which have at times captivated other literatures—most notably, the French. The age agreed generally with Pope "first [to] follow Nature," to which the rules of old conformed. But this conformity was insufficient. There remained "those freer beauties," which under the rules appeared "monstrous and mis-shap'd." These beauties could be reconciled to "form and grace," however, from a "due distance." This proper distance reconciled even irregularities in ancient writings:

Those oft are stratagems which errors seem
Nor is it Homer nods, but we that dream.[69]

As the man of letters was highly respected in the traditional republic of letters, so was the man of wit in the Republic of Wit. Dryden's influence at Will's coffeehouse and Johnson's large circle of friends of affluence indicate something of the attention paid to such cultivated gentlemen. The phrase "man of letters" was of course altered to suit the new age: "man of wit and sense," "man of wit and learning," "man of wit and judgment," or just "man of wit." The categories of learning were widened to include all gentlemen of learning—playwrights, churchmen, philosophers, writers of prose as well as poetry.

The appearance of the naturalist, the scientist per se, posed a problem, for here was a man with a more specialized knowledge than general learning. Learning had long been understood to be not only "the mother of vertue and perfection" but also "the knowledge of the arts and science."[70] But science in the older sense had meant the systematizing of knowledge in general. With the appearance of the natural sciences, which rejected all such systems, some effort was made to admit the scientist to the select company. Such an effort is evident in the aims of the journal *The Present State of the Republic of Letters* (1728). However, the humanities and natural sciences were not compatible within the concept of the republic. It is probable that the neoclassical culture was the final society in England dominated by the man of letters and his special approach to truth. Thereafter, the climate of opinion was determined increasingly by scientists and the empirical approach.

The literary community, centered in London, deplored the crudities of the rustic life which surrounded it. In matters of style, decorum cultivated *urbanitas* (i.e. city words, accents, and idiom), *facetus* (i.e. the grace and polished elegance of the learned), and other qualities of refined writing. The city boasted an atmosphere conducive to traditional learning. Thus *The Present State of the Republic of Letters* bragged: "No country in the world furnishes greater plenty of good materials . . . than England, as there is none where arts and sciences are cultivated with greater encouragement, or better success." The journal continued in praise of the lettered mind: "Here the greatest men in the State are often also the brightest ornaments of the Republic of Letters, and promote learning as much by their example, as by their protection."[71]

The phrase "Republic of Letters" occurred infrequently in the literature—the phrase "Republic of Wit" not at all, but the metaphor was regularly implicit. Swift's poem of dedication to wit, the "Ode to the Athenian Society," implied the concept of a Republic of Wit. Dennis assumed a continuing republic when he wrote to Steele:

> For all things of late Days have been manag'd by Cabal and Party; and there seems to have been a Conspiracy in the Commonwealth of Learning, among Fools of all Sorts, to exalt Folly at the Expence of Common-sense, and make Stupidity triumph over Merit in the very Dominions of Wit, which has been one of the Causes why Things are reduced to that deplorable State upon our British Parnassus. Apollo and the Muses seem to have abandon'd it; disdaining that their Divinities should honour a Place with their Songs, where Fools and Pedants, Buffoons, Eunuchs and Tumblers have so often met with Applause.[72]

Dennis's usual disdain for the popular use of wit did not prevent his acknowledging its significance in the literary community, which he refers to as the "Commonwealth of Learning" and the "Dominions of Wit" in the "British Parnassus."

The Republic of Wit in the Earl of Shaftesbury's Essay "Soliloquy: or, Advice to an Author"

One of the men who felt the reality of the Republic of Wit was Anthony Ashley Cooper, the third Earl of Shaftesbury. Born at Exeter House, London, in 1671, he was the grandson of the first earl, the would-be kingmaker. A Whig like his grandfather, Shaftesbury supported in his short political career the causes of liberty for the English citizen and independence for Parliament. Tutored by his grandfather's personal friend, John Locke, who had presided at his birth as a physician, he was imbued with many of the views of that great philosopher.

Shaftesbury is important in his own right as an ethical philosopher. Well-grounded in the classics, he could speak Greek and Latin fluently by the age of eleven. He borrowed from the ancients, especially Plato, the concept of a communion of enlightened minds, a communion to promote the harmony of the beautiful with the good. He believed in an instinct which attracts the individual to the race. In this idea he departed from his teacher, who would admit no innate ideas. Furthermore, Shaftesbury believed in immediate feeling and the play of the imagination, as opposed to the discursive reason and external sense-impressions. In this connection he advocated the secret power of wit, the *je ne sais quoi,* which could penetrate to the very source of the ridiculous and expose it. He opposed the egoistic doctrine of Thomas Hobbes, arguing in the wake of Locke for the natural goodness of man. He believed in a system of cosmic benevolence and thus was the first philosopher of feeling.

The strong Platonic flavor of his philosophy provided the necessary framework for the republic. He saw a sense of order and harmony in the universe, a moral coherence pervading man and his surroundings. This all-pervasive force was embodied in the classical concepts of truth and virtue, the achievements of learned men. Put another way, Truth and Virtue were the positive evidences of God in the universe. "Truth," as Shaftesbury asserted in "A Letter concerning Enthusiasm" (1708), "is the most powerful thing in the World." He accepted the techniques of wit—the inverted values of satire, humor, raillery, ridicule, and irony: "Expose any infirmity or vice," he maintained; by this means "Folly and Extravagance of every kind were more sharply inspected, or more wittily ridicul'd" (sect. ii).[73]

Several of Shaftesbury's essays develop the concept of the Republic of Wit. "A Letter concerning Enthusiasm" is the first essay in the collection of writings which he published in 1711 under the title, *Characteristicks.* The second essay, "*Sensus Communis:* An Essay on the Freedom of Wit and Humour" (1709), presents his "defence of Raillery" in a free society. Shaftesbury pleads for the freedom of public assembly where ridicule may have its opportunity for inquiry, "for without Wit and Humour, Reason can hardly have its proof, or be distinguish'd" (Part I, sect. v). One of the benefits from such inquiry is that "we shall grow better Reasoners, by reasoning pleasantly, and at our ease; taking, or laying down these Subjects, as we fancy" (Part I, sect. vi).

But not all reasoning or play of wit is pleasant, and Shaftesbury defends certain gentlemen who

> . . . speak as ill of themselves as they possibly can. If they have hard Thoughts of human Nature; 'tis a Proof still of their Humanity, that they give such Warning to the World. If they represent Men by Nature treacherous and wild, 'tis out of care for Mankind; lest by being too tame and trusting, they shou'd easily be caught.
>
> (Part II, sect. ii)

Shaftesbury defended the principles of wits as did Rochester and Swift.[74] He believed in the basic honesty of men, regardless of one's approach to truth: "A Man must be soundly ridiculous, who, with all the Wit imaginable, wou'd go about to ridicule Wisdom, or laugh at Honesty, or Good Manners" (Part IV, sect. i).

The third essay in the *Characteristicks,* entitled "Soliloquy: or, Advice to an Author" (1710), contains explicitly the metaphor of the Republic of Wit, specifically in Part II, Section 2. Shaftesbury traces the "Flourishing and Decay of Liberty and Letters," discussing first the decline of Rome and the invasion of the barbarians and "Gothicism," then the present "Age when Liberty is once again in its Ascendent." In the spirit of the ascendent liberty, he defended the men of wit:

> From these Considerations, I take upon me absolutely to condemn the fashionable and prevailing Custom of inveighing against Critics, as the Common Enemys, the Pests, and Incendiarys of the Commonwealth of Wit and Letters. I assert, on the contrary, that they are the Props and Pillars of this Building; and that without the Encouragement and Propagation of such a Race, we shou'd remain as Gothic Architects as ever.
>
> (Part II, sect. ii)

In order to determine the pertinence of the ancients for the modern republic, Shaftesbury examined certain writers of classic times, first of all Homer, the father-poet, who retained only what was "decent of the figurative or metaphorick Style, introduc'd the natural and simple; and turn'd his thoughts towards the real Beauty of Composition, the Unity of Design, the Truth of Characters, and the just Imitation of Nature in each particular" (Part II, sect. ii). Homer's style was copied in dramatic tragedy.

After the tragedies came the "witty Labours of an Aristophanes, and the other comick Poets." Their comedy, though lacking some fine points of the preceding literature, did

> . . . explode the false Sublime of early Poets. . . . The good Tragedians themselves cou'd hardly escape its Lashes. The pompous Orators were its never-failing Subjects. Every thing which might be imposing, by a false Gravity or Solemnity, was forc'd to endure the Trial of this Touchstone. Manners and Characters, as well as Speech and Writings, were discuss'd with the greatest freedom. Nothing cou'd be better fitted than this Genius of Wit, to unmask the face of things, and remove those Larvae naturally form'd from the Tragick Manner, and Pompous Style, which had preceded.

The general effect was a curb to excessiveness in various ways.

> The Comick Genius was apply'd, as a kind of Caustick, to those Exuberances and Fungus's of the swoln Dialect, and magnificent manner of Speech. But after a-while, even this Remedy it-self was found to turn into a Disease: as Medicines, we know, grow corrosive, when the fouler Matters on which they wrought are sufficiently purg'd, and the Obstructions remov'd.

Although the Athenian government found it necessary to curb by decree the public presentation of this caustic comedy, yet the overall effect was an improvement in realm of wit.

> Nothing therefore cou'd have been the Cause of these publick Decrees, and of this gradual Reform in the Commonwealth of Wit, beside the real Reform of Taste and Humour in the Commonwealth of Government it-self. . . . As this Intelligence in Life and Manners grew greater in that experienc'd People, so the Relish of Wit and Humour wou'd naturally in proportion be more refin'd. Thus Greece in general grew more and more polite; and as it advanc'd in this respect, was more averse to the obscene buffooning manner. The Athenians still went before the rest, and led the way in Elegance of every kind.
>
> (Part II, sect. ii)

Shaftesbury concluded his review of classical comedy with a brief discussion of Roman comedy and of Menander in particular.

Then the reader's attention was directed to the state of wit in England and to certain affinities it had with the earlier wit:

> In effect, we may observe, that in our own Nation, the most successful Criticism, or Method of Refutation, is that which borders most on the manner of the earliest Greek Comedy. The highly-rated burlesque Poem [*Hudibras*], written on the Subject of our Religious Controversys in the last Age, is a sufficient Token of this kind. And that justly admir'd Piece of Comick Wit [*The Rehearsal*], given us some time after by an Author of the highest Quality, has furnish'd our best Wits in all their Controversys, even in Religion and Politicks, as well as in the Affairs of Wit and Learning, with the most effectual and entertaining Method of exposing Folly, Pedantry, false Reason, and ill Writing. And without some such tolerated manner of Criticism as this, how grosly we might have been impos'd on, and shou'd continue to be, for the future, by many Pieces of dogmatical Rhetorick, and pedantick Wit, may easily be apprehended by those who know any thing of the State of Letters in our Nation, or are in the least fitted to judge of the Manner of the common Poets, or formal Authors of the Times.
>
> In what Form, or Manner soever, Criticism may appear amongst us, or Criticks chuse to exert their Talent; it can become none besides the grosly superstitious, or ignorant, to be alarm'd at this Spirit. For if it be ill manag'd, and with little Wit; it will be destroy'd by something wittier in the kind: If it be witty it-self, it must of necessity advance Wit.
>
> And thus from the Consideration of antient as well as modern Time, it appears that the Cause and Interest of Criticks is the same with that of Wit, Learning, and good Sense.
>
> (Part II, sect. ii)

In such manner did wit serve the ideal of the republic, exposing folly, pedantry, false reason, and ill writing; by this inverted technique the men of wit strove to illuminate the moral and spiritual truths, the essence of reality to the followers of Plato and Aristotle. The philosophy of the Earl of Shaftesbury was founded upon this idealism. He remarked upon the refusal of a workman to compromise his standards of workmanship, "This is Virtue! real virtue, and Love of Truth, independent of Opinion, and above the World."[75]

Such regard for ideals and spiritual values has ever challenged the intellects of mankind. Yet, the other side of the coin was turning up more and more frequently with the increasing success of the new sciences in physical truth. Although Shaftesbury's truth remained fairly much above the world, the new approach was very much in the world—the empirical world of fact. Its thoroughgoing materialism was a major factor in the ultimate destruction of the ideal of the Republic of letters, and of wit.

Summary

Wit served the Republic of Letters in a variety of ways. When Dryden heralded the "present age of wit," he had in mind the rhetorical effects of wit, in which "the language, wit, and conversation of our age, are improved and refined above the last."[76] But he believed that "moral truth" was as much the "mistress of the poet as of the philosopher." His effective expositions of wit as decorum and as secret grace described for his contemporaries two means of illuminating truth. His fellow poets agreed. To be sure, the approach of the men of wit was often negative rather than positive. In the manner of witty satire and criticism, they more often attempted to expose vice and ridicule folly than to dress truth and adorn nature. But their ultimate objective was the same, and moral seriousness underlay all of their major works.

The Republic of Wit is the culmination of the significance of wit in the age. The aims of the Republic motivated the concerted effort of the literature of the wits in the contentious years 1704 to 1729 to rectify the abuses of learning. When by mid-century the decline of wit was an accepted fact, it was natural for Richard Bentley, Esq., son of a famous father, to describe its decadent state against the background of the classical tradition:

> See all Parnassus mourn,
> Mute ev'ry Muse, see George's praise unsung,
> Their laurels scatter'd, and their lyres unstrung,
> Nay, Aganippe murmurs something sad.[77]

So we, grown penitent, on serious thinking,
Leave Whoring, and devoutly fall to Drinking.
Scowring the Watch grows out of fashion wit,
Now we set up for Tilting in the Pit,
Where 'tis agreed by Bullies, chicken-hearted,
To fright the Ladies first, and then be parted.
A fair Attempt has twice or thrice been made,
To hire Night-Murth'rers, and make Death a Trade.
When Murther's out, what Vice can we advance?

—JOHN DRYDEN, Prologue to *The Spanish Fryar* (1680)

7

The Caricature of Wit

THE QUALITY AND QUANTITY of literary productions of wit were greatest from 1704 to 1729, a period which began with the publications *A Tale of a Tub* and *The Battle of the Books* and ended with the Variorum Edition of *The Dunciad.* Concertedly, these publications attacked the "little Scriblers," and "critic Vermin," and the "Dunces." Wit enjoyed its greatest popular and critical esteem during these years: Swift, already dedicated to wit,[1] had written the *Tale* and *Battle* six to eight years before and continued turning out stinging wit through 1726 when *Gulliver's Travels* was published. Addison and Steele, writing in periodicals, sought to "enliven Morality with Wit, and temper Wit with Morality." Shaftesbury proposed to revitalize the "Commonwealth of Wit and Learning" with the free reign of wit and humor in the test of truth. Gay set ears a-tingle with his satire on the vicious practices of the time; and Pope perfected the Augustan mode of satire popularized by Dryden and gathered all modes and contexts of wit into one comprehensive essay on criticism.

Had these serious productions, written in the spirit of the Republic of Wit, been the only manifestations of wit, conceivably the future course of the republic would have been different. Under the impact of these attacks against pretension, stupidity, viciousness, and falsehood, wit gained its greatest eminence. Equally important is the fact that wit became so popular that it dictated most of the fashionable modes, and because of its eminence, some of its most severe critics softened their attacks. Blackmore, for instance, commended wit in 1716 in an essay tempered by more judgment and reason than his early diatribe, "The Plague of Wit."

However, because of its ascendancy, wit was known increasingly by a variety of manifestations, some of them grotesque. The propensity of wit to boundlessness was well known. The age observed how the ornamentation of wit tended always to extravagance, how psychological and aesthetic theory had constantly to supply imaginative wit with the control of judgment, how in spite of decorum the secret grace of wit was praised for its tendency to overflow and overreach art itself, and how even serious men of wit wrote *jeux d'esprit,* for which they later apologized.

Nevertheless, nowhere was the extravagance of wit more abundantly and ludicrously displayed than in those social evidences which accompanied its popularity. The standards of the great productions of wit were obscured by the racy and insolent gossip of the penny-catching poets and pamphleteers of Grub Street. The serious aims of the men of wit were burlesqued by the antics of frivolous and vulgar fops and their mistresses. The intellectual play of the wit degenerated popularly into the practical joke, midnight carousing, and slang. These social manifestations actually caricatured wit as it had developed in the concept of the republic. They debased it in the eyes of the morally serious and conservative middle-class citizenry. And this context of wit was to have a real influence upon the future of wit.

The Popularity of Wit

The social environment required for the maximum development of wit is evident in the milieu in which it thrived. For one thing, the "intellection" which Dr. Johnson noted demanded the stimulating culture of the city. Also, the intellectual weapons of wit were developed amid conflicting viewpoints in a skeptical and contentious age. Further, the elaborate rhetorical texture of Augustan poetry required an urbane tradition. Most of all, wit itself depended upon a facile mind, learned and fine-tempered.

While thriving in London society, wit spread beyond the confines of an intellectual milieu of urbanity and the facile, cultivated mind. Men who had little, if any, concept of the Republic of Wit mimicked the evidence of the wit with little or no perception of its purpose. But there is no substitute for intellect. Wit could never be sustained by mediocre minds which in their labors had to resort to imitation and pretense, only to appear stupid and inept. Evidences of debasement were to be found everywhere. One glaring instance was conversation.

Conversation was the *sine qua non* of Augustan society, and the qualities lent by fancy, invention, and ingenuity served wit excellently as conversational graces among the true wits. Dryden, defending wit against the attacks of Shadwell, called it the "very soul of conversation" and explained that the present age was superior to the last because "the wit of this age is much more courtly."[2] Courtliness would be presumably one level above urbanity. Bishop Sprat, more closely associated with the town, believed that "it is from the frequent conversations in Cities that the Humour and Wit and Variety and Elegance of Language are chiefly to be fetch'd."[3]

Conversation, as rationalized by the neoclassicist, was to be governed by proper words and thoughts. "Propriety of Words" was achieved, according to John Hughes, by a "diligent and careful Perusal of the most correct Writers of the Language in their various Kinds" and "with the Conversation of People of Fashion, that speak well and without Affection."[4] The ancients were used to set the standards of fashion in social and entertaining conversation. This influence is found in *An Essay on Entertainments* (1702) by Sir Charles Sedley, a Court wit and companion of the Earl of Rochester. Sedley explained the requirements for good company and talk, drawing heavily, he admitted, upon a treatise by Marcus Varro. The number at an elegant supper "ought not to be less than the Graces, nor greater than that of the Muses." Three principal requirements were listed for such a supper:

> The Guests must be Men of some Quality, well bred, and not ill drest. The Place must be well chosen; retir'd from publick View, and the common Disturbances of Passengers and Business; where they may hear no Noise, but what they make. The Time convenient, not too late, nor too early; for an early Supper comes too fast upon a late Dinner; and a late Supper takes too much of the Night from our natural Rest; and consequently too much of the next Day from Business.

Concerning the kind of company most conducive to a memorable evening, Sedley continued,

> Not all great talkers, nor too silent; but ingenious Men, knowing when to speak, and when to hear; rather facetious, witty and agreeable, than contentious, rhetorical, or eloquent: Eloquence is proper in the great Assembly or Senate; Contention for the Bar or Courts of Justice; but in private Company a shorter Way of Expression, and a quicker Turn of Wit is more acceptable. The Guests shou'd not be all old, nor all young Men: for old Men talk of nothing but what was done twenty Years ago; and young Fellows nothing but the Amours, the Disorders, and Debauches of last Week; the Old ought to put on as much Youth as they can on such Occasions; and the Young a temporary Gravity, that the two Extreams may meet in a third Point. Stories ought to be sparingly ventur'd upon, for they impose too long a Silence on the rest of the Company, and may offend three Ways, either by being tedious, common, or unpleasant. The Conversation shou'd not role or dwell upon State-affairs, private Business, or Matters of Interest, which Men are apt to dispute with more Heat, Concern, and Animosity, than is consistent with the good Humour and Mirth principally intended at such meetings; in which we shou'd rather talk of pleasant, chearful and delightful Subjects, such as Beauty, Painting, Musick, Poetry, and Writers of the past and present Age; whereby we may at once improve and refresh our Wits; not wrack or torture them with knotty, rugged and contradictory Disputes, occasion'd often by an Affection of Superiority, which is the worst Effect, and greatest Proof of Self-conceit.

Such were the ideal standards of decorous social conduct and conversation.

Actually, conversation seldom, if ever, conformed to so neat a decorum. Certainly, as popularly carried on, conversation was often an actual travesty of these standards. Criticism of popular conversation indicates a complete breakdown of decorum in public. As for elegant and proper expression, talk more often than not descended to vapid commonplaces and inconsequential banter. Swift's "A Compleat Collection of Genteel and Ingenious Conversation" affords excellent examples.[5] The "Collection" is purported to have been recorded as soon as possible after leaving an especially brilliant display. As a result of this new "art of polite conversing" (wrote Swift in his usual ironic vein), dull story-tellers need no longer be tolerated, for under the new "art" they will be interrupted with "some sudden surprizing piece of wit, that shall engage all the company in a loud laugh." The abhorrence with which polite company viewed the snigger and guffaw indicates the harsh sarcasm in this passage. Lord Chesterfield expressed a similar criticism in 1748, when he wrote in the letter dated May 10 of the mediocre observations which were "the common topics of witlings and coxcombs." Furthermore, he added, "those, who really have wit, have the utmost contempt for them, and scorn even to laugh at the pert things that those would-be wits say upon such subjects."

Not only was popular conversation pert, it was trivial. The frivolous and wanton use of wit inspired some of the most engaging satire in both the *Tatler* and the *Spectator*, especially from the pen of Steele. He, as well as Addison and members of the Scriblerus group, derided the unimportant chatter which passed daily for witty conversation. In the manner of his gentle raillery, he would print bits of this talk as little gems of repartee, letting the ludicrous result suffice of itself. He wrote in the *Tatler*, No. 3, of an evening spent with two young ladies:

> The first (Mistress Giddy) is very quick; but the second (Mrs. Slim) fell into Giddy's own style, and was as good company as she. Giddy happens to drop her glove; Slim reaches it to her: 'Madam,' says Giddy, 'I hope you'll have a better office.' Upon which Slim immediately repartees, and sits in her lap, and cries, 'Are you not sorry for my heaviness?' This sly wench pleased me to see how she

hit her height of understanding so well. We sat down to supper. Says Giddy, mighty prettily, 'Two hands in a dish and one in a purse': says Slim, 'Ay, madam, the more the merrier; but the fewer the better cheer.' I quickly took the hint, and was as witty and talkative as they. Says I,

> 'He that will not when he may
> When he will he shall have nay;'

and so helped myself. Giddy turns about, 'what, have you found your tongue?' 'Yes,' says I, 'it is manners to speak when I am spoken to; but your greatest talkers are little doers, and the still sow eats up all the broth.' 'Ha! Ha!' says Giddy, 'one would think he had nothing in him, and do you hear how he talks when he pleases! I grew immediately roguish and pleasant to a degree in the strain. Slim, who knew how good company we had been, cries, 'You'll certainly print this bright conversation.'

Steele then addressed his reader: "It is so; and hereby you may see how small an appearance the prettiest things said in company, make when in print."

Other abuses of conversation were affectation, familiarity, and slander, which accompanied the activities of the would-be wits. These fops and coxcombs made use of all the intellectual weapons available to wit: criticism, raillery, ridicule, satire, humor. True to tradition, these weapons alienated friends as well as enemies. A steady protest arose against them. Temple complained in 1690 of the recent "vein" of ridicule, which was not only helping to "Corrupt our modern Poesy" but was even entering conversation. The "Wits in Vogue . . . take up with that Part of it [ridicule] which were formerly left to those that were called Fools, and were used in great families only to make the Company Laugh."[6] Dennis felt that "that which they call Wit in Conversation, without good Sense, and without Judgment, is generally without good Sense, and without Judgment, is generally without Good-Nature likewise, and vents itself in Slander."[7] Steele wrote (*Tatler*, No. 218) of the abuse of familiarity in conversation, pointing out that "coxcombs will take upon them to be familiar with people whom they never saw before." He continued with the standard criticism of an adherent to decorum: "These people are the more dreadful, the more they have of what is usually called wit: for a lively imagination, when not governed by a good understanding, makes such miserable havoc both in conversation and business, that it lays you defenceless, and fearful to throw the least word in its way that may give it new matter for its further errors." The ludicrous effect of such "witty" conversation was brilliantly satirized by Boileau in a popular couplet:

> Thus one Fool lolls his Tongue out at another,
> And shakes his empty Noodle at his Brother.[8]

Not only did the popularity of wit debase the standards of conversation, it also assisted in debasing the standards of public entertainment in general. Despite the basic aim of wit to uphold truth by exposing vice and ridiculing folly, the prevalent hedonism and licentiousness proved too great for the necessary detachment. Figuratively speaking, serious wit often approached vice to condemn and remained to enjoy.

The extent to which the social force of wit could distort the aim of the man of wit is illustrated in the compromise which Dryden made with his age. His argument with Shadwell brought this compromise into full view. Dryden, caught up in the *Zeitgeist*, argued that the aim of the poet is to please the people and that since they demanded comedies, he would write such plays, realizing "that they are [not] always pleased with good plays, or that the plays which please them are [not] always good." He expressed his point of view candidly: "I confess my chief endeavours are to delight the age in which I live. If the humour of this be for low comedy, small accidents, and raillery, I will force my genius to obey it."[9]

Dryden undoubtedly was troubled by the necessity of writing inferior plays for public diversion. He knew the result: the debasing of the moral seriousness of a dedicated poet and wit with frivolity and licentiousness. Shadwell answered Dryden some months later in his prefatory "To the Reader" for the play *The Royal Shepherdesse* (1669):

I shall say little more of the Play, but that the Rules of Morality and good Manners are strictly observed in it: (Vertue being exalted, and Vice depressed) and perhaps it might have been better received had neither been done in it: for I find, it pleases most to see Vice incouraged, by bringing the Characters of debauch'd People upon the Stage, and making them pass for fine Gentlemen, who openly profess Swearing, Drinking, Whoring, breaking Windows, beating Constables, &c. . . . it is said, by some, that this pleases the people, and a Poet's business is only to endeavour that: But he debases himself to think of nothing but pleasing the Rabble, loses the dignity of a Poet, and becomes as little as a Jugler, or a Rope-Dancer.

Further evidence of the debasing of wit lay in the popular interest in vice rather than in virtue, in slander rather than in praise, in contention rather than in agreement. The extent of such debasement can be judged by serious-minded witnesses to it. So Defoe wrote:

> In vain a sober Thing, inspir'd with Wit,
> Writes Hymns and Histories from Sacred Writ;
> But let him Blasphemy and Baudy write,
> The Pious and the Modest both will buy it;
> The blushing Virgin's pleas'd, and loves to look,
> And plants the Poem next her Prayer-Book.[10]

The current vogue for detraction and gossip received the criticism of all serious men of wit. Dryden expressed the opinion sarcastically that

> Scandal, the Glory of the English Nation,
> Is worn to Rags, and scribbl'd out of Fashion.[11]

Wolseley observed the "Vein of Knavery that has of late years run through all Orders and Degrees of men among us, spreading itself like a pestilential Poyson." He discussed the ability of the Earl of Rochester to expose the "modern Sparks" with his wit and concluded, "Slander therefore is their Wit, and Dresse is their Learning; Pleasure their Principle, and Interest their God."[12] Sir William Temple complained of the new "Vein of Ridiculing," which he labeled "the Itch of our Age and Clymat."[13]

The vast difference between the ideal, decorous society and the superficial and vulgar London society served ever as a reminder to the serious men of wit of the need for more truth and virtue. The popular desire for the fashionable instead of the universal was often satirized. Charles Gildon in the dialogue of his *Complete Art of Poetry* (1718) had the frivolous Mrs. Lamode praise the latest fashions of wit in severely ironic tone:

> Give me the Wit and Poetry of Fashionable Turn, fine Things and fine Language. For, dear Laudon [Gildon], there's a Mode of Wit and Poetry, as well as of Cloaths; and he or she, that is out of the Fashion, makes a very ridiculous Figure, and is very scandalous Company. Wou'd it not be a very pretty Sight to have a young Lady come into the Drawing-room in a Ruff, and Farthingal? London, and Athens, are quite different places, and the Modes, and Manners of the People differ so much, that what was bright, and pleasing in Athens, must be dull, and insipid in London.[14]

Gildon here ridicules the popular heresy against the practices of the ancients and the ideals of the Republic of Letters. He felt strongly the mediocrity of the contemporary man of wit: "A modern Wit has a very great Aversion to Arts and Sciences, and with an Air of Sufficience, avows his Zeal for Ignorance. But as his Fancy only governs him, so are his Productions most commonly sad, crude, indigested things, like sick Mens Dreams, without either Head or Tail." Further than this, when one mentioned "Art" to such person, he would reply, "You are a Critic, an ill-natur'd Person," and would insist that "Nature is not to be ty'd up to Order, Harmony, Beauty of Design," as if, Gildon added, "Confusion were the only Perfection."[15]

One of the perceptive observers of fashion and manners and at the same time one enslaved to them by a sense of duty was Philip Dormer Stanhope, the fourth Earl of Chesterfield. As a politician, wit, and letter writer, he lived in the very thick of fashion. He felt it important to advise his son in a letter (October 29, 1748) to "perceive the little weaknesses, and the idle but innocent affectations of the company," but at the same time "even to flatter them" as a "sort of polite duty." How to do this he discussed at some length:

For instance: you will find, in every *groupe* of company, two principal figures, viz. the fine lady and the fine gentleman who absolutely give the law of wit, language, fashion, and taste, to the rest of that society. There is always a strict, and often for the time being, a tender alliance between these two figures. The lady looks upon her empire as founded upon the divine right of beauty (and full as good a divine right it is as any king, emperor, or pope, can pretend to); she requires, and commonly meets with, unlimited passive obedience. And why should she not meet with it? Her demands go no higher than to have her unquestioned pre-eminence in beauty, wit, and fashion, firmly established. Few sovereigns (by the way) are so reasonable. The fine gentleman's claims of right are, *mutatis mutandis,* the same; and though, indeed, he is not always a wit *de jure,* yet, as he is the wit *de facto* of that company, he is entitled to a share of your allegiance, and everybody expects at least as much as they are entitled to, if not something more. Prudence bids you make your court to these joint sovereigns; and no duty, that I know of, forbids it. Rebellion here is exceedingly dangerous, and inevitably punished by banishment, and immediately forfeiture of all your wit, manners, taste, and fashion; as, on the other hand, a cheerful submission, not without some flattery, is sure to procure you a strong recommendation and most effectual pass, throughout all their, and probably the neighboring, dominions.

This was the decadent and sterile system of social, fashionable wit at mid-century, a culmination of many years of development. In 1690 Temple had deplored the situation in which "a mean Wit or Beauty may pass in a Room, where the rest of the Company are allowed to have none." He added, " 'Tis something to sparkle among Diamonds, but to shine among Pebbles is neither Credit nor Value worth the pretending."[16] Clearly, the fine lady and fine gentleman stand out ludicrously as grotesque imitations of true wit—of Dryden, for example, who dominated conversation at Will's through sheer intellectual brilliance. One may well look more closely at these social wits, both women and men.

Women as Wits

Women were not usually accorded the capacity for genuine wit; furthermore, they were not considered to have a serious role in the Republic of Wit. Therefore, women who aspired to the role of a wit present one aspect of its caricature. Nevertheless, women had a considerable influence upon the fortunes of wit, and a few were accorded the honor of sharing its distinction. Women were beginning for the first time to enter the arts in some numbers, particularly acting and writing. Although their greatest influence was social, a few were recognized for literary or intellectual achievements. The inscription on the marble stone covering the grave of Aphra Behn in Westminister Abbey offers mute testimony to her ability:

> Here lies proof that wit can never be
> Defense enough against mortality.[17]

The Age of Wit, however, was a man's age; only a few women were recognized as wits, and then usually with severe qualifications. Abercromby's estimate found general agreement:

> I pretend not by this discourse to puff Women up with Pride, for they are but too proud already; my design only is to show that they ought not to be undervalued by Men, as if they were little better than Fools, and had no kind of real Wit; since their very Malice and Tricks do demonstrate the contrary. But nevertheless, though it may be allowable to call some Women fine Wits, because of some peculiar vivacity they are gifted with; yet few of them can pretend to be great Wits, such a Character requiring a constant temper of the Soul, which they, because of their changeable humour, are not capable of.[18]

This guarded admission with its air of condescension is found also in the remarks of Steele in the *Tatler,* No. 19, on the occasion of the production of Mrs. Centilivre's play *The Busy Body* (1709): "On Saturday last was presented, 'The Busy Body,' a comedy, written (as I heretofore remarked) by a woman. The plot and incidents of the play are laid with that subtlety of spirit which is peculiar to females of wit, and is very seldom well performed by those of the other sex, in whom craft in love is an act of invention, and not, as with women, the effect of nature and instinct." The Earl of Chesterfield, writing to his son on September 5, 1748, called women simply "children of a larger growth" who possess "entertaining tattle" but only "sometimes wit." He confessed never to have seen a woman with solid reasoning or good sense for any one twenty-four hours. "Some little passion or humour always breaks upon their best resolutions." Women were governed too much by imagination or fancy, but wit was not ruled out entirely. They did have moments of clear reasoning.

Grudgingly as women might be admitted to possess real wit, some witty women enjoyed equal status with men in literary friendships. In correspondence and conversation, they indulged in greater freedom and wit than usually existed between husband and wife;[19] wit, after all, seemed sharper—certainly more inspired—when directed at someone else's spouse. The age produced a number of noteworthy women wits, among them Margaret, Duchess of Newcastle; Dorothy Osborne; Molly Lepell; Lady Mary Wortley Montagu; Mary Astell; and Henrietta, Countess of Suffolk.

Men of wit found it advantageous for a variety of reasons to cultivate these ladies. Swift corresponded with Lady Suffolk and Mrs. Clayton for social prestige and preferments, with Estella (Esther Johnson) and Vanessa (Hester Vanhomrigh) for friendship and intellectual pleasure. Pope wrote variously to Lady Wortley Montagu, Lady Suffolk, Martha Blount, and others for similar reasons. Although a bachelor, he occasionally pretended facetiously the role of husband. In one letter to Lady Rich in July, 1716, Pope remarked upon the prosaic effect of marriage upon wit, for it was commonly believed that indulgence in wit destroyed the respect of husband and wife for each other. In his words, "The wits would say, that this must needs be a dull letter, because it is a married one." He modestly admitted that the husband's (in this instance, Pope's) share of his wife is the dullest. When he did not assume this rhetorical role of husband, Pope was as capable of risqué and salacious wit as any young gallant. He wrote in November, 1716, to Lady Mary Wortley Montagu, while she was traveling through eastern Europe and Asia Minor:

> The court of Vienna is really very edifying: the ladies, with respect to their husbands, seem to understand that text very literally, that

commands us to *bear one another's burthens:* but I fancy many a man there is, like Issacher, *an ass between two burthens.* I shall look upon you no longer as a Christian when you pass from that charitable court to the land of jealousy, where the unhappy women converse with none but eunuchs, and where the very cucumbers are brought to them cut.

Insofar as the wit between women and men was considered inimical to the ideals of the Republic of Wit, it was caricature. Furthermore, wit in women was generally considered reprehensible. A husband neither looked for nor desired wit in his wife. As a sixteenth-century poem, "The Bachelor's Choice of a Wife," runs:

> If e'er I wed, my wife shall not be old,
> Deform'd, nor ugly, handsome, nor a scold;
> She shan't be pale, nor red, nor shall she paint;
> Shall be religious too, but not a saint;
> She shall have sense; if not a wit, I'll take her:
> Give such a wife, ye Gods, I'll ne'er forsake her.[20]

Addison and Steele joined talents in the *Tatler,* No. 75, to describe in detail some of the awesome aspects of a "female of wit": Isaac Bickerstaff had promised to provide a husband for his sister Jenny, if she "kept her honour, and behaved herself in such manner as became the Bickerstaffs." As a result, wrote Isaac, the unmarried Jenny

> . . . sits with her nose full of snuff, and a man's nightcap on her head, reading plays and romances. Her wit she thinks her distinction; therefore knows nothing of the skill of dress, or making her person agreeable. It would make you laugh to see me often with my spectacles on lacing her stays; for she is so very a wit, that she understands no ordinary thing in the world.

Here is the eighteenth-century caricature of the intellectual woman. Because of her impracticality, Isaac married her to a "man of business, who soon let her see, that to be well dressed, in good humour, and cheerful in the command of her family, are the arts and sciences of female life." She could have been married to "a fine gentleman, who extremely admired her wit, and would have given her a coach and six," but Isaac found it "absolutely necessary to cross the strain," for, he explained, "had they met, they had eternally been rivals in discourse, and in continual contention for the superiority of understanding, and brought forth critics, pedants, and pretty good poets. As it is, I expect an offspring fit for the habitation of city, town or country; creatures that are docile and tractable in whatever we put them to."

Wit, then, between the sexes was popularly considered to exist without the confines of marriage. The formalities of love-making were believed to bring out the wit in both parties, if indeed they possessed any. One dialogue in William Wycherley's *The Country Wife* (II, i) runs as follows:

SPARKISH. (speaking of Alithea, his mistress): Prithee, Frank, dost think that my wife shall be a fine person?
HARCOURT. I could gaze upon her till I became as blind as you are.
SPARKISH. How as I am? How?
HARCOURT. Because you are a lover, and true lovers are blind, stock blind.
SPARKISH. True, true; but by the world she has wit too, as well as beauty: go, go with her into a corner, and try if she has wit; talk to her anything, she's bashful before me.
HARCOURT. Indeed if a woman wants wit in a corner, she has it nowhere.

One stock situation in Restoration and later comedy for the display of wit was the love scene in which each partner used his most brilliant thrusts and parries. Congreve employed wit very effectively in the bargaining scene between Mirabell and Mrs. Millamant in *The Way of the World* (IV, i).

This particular aptitude in wit was used consequently as a prelude to seduction. Pepys acknowledged this use, although admitting ineptness in it. He confided that one evening (April 1, 1667) while walking to Deptford and back on business he was "pleased with a jolly femme that I saw going and coming in the way, which je could avoir been contented pour avoir staid with if I could have gained acquaintance con elle, but at such times as these I am at a great loss, having not confidence, no alcune ready wit. So home and to the office, where late, and then home to supper and bed."

The actual conversations of love-making were often ridiculed, especially in the journals, where social manifestations of wit were parodied.[21] Women's activities as wits were largely confined to social activities, to which the love game was central. These activities were manifestly ludicrous imitations of serious wit. Men's social activities, on the other hand, were more varied but nevertheless no more intellectual or serious.

The Little Wits and Pretenders

The popular appeal of wit among men seems to have touched all social levels of Englishmen but was a greater stimulation to those of some education in the middle and upper classes. The requirements for real wit were severe, and as Swift noted, "millions miss, for one that hits."[22] The little wits and pretenders were those who aimed but missed. The distinction between the true men of wit and the lesser ones was a matter of degrees of success and seriousness of purpose. Certainly many of the fops and coxcombs were men of substantial intellect and education.

The Court wits of the Restoration, who set the behavior patterns for succeeding men of wit and pleasure about town, were gentlemen of the best education.[23] Five of these favorites of Charles II were wealthy: Sedley, Mulgrave, Vaughan, Buckhurst, and Buckingham, though the last had wasted practically all of his patrimony by the time of his death. The wealth of Rochester and Etherege consisted largely of a family name, but both married well and so thrived moderately. Killigrew and Bulkeley, like some of the others, held remunerative Court appointments. Wycherley was the only one who suffered financially through the years. Intellectually, these wits were acquainted with the new scientific discoveries, read the philosophy of their personal friend Thomas Hobbes, and accepted the implications of the growing empirical approach to reality. They used the new knowledge as a justification of their way of life.[24] Their successes as wits varied widely, as did their abilities and interests. The more intellectual and literary of them produced a notable body of literature. The more sensual produced mostly scandal and progeny to attest to their wit.

The social wits who came after were of a lesser breed, having neither the Court position nor the intellectuality to command respect in the Republic of Wit. They were primarily men of fashion and pleasure, unchallenged by the pursuit of truth and virtue. They were the dilettanti, content to imitate and pretend in a milieu beyond their capacities. There were two groups, most often designated little wits and pretenders to wit, but their differences were not always distinct.

The limitations of the little wits were obvious to the true wit. Their achievements would never rise above mediocrity. Their major characteristic was dullness. Robert Wolseley wrote of the impotence of the "polish'd Dullness" of the "little Witlings of the Town," who knew only the form of poetry without conceiving its power. Without genius they could not transcend the rules of poetics. In his "Essay" Pope advised critics to let the dull try to write without censure, for it was better for them to be thus occupied than to criticize:

> 'Tis best sometimes your censure to restrain,
> And charitably let the dull be vain:
> Your silence there is better than your spite,
> For who can rail so long as they can write?
> (ll. 596–599)

When they turn critics, they

> Still run on poets, in a raging vein,
> Ev'n to the dregs and squeezings of the brain,
> Strain out the last dull droppings of their sense,
> And rhyme with all the rage of impotence.
> (ll. 606–609)

The straining "out the last dull droppings of their sense" recalls Dryden's discussion of the "middling" genius, whose "mean fortune" of ability is managed "with extreme frugality, or rather parsimony." These were the little wits of limited endowments.

Swift, with the same concept of the dullards, wrote of "a Brain that will endure but one scumming: Let the Owner gather it with Discretion, and manage his little Stock with Husbandry"; above all, "let him beware of bringing it under the Lash of his Betters; because, That will make it all bubble up into Impertinence, and he will find no new Supply." He extended the metaphor of their particular limitation further: "Wit, without knowledge, being a Sort of Cream, which gathers in the Night to the Top, and by a skilful Hand, may be soon whipt into Froth; but, once scumm'd away, what appears underneath will be fit for nothing, but to be thrown to the Hogs."[25] Another member of the Scriblerus group alluded to this passage. John Gay in *The Present State of Wit* (1711) alluded to the "Poor REVIEW," written by Daniel Defoe, who was "a lively instance of those Wits, who, as an Ingenious Author says, will endure but one Skimming."

The taste of the little wits was notoriously inferior. Dryden called them "*Les Petits Esprits* . . . who like nothing but the husk and rind of wit; prefer a quibble, a conceit, an epigram, before solid sense, and elegant expression."[26] To Addison, they could "laugh at an indecency but not relish the sublime." Pope wrote of them as "half-learn'd witlings."[27] Addison described in the *Tatler*, No. 239, their need to borrow their wit; the witlings have "no other method of showing their parts, but by little variations and repetitions of the man's words whom they attack."

If the little wits were laughed at, the pretenders to wit were detested. The pretender might have little or no wit, but his crime against morality and ethics was that of appearing to have more wit than he did. Abercromby discussed this dishonesty:

> I mean not by a Pretender to Wit a meer Fool, but rather one that hath some share in this Noble Endowment of the Mind. Far less do I understand any of those Learned Societies, that make a peculiar profession of promoting real Knowledge: For we must needs confess several of their Members not to be meer Pretenders of Learning, but eminent Virtuoso's, and great Wits, I mean then by this somewhat ambiguous Word, All such as foolishly pretend to more Wit than God and Nature have really allowed them.[28]

Wolseley agreed with Abercromby on this pretension. The pretenders were in "no way to be remarkable above the ordinary Level of Mankind but by being singular." They were "Men who, like old Lovers, are curst with a strong Inclination and weak Abilities, to whom nothing is more unlucky than an opportunity to satisfie their unnatural longings." Wolseley had in mind the would-be poets and critics who moved in both social and literary circles: "fatal to them is the Favour of their Muse," particularly if they attempt satire, for "when most they wou'd serve the Lust of their Spite, they do but betray the Impotence of their Wit." They were the "Well-wishers to Verse and men that are towards Wit."[29]

Differences between little wits and pretenders were so slight that the terms were practically synonymous. Both often passed for true wits in society and were, in effect, social instead of intellectual wits—a source of chagrin and alarm to the men of real wit. Wolseley explained the major concern of the Earl of Rochester with the "growing Fopperies of the Times," and Abel Boyer described their brand of wit: "Some pert Coxcombs so violently affect the Reputations of Wits, that not a French Journal, *Mercury, Farce,* or *Opera,* can escape their Pillaging: yet the utmost they arrive at, is but a sort of Jack-a-Lanthorn Wit, that like the Sun-shine which wanton Boys with fragments of Looking-glass reflect in Men's Eyes, dazzles the Weak-sighted, and troubles the strong."[30] Boyer recognized the distortion of the genuine critical powers of the true wit in the petty carping of the "critic Vermin." Their immaturity in wit fitted them only to catch scraps from the tables of the great and pawn them off secondhand. Their self-assurance in spite of their ignorance appalled spectators. Abercromby wrote of them:

> They are only capable to judge of a polite Expression, of a Word *A-la-mode,* and other such like Childish nicities. They have, I confess, some confused Notions of every thing, which emboldens them to debate things that are beyond the reach of their Capacity. They are the professed Censurers of Mankind, and can speak good of none, themselves only excepted: I conceive them to be ever without Rest and Repose, yea, and the most miserable of all Men, because most obnoxious, not to be envyed, but to envy others.[31]

Swift burlesqued this envy and contention in his Preface to *A Tale of a Tub:* "I cannot imagine why we should be at expense to furnish wit for succeeding ages, when the former have made no sort of provision for ours." His every effort was directed at the very opposite.

These social wits, posing as authorities, often became the popular critics and purveyors of taste. Their contributions were negative and vicious, involving detraction of personality and of character. Ned Ward, a petty scribbler thoroughly acquainted with the pamphleteering standards of the day, described the techniques used in politics:

> For he that writes in such an Age,
> When Parties do for pow'r engage,
> Ought to chuse one Side for the Right,
> And then, with all his Wit and Spite,
> Blacken and vex the Opposite. . . .
> Scurrility's a useful Trick,
> Approv'd by the most Politic,
> Fling Dirt enough, and some will Stick.[32]

Dirt-flinging begets dirt-flinging. Both pretenders and true wits frequently engaged in personal attacks, and charges and counter-charges were constantly hurled through the years. John Oldmixon attributed this practice to the "Itch for Answering." He explained that the very titles of the publications reflected the modesty of these "Answerers." The first answer would begin with the title "The best Answer that ever was," which would be answered with "A better Answer than the best Answer," which would then inspire "The Unanswerable Answer." Indeed, this itch had gone so far, he noted, that "some Authors have taken it in Dudgeon, not to have been thought worthy of an Answer; and to prevent such Disgrace a second Time, have written on Purpose that they might answer themselves."[33] This was, of course, standard practice among the wits.

The social wits brazenly took over conversation and held the center of attention with risqué witticisms, referred to as "brisk" talk. The word brisk was appropriate as a kind of mediocre false wit. Shadwell, discussing the "smart reparties" of the new comedies, said that "their chief Subject is bawdy and profaness, which they call brisk writing."[34] In his Prologue to *The Royal Shepherdesse,* he alluded to the comic heroines as "Ayery, Witty, Brisk, and Wild, But, with their Favours, those are terms too mild," indicating the quality of licentiousness in the names. Dennis remarked of the character of Novel in *The Plain Dealer,* "He says nothing but what a brisk Coxcomb may very well be suppos'd to say who will venture at all, and who having a good Memory keeps the top Company in a Town over-run with Wit."[35]

The brash egocentricism of the extravert motivated these gay blades. Yet even with their substitution of bawdy and slang for true wit, they were judged dull. The Prologue to *The Rehearsal,* which pretends to cater to the current demand for such "stuff," remarks:

> Here brisk insipid Rogues, for wit, let fall
> Sometimes dull sence; but oft'ner none at all.

Sir Charles Sedley addressed the gallants in the Prologue to *Bellamira,* advising them to bring their "own brisk wit from home," a wit which he called false. And Steele in the *Tatler,* No. 29, described two pretenders to wit "by profession" as follows: "Spondee is dull, and seems dull; but Dactyle is heavy with a brisk face. It must be owned also, that Dactyle has almost vigour enough to be a coxcomb; but Spondee, by the lowness of his constitution, is only a blockhead." Briskness did possess apparently a certain liveliness faintly reminiscent of wit.

Wit of Mind and Wit of Action

It is obvious from a study of these *sol-disant* wits that their antics exhibit a distortion of the very essence of wit as the republic used it. The little wits and pretenders, in their attempts to imitate true wit, often substituted physical activity for intellectual effort. The result was a caricature of the concept of wit itself.

Although little wits and pretenders were products of the Age of Wit, they had precedents in all ages, known as rogues, clowns, buffoons, wags, *beaux esprit,* fools, madcaps. Their comedy is low, farcical, and physical. William Cartwright wrote of earlier wits:

> Old fashioned Wit, which walked from town to town
> In turned hose, which our fathers called the clown;
> Whose wit our nice times would obsceneness call,
> And which made bawdry pass for comical.[36]

Even the Greeks had difficulty in keeping fun in bounds. Aristotle distinguished in his *Nicomachean Ethics* between the wit and the buffoon:

> People whose fun is in good taste are called witty, a name which implies the happy turns of their art. . . . But as it is never necessary to look far for subjects of ridicule and as an excessive fondness for fun and mockery is pretty universal, it happens that not only true wits but buffoons are described as witty, because they are amusing. But it is clear from what has been said that there is a difference, and indeed a wide difference between the two. (IV, 14)

The quality which distinguished for Aristotle the fun of the gentleman from that of a boor was tact. The problem of controlling wit is an old one.

Low comedy, wherever found, has sought its release in excesses, indulging in topics and antics of universal appeal which are usually scorned publicly but enjoyed privately. In the *Spectator,* No. 47, there is an account of a current type so much admired by the common people of all countries that these people "could eat them, according to the old proverb." The type referred to was the "Set of merry Drolls."

> I mean those circumfornaeous Wits whom every Nation calls by the name of that Dish of Meat which it loves best. In Holland they are termed Pickled Herrings; in France, Jean Pottages; in Italy, Marcaronies; and in Great Britain, Jack Puddings. These merry Wags . . . that they make their Audiences laugh, always appear in a Fool's Coat, and commit such Blunders and Mistakes in every step they take, and every Word they utter, as those who listen to them would be ashamed of.

There were social wits for all levels of society, and their attraction was great, nuisances though they often were.

The preoccupation with bawdry in conversation indicates the social wits' interest in carousing and gaming. Even sober minds, who viewed these activities with disgust, could also show a passing interest in them. Samuel Pepys, who enjoyed his own pleasures, related with surprise and aversion the events of one evening (May 30, 1668) when he happened to join with some of the young wits: "There fell into the company of Harry Killigrew, a rogue newly come back out of France, but still in disgrace at our Court, and young Newport and others, as very rogues as any in the town, who were ready to take hold of every woman that came by them. And so to supper in an arbour: but, Lord! their mad bawdy talk did make my heart ake!" He continued with comments upon similar groups of some notoriety, including "Lady" Bennet, a well-known procuress to whom Wycherley satirically dedicated his play *The Plain Dealer*. Pepys concluded, "And here I first understood by their talk the meaning of the company that lately were called Ballers; Harris telling how it was by a meeting of some young blades; and their there dancing naked, and all the roguish things in the world. But, Lord! what loose cursed company was this, that I was in tonight, though full of wit; and worth a man's being in for once, to know the nature of it, and their manner of talk, and lives."

These were the notorious "men of Wit and Pleasure about Town."[37] The Renaissance had had its Bully Ruffs. The Age of Wit viewed in succession and with alarm the Ballers (mentioned above), the Nickers, the Hectors, the Scowrers—and then the Mohawks. The Mohawks refined the merrymaking and obscenities of the earlier groups into physical attacks upon defenseless citizens and assaults upon unescorted women. Their activities included slicing street-chair covers, stabbing with pocketknives, and slitting noses. The new slang of such wits was noted in 1700 by Tom Brown: "A huge great muff, and a gaudy ribbon hanging at a bully's backside, is an excellent jest, and new-invented curses, as *Stap my vitals, damn my diaphragm, slit my wind pipe, sink me ten thousand phatham deep, rip up a new beau.*"[38] Addison and Steele reviewed several of the fashions of past years in the *Tatler*, No. 77.

The popular hours of these men of wit and pleasure were the late, dark hours, the so-called "witty Hours of the Night" (*Spectator*, No. 358), when they indulged in their games. One new one was known as the "Frolick," which was described in the *Spectator*, No. 358, as follows:

> I have heard of some very merry Fellows, among whom the Frolick was started, and passed by a great Majority, that every Man should immediately draw a Tooth; after which they have gone in a Body and smoked a Cobler. The same Company, at another Night, has each Man burnt his Cravat; and one perhaps, whose Estate would bear it, has thrown a long Wigg and laced Hat into the same Fire. Thus they have jested themselves stark naked, and ran into the Streets, and frighted Women very successfully.

It was Steele's opinion that anyone who lived in the vicinity of Covent Garden could tell of a hundred such Frolicks. A private and more lascivious game was called "Quadrille."[39]

As is evident in these activities, wit of action centered often on the perennial game of wenching, so often in fact that Steele could refer sarcastically in the *Spectator*, No. 190, to wenching as an act of wit. Indeed, promiscuous behavior appeared to absorb such attention that Steele had been moved to state in the *Tatler*, No. 84, that "there are more than ordinary crowds of women at the Old Bailey when a rape is to be tried." However, he justified this interest, women "being the only persons liable to such insults. Nor indeed do I think it more unreasonable that they should be inquisitive on such occasions, than men of honour when one is tried for killing another in a duel. It is very natural to inquire how the fatal pass was made, that we may the better defend ourselves when we come to be attacked."

Promiscuity was carried on in public as well as private places, and the social wits were prominent participants. Theaters were second only to coffeehouses as meeting places and were, in fact, referred to as the "seat of wit" (*Tatler*, No. 12). The concentration of little wits in theaters exerted a potent influence upon audience reaction and opinion. A standard convention of the prologue and epilogue of plays was to throw out sops for these would-be critics, pleading not only for favorable criticisms but for decent behavior. Dryden requested facetiously that they leave the women actors alone:

> Alas, our Women are but washy Toys,
> And wholly taken up in Stage employs:
> Poor willing Tits they are: but yet I doubt
> This double Duty soon will wear 'em out.[40]

But offense came not only from the male wits in the audience, for women in the pit were carrying on competition with the women on the stage for the attentions of the fops. The Epilogue to Thomas Otway's *The City Heiress, or Sir Timothy Treatall,* delivered by the actress Mrs. Butler, criticized the competitors in the pit, who, it charged,

> Invade Fop-Corner with your glaring Beauties,
> And tice our Loyal Subjects from their Duties.
> Pray, Ladies, Leave that Province to our care,
> A Fool is the Fee-simple of a Player,
> In which we Women [actors] claim a double share.
> In other things the Men are Rulers made;
> But catching Woodcocks is our proper Trade.

These popular diversions go far to explain the demand for bawdry and obscenity in the plays.

Promiscuity and wenching prompted the view expressed in the *Spectator,* No. 151, that the "Man of Wit and Pleasure" was "either a Drunkard too old for Wenching, or a young lewd Fellow with some Liveliness, who would converse with you, receive kind Offices of you, and at the same time debauch your Sister or Lye with your Wife." The *Spectator,* No. 190, printed a letter designed either to laugh or to weep these vices out of existence, depending upon the reader's disposition:

> Mr. Spectator,
> I am to complain to you a Set of impertinent Coxcombs, who visit the Apartments of us Women of the Town, only, as they call it,

to see the World. I must confess to you, this to Men of Delicacy might have an Effect to cure them; but as they are stupid, noisy, and drunken Fellows, it tends only to make Vice in themselves, as they think, pleasant and humorous, and at the same Time nauseous in us. I shall, Sir, hereafter from Time to Time give you the Names of these Wretches who pretend to enter our Houses meerly as Spectators. These Men think it Wit to use us ill: Pray tell them however worthy we are of such Treatment, it is unworthy them to be guilty of it towards us. Pray, Sir, take Notice of this, and pity the Oppressed: I wish we could add to it, the Innocent.

Some social diversions afforded every opportunity for genuine wit and were enjoyed on various levels, depending upon the abilities of the participants. One which worked equally well for practical joking and for play of the intellect was "biting." Swift, conveying the latest amusements of the city, explained it to a friend.

I'll teach you a way to outwit Mrs. Johnson; it is a new fashioned way of being witty, and they call it a bite. You must ask a bantering question, or tell some damned lie in a serious manner, then she will answer, or speak as if you were in earnest, and then cry you, 'Madam, there's a bite.' I would not have you undervalue this, for it is the constant amusement in Court, and everywhere else among the great people; and I let you know it, in order to have it obtain among you, and to teach you a new refinement.[41]

Steele ventured an explanation of its origin in the *Spectator,* No. 504:

This Way of Wit is called Biting, by a Metaphor taken from Beasts of Prey, which devour harmless and unarm'd Animals, and look upon them as their Food wherever they meet them. The Sharpers about Town very ingeniously understood themselves to be to the undersigning Part of Mankind what Foxes are to Lambs, and therefore used the Word *Biting* to express an Exploit wherein they had over-reach'd any innocent and inadvertent Man of his Purse. . . . Shallow Fops, who are govern'd by the Eye, and admire every Thing that struts in Vogue, took up from the Sharpers the phrase of Biting, and used it upon all Occasions.

A typical example had been afforded earlier in the *Tatler*, No. 12. Here the participants are pretenders to wit:

White's Chocolate-house, May 5.

[*Enter Pip, Trim and Acorn*]

ACORN. What's the matter gentlemen? What! Take no notice of an old friend?

PIP. Pox on it! Don't talk to me, I am voweled by the Count, and cursedly out of humour.

ACORN. Voweled! Prithee, Trimmer, what does he mean by that?

TRIMMER. Have a care, Harry, speak softly; don't show your ignorance: If you do, they'll bite you where-e'er they meet you; they are such cursed curs, the present wits.

ACORN. Bite me! What do you mean?

PIP. Why! Don't you know what biting is? Nay, you are in the right on it. However, one would learn it only to defend oneself against men of wit, as one would know the tricks of play, to be secure against the cheats. But don't you hear, Acorn, that report, that some potentates of the Alliance have taken care of themselves, exclusive of us?

ACORN. How! Heaven forbid! After all our glorious victories; all of this expense of blood and treasure!

PIP. Bite—

ACORN. Bite! How?

TRIMMER. Nay, he has bit you fairly enough; that's certain.

ACORN. Pox! I don't feel it—How? Where?

[*Exit Pip and Trimmer, laughing*]

This is the traditional joking of April Fools Day. In the above discussion in the *Tatler*, biters are called "an ingenious Tribe of Men sprung up of late Years, who are for making April Fools every Day of the Year," instead of on the customary one day. In this special "Art of Wit," biters were "perpetually employed in laughing at those Mistakes which are their own Productions." There were orders among such wits: "in proportion as one Man is more refined than another, he chuses his Fool out of a lower or higher Class of Mankind." At the bottom of the orders was the "butt," he who "gets the Laugh on his Side, and turns the Ridicule upon him that attacks him."

Sir John Falstaff was an Hero of this Species, and gives a good description of himself in his Capacity of a Butt, after the following manner; *Men of all Sorts* (says that merry Knight) *take a Pride to gird at me. The Brain of Man is not able to invent any thing that tends to Laughter more than I invent, or is invented on me. I am not only Witty in my self, but the Cause that Wit is in other Men.*

The quotation in the *Tatler* from *King Henry IV*, Part II (I, ii), bears testimony to the age of this kind of wit.

Swift made the bite a literary device in much of his writings.[42] He used it with grim success as the denouement in his poem "The Day of Judgment." The opening lines state that the poem is of a "horrid Vision" of the opening graves on the day of judgment:

Jove, arm'd with Terrors, burst the Skies,
And Thunder roars, and Light'ning flies!
Amaz'd, confus'd, its Fate unknown,
The World stands trembling at his Throne.
While each pale Sinner hangs his Head,
Jove, nodding, shook the Heav'ns and said,
"Offending Race of Human kind,
By Nature, Reason, Learning, blind;
You who thro' Frailty step'd aside,
And you who never fell—thro' Pride;
You who in different Sects have shamm'd,
And come to see each other damn'd;
(So some Folks told you, but they knew
No more of Jove's Designs than you)
The World's mad Business now is o'er,
And I resent these Pranks no more.
I to such Blockheads set my Wit!
I damn such Fools!—Go, go, you're bit."

The caricature of wit, whatever its nature, was disturbing to the concept of the republic. It was of two kinds. On the one hand, caricature resulted from a reproduction of the intellectual play of the true wit: poetizing, writing criticisms of the latest plays, parroting the latest witticisms, frequenting the popular coffeehouses to bask in the light of the true wits. On the other hand, caricature resulted from the interpretation of wit as physical activity: practical joking, fighting, dressing fashionably, swearing, wenching.

Social Meaning of False Wit

The public was sometimes amused, often antagonized, and generally confused over the nature of this wit, but the serious-minded citizen recognized the spectacle for what it was and unanimously condemned it as bad behavior and false wit. Its opponents understood it to be just another exhibition of unchecked imagination. Blackmore explained ill manners as a lack of judgment: "Persons of facetious Talents and agreeable Humour," who lack judgment and discretion, "are more inclin'd than others to Levity and dissolute Manners." Furthermore, a lively imagination encourages such manners: "The same swiftness of Thought, and sprightliness of Imagination, that qualifies them for ingenious Conversation, Sports of Fancy and Comick Writing, do likewise give them an exquisite Taste of sensual Pleasures, and expose them to the prevailing Power of Tempting, the forbidden Enjoyments."[43]

Regardless of the psychology of this kind of wit, most citizens agreed with Steele in the *Spectator*, No. 358, that games like Frolicks were "better performed by other Animals than Man." He felt that "it is not to rid much Ground, or do much Mischief, that should dominate a pleasant Fellow; but that is truly Frolick which is the Play of the Mind, and consists of various and unforced Sallies of Imagination." Steele protested against such distortions of wit: "I am humbly of Opinion, that a Man may be a very Witty Man, and never offend one Statute of this Kingdom, not excepting even that of Stabbing." A similar view was held by Lord Chesterfield, who in his letter of August 20, 1749, to his son, placed all physical actions outside the nature of true wit: "Horse-play, romping, frequent and loud fits of laughter, jokes, waggery, and indiscriminate familiarity, will sink both merit and knowledge into a degree of contempt." He added that "a joker is near akin to a buffoon; and neither of them is the least related to wit." His evident feeling for the butt of a joke shows the effects of the cult of sensibility, which by 1749 was well developed.

Knowledge of the social context for false wit is essential to passing critical judgment upon opinions of the men of wit themselves. Without it one may quote their own statements against them or interpret such statements erroneously. A passage by Addison will illustrate this. He was concerned in the *Spectator*, No. 249, with the vicious "talent of turning Men into Ridicule," a concern rampant in 1711. "What an absurd thing it is," he felt, "to pass over all the valuable Parts of a Man and fix our Attention on his Infirmities; to observe his Imperfections more than his Virtues." Addison continued his argument thus:

> We therefore very often find that Persons the most accomplished in Ridicule, are those who are very shrewd at hitting a Blot, without exerting any thing Masterly in themselves. As there are many eminent Criticks who never writ a good Line, there are many admirable Buffoons that animadvert upon every single Defect in another, without ever discovering the least Beauty of their own. By this Means these unlucky little Wits often gain Reputation in the Esteem of vulgar Minds and raise themselves above Persons of much more laudable Characters.
>
> If the talent of Ridicule were employed to laugh Men out of Vice and Folly, it might be of some Use to the World; but instead of this, we find that it is generally made Use of to laugh Men out of Virtue and good Sense, by attacking every thing that is Solemn and Serious, Decent and Praise-worthy in human Life.
>
> . . . And it is very remarkable, that notwithstanding we fall short at present of the Ancients in Poetry, Painting, Oratory, History, Architecture, and all the noble Arts and Sciences which depend more upon Genius than Experience, we exceed them as much in Doggerel, Humour, Burlesque, and all the trivial Arts of Ridicule. We meet with more Raillery among the Moderns, but more good Sense among the Ancients.

This argument is easily misunderstood. In view of only the specialized "Arts" developed by the moderns—"Doggerel, Humour, Burlesque," not to mention "the trivial Arts of Ridicule," one might conclude that the wit of 1711 was indeed "degraded."[44]

However, Addison was not writing of "eminent Criticks" but of "admirable Buffoons." His "unlucky little Wits" are in the same category as the pretenders that Swift called the "critic vermin." Both appealed to "vulgar Minds." If Addison's opinion were an estimate of the status of wit in the year 1711, then logically he was judging himself as one of the "unlucky little Wits." But we know that Addison considered himself a true wit, having set for himself a high purpose commensurate with the aims of the republic. Wit was to him the male deity at the right hand of truth. The fact is that Addison was not considering wit in general or attempting to evaluate the true wit of his day. What he had in mind was the social caricature in the taste of little wits and pretenders, from whom the realms of true wit were forever removed.

John Gay turned for protection against these social wits to the new publication, the *Spectator,* which he called in 1711 "our Shelter from that Flood of False Wit and Impertinence which was breaking in upon us."[45] The affection of genuine wit by means of worn out rhetorical devices was the stock-in-trade of what Wolseley had called the "Purloiners of Wit," who were the "vainest Pretenders." If they wrote poetry, " 'twas with the same secrecy that others make Love," in the vain hope of passing for real wits. Much attention is given by Pope in the "Essay on Criticism" to this abuse of true wit. Like Abercromby, he detested the pretension to "more Wit than God and Nature had really allowed them." He commented upon the "half-learn'd witlings" and returned later to their practice of catching the "spreading notion of the town":

> They reason and conclude by precedent,
> And own stale nonsense which they ne'er invent.
> Some judge of authors' names, not works, and then
> Nor praise nor blame the writings, but the men.
> Of all this servile herd, the worst is he
> That in proud dullness joins with quality.
> A constant critic at the great man's board,
> To fetch and carry nonsense for my lord.
> What woeful stuff this madrigal would be,
> In some starv'd hackney sonneteer, or me!

But let a lord once own the happy lines,
How the wit brightens! how the style refines!
Before his sacred name flies ev'ry fault,
And each exalted stanza teems with thought!

(ll. 410–422)

His concluding words, "The vulgar thus through imitation err," indicate the real distance between the true wit and the social wit. Real wit was, as Pope stated, "by knaves undone."

The Caricature of Wit in Wycherley's Play *The Country Wife*

The attractions of wit in its many social implications were manifested early, completely, and extraordinarily in the Court wits during the reign of Charles II. The literature of these gentlemen exhibits all of the social implications of wit. This is particularly true of William Wycherley's *The Country Wife*, produced in 1675.

The Country Wife, salacious and libertine in content, depicted the scheming wit and easy morality which the hedonistic theater audiences so much enjoyed viewing. The leading rake of the play, Horner, specializes in cuckolding husbands. His current technique in seduction is a pretended impotence, a ruse he adopts to become the trusted companion of pretty wives, an association encouraged by nervous husbands who believe the rumor and wish security for their wives from young gallants. The mistresses Horner inveigles are Mrs. Squeamish, Mrs. Dainty Fidget, and Lady Fidget, the last well known by her associates for her nymphomania. The two men who know her best—her husband (Sir Jasper), who speaks flatteringly and superficially to her, and her paramour (Horner), who speaks aside honestly and intimately about her—pose neatly the crucial duplicity of the play with these comments:

SIR JASPER. Ay, my dear, dear of honour, thou hast still so much honour in thy mouth—
HORNER [*aside*]. That she has none elsewhere (II, i).

Horner's latest conquest is the country wife, innocent and virginal Mrs. Pinchwife, wed to an old, sated, and jealous rake. In the denouement, when the truth, by all odds, should break out and reveal the deception of Horner and his mistresses and destroy the honor of the country wife, the hoax of impotence is preserved by general conspiracy. In the conversation below the aroused suspicions of the gullible Mr. Pinchwife, who has just caught his wife in Horner's china room, are allayed by all present, even to the point of hushing the naive and impulsive Mrs. Pinchwife:

DORILANT. Why, thou jealous fool, dost thou doubt it? He's an arrant French capon.
MRS. PINCHWIFE. 'Tis false, sir, you shall not disparage poor Mr. Horner, for to my certain knowledge—
LUCY. O, hold!
MRS. SQUEAMISH [*aside to Lucy*]. Stop her mouth!
LADY FIDGET [*to Mr. Pinchwife*]. Upon my honour, Sir, 'tis as true— (V, iv).

And so truth is smothered to perpetuate an infamous fraud. At the end of the play Mrs. Pinchwife, once innocent, lies overtly, taking up the morals of her companions, and the action ends with a dance of the cuckolds.

The comedy, plain-dealing in its interpretation of Restoration society and of human nature in general, is perfectly executed. Its lines shimmer with true wit as its action reveals much of the caricature of wit. Several kinds of wits and pretenders are included: the true wit, Horner; the pretender to wit, Sparkish; and the fool with no wit, Sir Jasper Fidget. The social force of wit is depicted in various situations. For instance, extramarital love is a stimulant to wit; as Pinchwife asserts, "What is wit in a wife good for, but to make a man a cuckold" (I, i). Horner is the embodiment of this aspect of social wit. Years later, Richard Steele, after attending a revival of the play in 1709, explained in the *Tatler*, No. 3, that the character of Horner was a good representation of the age when "love and wenching were the business of life, and the gallant manner of pursuing women was the best recommendation at Court." But there is more in the play than the pursuit of women. The women themselves become the pursuers. Even the country wife catches "the London disease they call love":

> I am sick of my husband, and for my gallant. I have heard this distemper called a fever, but methinks 'tis like an ague; for when I think of my husband, I tremble, and am in a cold sweat, and have inclinations to vomit; but when I think of my gallant, dear Mr. Horner, my hot fit comes, and I am all in a fever indeed; and, as in other fevers, my own chamber is tedious to me, and I would fain be removed to his, and then me thinks I should be well. (IV, iv)

Sparkish, whose name signifies his limitation (faint wit), always sits in "wit's row" at the opening of each new play. In the following scene (III, ii), three young men of wit and pleasure about town—Horner, Harcourt, and Dorilant—have fun with the pretender Sparkish:

SPARKISH. But we are some of us beforehand with you to-day at the play. The wits were something bold with you, sir; did you not hear us laugh?

HORNER. Yes; but I thought you had gone to plays to laugh at the poet's wit, not at your own.

SPARKISH. Your servant, sir: no, I thank you. 'Gad I go to a play as to a country treat; I carry my own wine to one, and my own wit to t'other, or else I'm sure I should not be merry at either. And the reason why we are so often louder than the players, is, because we think we speak more wit, and so become the poet's rivals in his audience: for to tell you the truth, we hate the silly rogues; nay, so much, that we find fault even with their bawdy upon the stage, whilst we talk nothing else in the pit as loud.

HORNER. But why shouldst thou hate the silly poets? Thou hast too much wit to be one; and they, like whores, are only hated by each other: and thou dost scorn writing, I'm sure.

SPARKISH. Yes; I'd have you to know I scorn writing: but women, women, that make men do all foolish things, make 'em write songs too. Everybody does it. 'Tis even as common with lovers, as playing with fans; and you can no more help rhyming to your Phillis, than drinking to your Phillis.

HARCOURT. Nay, poetry in love is no more to be avoided than jealousy.

DORILANT. But the poets damned your songs, did they?

SPARKISH. Damn the poets! they have turned 'em into burlesque, as they call it. That burlesque is a hocus-pocus trick they have got, which, by the virtue of *Hictius doctius topsy turvy,* they make a wise and witty man in the world, a fool upon the stage you know not how: and 'tis therefore I hate 'em too, for I know not but it may be my own case; for they'll put a man into a play for looking asquint. Their predecessors were contented to make servingmen only their stage-fools: but these rogues must have gentlemen, with a pox to 'em, nay, knights; and, indeed, you shall hardly see a fool upon the stage but he's a knight. And to tell you the truth, they have kept me these six years from being a knight in earnest, for fear of being knighted in a play, and dubbed a fool.

DORILANT. Blame 'em not, they must follow their copy, the age.

HARCOURT. But why shouldst thou be afraid of being in a play, who expose yourself every day in the play-houses, and at public places?

HORNER. 'Tis but being on the stage, instead of standing on a bench in the pit.

DORILANT. Don't you give money to painters to draw your like? and are you afraid of your pictures at length in a playhouse, where all your mistresses may see you?

SPARKISH. A pox! painters don't draw the small-pox or pimples in one's face. Come, damn all your silly authors whatever, all books and booksellers, by the world; and all readers, courteous or uncourteous!

It was Wycherley's desire to show up the defects, the small-pox and pimples, in his characters, especially those who receive his implicit criticism: Lady Fidget's grotesque sense of honor, Sparkish's futile attempts at wit, the sham marriage between Pinchwife and his wife, and the stupidity of the cuckolded Sir Jasper Fidget.

There is the question of Wycherley's intent in this satire. The argument lies between those who interpret his plays as moralistic comedies of manners and those who interpret them as naturalistic comedies of wit. Wycherley was undoubtedly a naturalist in philosophy and ethics, a view that would argue against a strong moralistic purpose of his satiric wit.

Wycherley presented mankind as hopelessly corrupt and stripped human nature to its basic elements. Perverse standards were set up for satiric purposes as he held up his mirror to the life he knew. In so doing, he made life ugly, a phase of the ridiculous. The result may be emetic but never aphrodisaic. Thus he refers to the "naughty town-women, who only hate their husbands, and love every man else" (II, i). There is Pinchwife's summation of town behavior: "Be a pander to your own wife! bring men to her! let 'em make love before your face! thrust 'em into a corner together, then leave 'em in private! is this your town wit and conduct?" (II, i). Then, the remark by Sparkish: "Virtue makes a woman as troublesome as a little reading or learning" (II, ii). Or Harcourt's probing of truth: "Have women only constancy when 'tis a vice, and are, like Fortune, only true to fools?" (III, ii). And Lucy's insight: "No, madam, marrying to increase love is like gaming to become rich; alas! you only lose what little stock you had before" (IV, i). Lady Fidget's frequent remarks on the nature of honor simply reinforce her final comment that it is "the jewel of most value and use, which shines yet to the world unsuspected, though it be counterfeit" (V, iv). This reversal of values prepares for the ironic climax in which the confused Mrs. Pinchwife is forced to lie to preserve her honor—which does not exist.

But one may say of Wycherley as was said of Touchstone in *As You Like It* (V, iv, ll. 111–12): "He uses his folly like a stalking-horse and under the presentation of that he shoots his wit." Wycherley's mirror presents a reversed view of life, life's underside, either that life lurking in the dark recesses of the mind or that life diametrically opposed to conventions. All of the characters inhabit a topsy-turvy world. Horner most nearly voiced values held by Wycherley, especially those of natural actions and plain-dealing, at the price of conventional morals. Such values, however, led Wycherley squarely against the middle-class morality, with which any public form of entertainment must come to terms.

Wycherley and the rest of the Restoration dramatists received the brunt of public outrage, exemplified in the attacks of Jeremy Collier. The middle-class mind could find no redeeming element of value in the frankly sexual *double entendre* of the china-scene (IV, iii). Equally unacceptable and shocking must have been the scene in which Horner and his mistresses discuss the relationships between men and women. Their frankness is clear from the opening speech addressed to Horner (V, iv):

MRS. DAINTY. Dear brimmer! Well, in token of our openness and plain-dealing, let us throw our masks over our heads.

HORNER [*aside*]. So, 'twill come to the [china] glasses anon.

MRS. SQUEAMISH. Lovely brimmer! Let me enjoy him first.

LADY FIDGET. No, I never part with a gallant till I've tried him. Dear brimmer! that makest our husbands short-sighted.

MRS. DAINTY. And our bashful gallants bold.

MRS. SQUEAMISH. And, for want of a gallant, the butler lovely in our eyes.—Drink, eunuch.

LADY FIDGET. Drink, thou representative of a husband.—Damn a husband!

MRS. DAINTY. And, as it were a husband, an old keeper.

MRS. SQUEAMISH. And an old grandmother.

HORNER. And an English bawd, and a French surgeon.

LADY FIDGET. Ay, we have all reason to curse 'em.

HORNER. For my sake, ladies?

LADY FIDGET. No, for our own; for the first spoils all young gallants' industry.

MRS. DAINTY. And the other's art makes 'em bold only with common women.

MRS. SQUEAMISH. And rather run the hazard of the vile distemper amongst them, than of a denial amongst us.

MRS. DAINTY. The filthy toads choose mistresses now as they do stuffs, for having been fancied and worn by others.

MRS. SQUEAMISH. For being common and cheap.

LADY FIDGET. Whilst women of quality, like the richest stuffs, lie untumbled, and unasked for.

HORNER. Ay, neat, and cheap, and new, often they think best.

MRS. DAINTY. No, sir, the beasts will be known by a mistress longer than by a suit.

MRS. SQUEAMISH. And 'tis not for cheapness neither.

LADY FIDGET. No; for the vain fops will take up druggets, and embroider 'em. But I wonder at the depraved appetites of witty men; they use to be out of the common road, and hate imitation. Pray tell me, beast, when you were a man, why you rather chose to club with a multitude in a common house for an entertainment, than to be the only guest at a good table.

HORNER. Why, faith, ceremony and expectation are unsufferable to those that are sharp bent. People always eat with the best stomach at an ordinary, where every man is snatching for the best bit.

LADY FIDGET. Though he get a cut over the fingers.—But I have heard, that people eat most heartily of another man's meat, that is, what they do not pay for.

HORNER. When they are sure of their welcome and freedom; for ceremony in love and eating is as ridiculous as in fighting; falling on briskly is all should be done on those occasions.

LADY FIDGET. Well then, let me tell you, sir, there is no where more freedom than in our houses; and we take freedom from a young person as a sign of good breeding; and a person may be as free as he pleases with us, as frolic, as gamesome, as wild as he will.

HORNER. Han't I heard you all declaim against wild men?

LADY FIDGET. Yes; but for all that, we think wildness in a man as desirable a quality as in a duck or rabbit: a tame man! foh!

HORNER. I know not, but your reputations frightened me as much as your faces invited me.

LADY FIDGET. Our reputation! Lord, why should you not think that we women make use of our reputation, as you men of yours, only to deceive the world with less suspicion? Our virtue is like the statesman's religion, the quaker's word, the gamester's oath, and the great man's honour; but to cheat those that trust us.

MRS. SQUEAMISH. And that demureness, coyness, and modesty, that you see in our faces in the boxes at plays, is as much a sign of a kind woman, as a vizard-mask in the pit.

MRS. DAINTY. For, I assure you, women are least masked when they have the velvet vizard on.

LADY FIDGET. You would have found us modest women in our denials only.

MRS. SQUEAMISH. Our bashfulness is only the reflection of the men's.

MRS. FIDGET. We blush when they are shamefaced.

HORNER. I beg your pardon, ladies, I was deceived in you devilishly. But why that mighty pretence to honour?

LADY FIDGET. We have told you; but sometimes 'twas for the same reason you men pretend business often, to avoid ill company, to enjoy the better and more privately those you love.

HORNER. But why would you ne'er give a friend a wink then?

LADY FIDGET. Faith, your reputation frightened us, as much as ours did you, you were so notoriously lewd.

HORNER. And you so seemingly honest.

LADY FIDGET. Was that all that deterred you?

HORNER. And so expensive—you allow freedom, you say.

LADY FIDGET. Ay, ay.

HORNER. That I was afraid of losing my little money, as well as my little time, both which my other pleasures required.

LADY FIDGET. Money! foh! you talk like a little fellow now: do such as we expect money?

HORNER. I beg your pardon, madam, I must confess, I have heard that great ladies, like great merchants, set but the higher prices upon what they have, because they are not in necessity of taking the first offer.

MRS. DAINTY. Such as we make sale of our hearts?

MRS. SQUEAMISH. We bribed for our love? foh!

HORNER. With your pardon ladies, I know, like great men in offices, you seem to exact flattery and attendance only from your followers; but you have receivers about you, and such fees to pay, a man is afraid to pass your grants. Besides, we must let you win at cards, or we lose your hearts; and if you make an assignation, 'tis at a goldsmith's, jeweller's, or china-house; where for your honour you deposit to him, he must pawn his to the punctual cit, and so paying for what you take up, pays for what he takes up.

MRS. DAINTY. Would you not have us assured of our gallants' love?

MRS. SQUEAMISH. For love is better known by liberality than by jealousy.

LADY FIDGET. For one may be dissembled, the other not.—[*aside*] But my jealousy can be no longer dissembled, and they are telling ripe.—[*aloud*]—Come, here's to our gallants in waiting, whom we must name, and I'll begin. This is my false rogue.

[*Claps him on the back.*]

MRS. SQUEAMISH. How!

HORNER. [*aside*] So, all will out now.

MRS. SQUEAMISH. [*aside to Horner*] Did you not tell me, 'twas for my sake only you reported yourself no man?

MRS. DAINTY. [*aside to Horner*] Oh, wretch! did you not swear to me, 'twas for my love and honour you passed for that thing you do?

HORNER. So, so.

LADY FIDGET. Come, speak, ladies: this is my false villain.

MRS. SQUEAMISH. And mine too.

MRS. DAINTY. And mine.

HORNER. Well then, you are all three my false rogues too, and there's an end on't.

LADY FIDGET. Well then, there's no remedy; sister sharers, let us not fall out, but have a care of our honour.

Modern as this conversation is in its frank presentation of relationships between men and women and with its basic metaphors of beastliness, sexuality, and hypocrisy in human behavior, the scene did not receive real illumination until the advent of modern psychology. It merely convinced the conservative keepers of public morals during the Restoration of the corrupt nature of social wit. And brilliant though *The Country Wife* is in wittiness, the play appeared even to some serious wits as a caricature of the high aims of the Republic.

Summary

The social caricature of wit altered the impact of true wit. The concern with vice rather than with virtue, the misuse of the intellectual weapons of wit, the substitution of wit of action for wit of mind—all served to discredit wit and divert public attention from its high aims. Obviously, the indirection in method contributed to this confusion. In the social context, wit was not intended to test truth or attain the sublime but to entertain.

Dryden, upon whom this social distortion was a major influence, steadily modified his view toward wit, revealed in his changes in purpose. When he was most enthusiastic toward wit, his aim was to "please" or "delight" first, and then to "instruct."[46] By 1677 he had reversed these aims, for now comedy aimed first to instruct and next to please.[47] Two years later, his aim had become to instruct delightfully.[48] In 1700 he was apologizing for having placed pleasure before instruction.[49] This same shift is evident in his opinion of wit. Whereas he had early emphasized the importance of the secret graces which violated the rules, by the mid-eighties he was stressing propriety and decorum. Dryden had, in fact, re-evaluated the Age of Wit, which he had proudly proclaimed in 1672. He wrote to his young friend William Congreve in 1694:

> Our age was cultivated thus at length,
> But what we gained in skill we lost in Strength.
> Our Builders were with Want of Genius curst;
> The second Temple was not like the first.

Dryden had come to regret his participation in the social distortions of wit, which were judged degenerative and vicious by morally indignant men: notably Collier, Shadwell, Rymer, and Blackmore. Dryden had been singled out as mainly responsible, and he made his peace with his detractors in 1700 in the Preface to *The Fables.* A part of his remarks follows: "I shall say the less of Mr. Collier, because in many things he has taxed me justly; and I have pleaded guilty to all thoughts and expressions of mind, which can be truly argued of obscenity, profaneness, or immorality, and retract them. If he be my enemy, let him triumph; if he be my friend, as I have given him no personal occasion to be otherwise, he will be glad of my repentance." In this way Dryden repudiated the falseness of his wit in social context. His contemporaries understood this. In June, 1700, Sir John Vanburgh revised and produced Fletcher's *The Pilgrim,* to which Dryden wrote the Prologue and Epilogue. Colley Cibber, commenting soon after on the "Immoralities of the Stage" in the time of Charles II, wrote: "Nothing that was loose could then be too low for [the stage]. . . . In this almost general Corruption, Dryden, whose Plays were *more fam'd for their Wit than their Chastity,* led the way, which he fairly confesses, and endeavours to excuse in his Epilogue to the Pilgrim, revived in 1700 for his Benefit, in his declining Age and Fortune."[50]

All men of wit felt the ill effects and the handicaps of social wit. Not only did some of them come to reject their roles as wits, but slowly the attitude of the whole community turned against the wit himself. This change in attitude can be seen in an essay on the contrasts between wit and learning which Samuel Johnson published in the *Rambler,* No. 22, in 1750. In making such contrasts Johnson separated terms which had characterized men of letters during the preceding years. He began by recognizing both wit and learning as children of Apollo. Wit was allied with cheerfulness and vivacity, and Learning with seriousness and caution. Their opposition continued when they were "of age to be received into the apartments of the other celestials" upon Mount Olympus; Wit preferred to "entertain Venus at her toilet, by aping the solemnity of Learning" while Learning sought to "divert Minerva at her loom, by exposing the blunders and ignorance of Wit." Other differences lay in the fact that "Novelty" was Wit's darling while "Antiquity" was the favorite of Learning and in the fact that "To Wit, all that was new was specious," whereas "to Learning, whatever was ancient was venerable." Johnson credited the use of satire in wit with further degeneration:

> Wit, cohabiting with Malice, had a son named Satyr, who followed him, carrying a quiver filled with poisoned arrows, which, where they once drew blood, could by no skill be extracted. These arrows he frequently shot at Learning, when she was most earnestly or usefully employed, engaged in abstruse inquiries, or giving instructions to her followers. Minerva, therefore, desputed Criticism to her aid, who generally broke the point of Satyr's arrow's, turned them aside, or retorted them on himself.

Johnson envisioned an ultimate reconciliation of the two in their future life together on the heights of Olympus, where they "joined their hands, and renewed their flight." In this future relationship, "Learning was borne up by the vigour of Wit, and Wit guided by the perspicacity of Learning. They soon reached the dwellings of Jupiter, and were so endeared to each other, that they lived afterwards in perpetual concord. Wit persuaded Learning to converse with the Graces, and Learning engaged Wit in the service of the virtues."

Altogether, Johnson's discussion reveals the ravages of wit which the social wits accomplished. In one sense, wit's entertainment of Venus refers to the pursuit of verbal loveliness, i.e. the quality of *venusta,* a pursuit alluded to as a "converse with the Graces." As mere gracefulness in fine writing, wit was accused of aping the seriousness of learning. In another sense, Johnson indicates, by Wit's attraction to Venus, the licentious concern with the temporal and physical aspects of life, called the "blunders and ignorance of Wit," as manifested in the antics of the social wits. The designation of novelty as "the darling of Wit" reflects the distortion of the new aesthetic interest in uniqueness and individuality, a distortion seldom rising above the cultivation of fads and slang. Johnson's allusion to the poisoned arrows used against learning harks back to the air of contention and the "itch for answering," which, because of the limited vision of the social wits, subverted the search for truth. In these manifestations of the past hundred years, Johnson observed the separation of wit and learning. This separation developed largely through the caricature in social context of the aims and means of true wit. Only on some future Olympia could the disparagement be corrected.

The social caricature was instrumental in diminishing the dignity of wit, but the phenomenon of decline defies any simple explanation. Many other factors contributed to its decay, accompanied by not only charges and countercharges but also by a final ironic reaction which signalled its destruction—the stigma of wit.

> I must recommend to you an affair which has given me some small palpitations of the heart, which is, that you should not wrap up old shoes or neglected sermons, in my letters, but that what of them have been spared from going towards making gin for the ladies, may henceforth be committed instantly to the flames; for, you being stigmatized with the name of wit, Mr. Curll will rake to the dunghills for your correspondence.
>
> —LADY ELIZABETH GERMAINE to Jonathan Swift, May 27, 1735

8

The Stigma of Wit

ONE CANNOT READ the literature and lives of the men of wit without perceiving the stigma attached to their role. These men, in commenting publicly upon wit's influences in society, might choose to overlook the stigma, but each felt it. When Pope wrote the lines in the "Essay" (ll. 438–439) describing the early years in the reign of Charles II,

> Jilts rul'd the state, and statesmen farces writ;
> Nay, wits had pensions, and young lords had wit,

Dennis, in a contentious mood, pounced upon this couplet: "There was then indeed a favourable regard shown Wit, but no real encouragement. Butler was starv'd at the same time the King had his Book [*Hudibras*] in his Pocket. Another great Wit [Wycherley] lay seven Years in Prison for an inconsiderable Debt, and Otway dar'd not to shew his Head for fear of the same Fate. These are some of the Glories of that Reign according to this author."[1] These corrections by Dennis call attention to the adversities which the wits experienced.

The nature of the adversity varied with the social and economic status of the wit. The independent positions of the earls of Rochester and Sedley protected them from the misfortunes of Wycherley and Otway, but they were still subject to the ill will and criticism which the role of wit brought and which were showered upon Butler, Dryden, and others during the Restoration.

Over and over, the man of wit felt it necessary to make some public accounting. The condemnation of Rochester was so great that he was defended posthumously by Robert Wolseley. As has been noted, criticisms of Dryden's activities in wit compelled him to publish a retraction of his "loose writings" near the end of his life. Included in the preface to a collection of Chaucer's tales, it reads in part:

> May I have leave to do myself the justice, (since my enemies will do me none, and are so far from granting me to be a good poet, that they will not allow me so much as to be a Christian, or a moral man), may I have leave, I say, to inform my reader that I have confined my choice to such tales of Chaucer as savour nothing of immodesty. If I had desired more to please than instruct, the Reeve, the Miller, the Shipman, the Merchant, the Sumner, and above all, the Wife of Bath, in the Prologue to her Tale, would have procured me as many friends and readers, as there are beaux and ladies of pleasure in the town. But I will no more offend against good manners: I am sensible as I ought to be of the scandal I have given by my loose writings; and make what reparation I am able, by this public acknowledgement. If anything of this nature, or of profaneness, be crept into these poems, I am so far from defending it, that I disown it.[2]

This public accounting of and apologizing for one's participation in the Republic of Wit continued through the Augustan period. Steele's concluding words in the last *Tatler*, No. 271, are to the point:

> I never designed in it to give any man any secret wound by my concealment, but spoke in the character of an old man, a philosopher, a humourist, an astrologer, and a censor, to allure my reader with the variety of my subjects, and insinuate, if I could, the weight of reason with the agreeableness of wit. The general purpose of the whole has been to recommend truth, innocence, honour, and virtue, as the chief ornaments of life; but I considered, that severity of manners was absolutely necessary to him who censure others, and for that reason, and that only, chose to talk in a mask. I shall not carry my humility

so far as to call myself a vicious man; but at the same time must confess, my life is at best pardonable.

If this is not a public apology, it is certainly an admission of accountability for his wit. To the mild criticism of Blackmore in 1716, Addison felt it necessary to defend his writings at some length in *The Free-Holder,* No. 45, though he could find no tangible evidence of benefit to society.

Pope always had mixed feelings toward wit, admiring true wit as he saw it, even enjoying his reputation as the "wasp of Twickenham," but fearing the stigma. His early correspondence with Wycherley[3] reveals a conservative view of wit as decorous truth, with which he opposed Wycherley's concept of wit as secret grace. However, although he corrected Wycherley, he was troubled by the popular debasing of wit, which was prejudicing the cause to which he was dedicated. He often criticized the little wits, corruptors of literature and manners. He wrote to Caryll on July 31, 1710, "I know no condition so miserable and blind as that of a young fellow who labours under the misfortune of being thought to think himself a wit. He must from that moment expect to hear no more truth than a prince or an emperor," for thereafter praise, "if given to his face," cannot be distinguished from flattery, and if behind his back, how can he "be certain of it?" Two years later he apologized to Caryll (November 19, 1712) for the undressed style he used with his friends; one should not display his wit in personal letters or in other indiscriminate ways: "Some people are wits all over, to that degree that they are fools all over. They are wits in the church, wits in the streets, wits at a funeral, nay, the unmannerly creatures are wits before women. There is nothing more wrong than to appear always in the *Pontificalibus* of one's profession, whatever it be." In this mood he added that wit was only one of the several roles he wished to be known by.

Pope was sensitive to the public reaction to both his wit and his role as a wit. His "Essay on Criticism" marked the zenith of his public support of both. Thereafter, he frequently hedged on his share in the republic. His sensitivity is found in many of the letters he carefully nurtured and edited. On December 8, 1713, he wrote Swift concerning the latter's salvation, since he "must certainly be damned to all eternity" for having "composed more libels than sermons." Though written in a friendly air of drollery, the letter undoubtedly contained more seriousness than is generally recognized.

Pope's sensitivity is borne out by a change in attitude which occurred during the four years from publication of the "Essay" to his Preface to the *Iliad* (1715). Examination of the Preface shows that he avoided the use of the word "wit" almost entirely, substituting the word "invention." The exchange was easy, because of their synonymous meanings. In 1715 it is invention that "distinguishes all great Genius's." Not even "the utmost Stretch of human Study, Learning, and Industry, which masters every thing besides," can equal invention. "It furnishes Art with all her Materials, and without it Judgment itself can at best but steal wisely: For Art is only like a prudent Steward that lives on managing the Riches of Nature." Pope concluded this passage: "Whatever Praises may be given to Works of Judgment, there is not even a single Beauty in them but is owing to the Invention: As in the most regular Gardens, however Art may carry the greatest Appearance, there is not a Plant or Flower but is the Gift of Nature." This beauty contributed by invention, rising as it does above the powers of the judgment, has now been substituted for the grace beyond the reach of art, which was the distinctive contribution by wit. Ironically, it was Homer whom Pope had used four years before as illustrative of those "great Wits" who "sometimes may gloriously offend,/To rise to faults true critics dare not mend." The substitution of invention for wit[4] is all the more evident when one considers how the great wits discussed their favorite subject at all appropriate opportunities; this was certainly one such opportunity. Pope was, surely, suffering one of his periodic misgivings over the stigma of his wit, misgivings which were to become more frequent in later years.

Pope and Henry St. John, Viscount Bolingbroke, wrote to Swift on December 14, 1725, preparing him for the ill reception which he and his works would receive in England, reflecting at the same time on the stigma which his role had brought him: "We your true acquaintances will look upon you as a good man, and love you; others will look upon you as a wit, and hate you. So you know the worst." Yet, though aware of this stigma, Pope was himself influenced by his friends. His *Dunciad,* Books I–III (1728–29) was the most sustained vicious satire of a personal nature that he produced, largely because he could not forget personal grievances. He worked under the inspiration of the Scriblerus group, particularly Swift, who "put Mr. Pope on writing a poem, called the *Dunciad*" in order to "hale those scoundrels out of their obscurity by telling their names at length, their works, their adventures, sometimes their lodgings, and their lineage."[5]

Like Dryden, Pope regretted in his old age his loose writings, though he discussed them only privately with his friends. In a letter to Swift on February 16, 1733, in which he reaffirmed his concept of the true man of wit, he wrote;

> There is nothing of late which I think of more than morality, and what you mention, of collecting the best monuments we can of our friends,—their own images in their writings; for those are the best, when their minds are such as Mr. Gay's was, and as yours is. I am preparing also for my own, and having nothing so much at heart as to show the silly world that men of wit, or even poets, may be the most moral of mankind. A few loose things sometimes fall from them, by which censorious fools judge as ill of them as possibly they can, for their own comfort: and indeed, when such unguarded and trifling *jeux d'esprit* have once got abroad, all that prudence or repentance can do, since they cannot be denied, is to put them fairly upon that foot, and teach the public, as we have done in the preface to the four volumes of Miscellanies, to distinguish betwixt our studies and our idlenesses, our works and our weaknesses.

Pope's sense of the importance of the man of wit is evident in his concession that "*even* poets" may equal men of wit as the most moral beings. But he sought to abandon the role of wit. He would seek truth by other means, as he explained in his communication to Swift in April, 1733:

> You are sensible with what decency and justice I paid homage to the royal family, at the same time that I satirized false courtiers and spies, etc., about them. I have not the courage, however, to be such a satirist as you, but I would be as much, or more, a philosopher. You

call your satires, libels; I would rather call my satires, epistles. They will consist more of morality than of wit, and grow graver, which you will call duller. I shall leave it to my antagonists to be witty, if they can, and content myself to be useful, and in the right.

Pope's moodiness even turned him against his new role of moralist. He wrote to Swift in December, 1734, "I am almost at the end of my morals, as I have been long ago of my wit. My system is a short one, and my circle narrow." In his late maturity, he even questioned the possibility of finding truth: "Where one is confined to truth, or, to speak more like a human creature, to the appearances of truth, we soon find the shortness of our tether."

Even though his tether was short and his spirit for wit weak, his waspishness continued through much of his life to his quarrel with Colley Cibber in 1742, when Pope elevated his old enemy and made him the hero of the new *Dunciad.* But even here some of the sting is gone, the tone of the wit different. Book IV, the new portion of the work, contains a change in approach to the material, less personal and abusive—altogether a more subtle kind of satire. Cibber's reaction and the resulting outpour of scurrilous vindictiveness against Pope simply confirmed in his own mind the stigma which usually accrued to the man of wit.

The stigma of wit is the final context of meanings in the Age of Wit. It developed from a wide variety of circumstances and developments. Very important was the social caricature, for it conditioned the thinking of the average citizen. The influence of caricature is manifest in the defense of Rochester's bawdy, in Dryden's apology for profaneness and obscenity, and in Pope's substitution of morality for wit. However, these reactions reflect more than just the context of caricature.

Chief Charges Against Wit

The opposition to wit was present from the beginning of the age and took many forms—some valid and some purely academic. Opponents, striving only for effect, argued sometimes from traditional positions no longer valid. For example, the charge that wit was a disease became academic with the dissolution of the theory of the humors. One of the most persistent conventional arguments, and one of the hoariest, was that wit was a form of madness. Many wits, including the Earl of Rochester, Dryden, and Swift, were accused of this malady.

The charge of madness was quite logical in terms of faculty psychology. Carleton, elaborating upon the views of Hobbes, explained that "from Celerity of Imagination there ariseth a twofold difference of Wit." One kind of mind fixed itself upon one object and examined it closely; the second kind indulged in the "liberty of Ranging" and was "allowed to have *Laudabilem Phantasiam*" and "a Genius disposed to Poesy and Invention." The danger in the latter mind is that if its fancy is "immoderately quick and ranging," then it "passes into Folly, such as theirs, who are not able to finish the discourse they have begun, being suddenly taken off and carryed away by new thoughts altogether impertinent." This "undecent shifting of thoughts," a form of extravagance, was a main weakness in wit. And extravagance was "a degree of Madness."[6] Put another way, "without Judgment, Fancy is but mad."[7] As could be observed at Bedlam, "In fancy mad men equal, if not excell all others."[8] Further, without control by judgment, reason was lost—another evidence of madness.[9]

Dryden, accepting the importance of the fancy in his poetical theory, met this traditional belief in the rationalistic manner of the age: "They who would justify the madness of Poetry from the authority of Aristotle, have mistaken the test, and consequently the interpretation: I imagine it to be false read, where he says of Poetry, that it is Εμφυους ἤ Μανικον, that it had always somewhat in it either of a genius, or of a madman, 'Tis more probable that the original ran thus, that Poetry was Εὐφυοῦς ου Μανικον, that it belongs to a witty man, but not to a madman."[10] Dryden's wish for the "right" meaning of the Greek did not father a valid thought, and, wit, as a product of fancy, came by madness naturally. Sedley could refer jestingly in the Prologue to his *Antony and Cleopatra* (1677) to this association:

'Tis well most Wits have something of the Mad,
Or where shou'd Poets for the Stage be had?

But to Blackmore the madness of wit was no jesting matter:

The Plague of Wit prevails; I fear 'tis vain
Now to attempt its Fury to restrain.
It takes Men in the Head, and in the Fit
They lose their Senses and are gone in Wit.[11]

Other critics commonly noted the relationship. Boyer could see "somewhat that borders upon Madness in every exalted Wit,"[12] and Arthur Mainwaring, in considering the actions of wit, specifically drinking, felt that wine "has great Efficacy in Matters of Wit and Eloquence." He added archly, "Wine is therefore call'd Generous, and is as nearly ally'd to Wit, as Wit is to Madness."[13] So went this academic argument.

More substantial and convincing charges against wit were made than that of madness. Public reaction brought three general charges: wit was irreligious and immoral; wit actually betrayed truth; wit was abusive and ill-natured.

Wit as Irreligious and Immoral

Early accusations of irreligion and immorality appeared amid allegations that wit confounded the chief aim of poetry, which to the moralist was to teach. Dryden and Shadwell had argued the question over a period of years, Shadwell aggressively berating wit. In the following decades, Blackmore assumed a major role in championing the cause of morality. His Preface to *Prince Arthur* (1695) began a series of attacks upon wit. This Preface stated his position clearly:

'Tis true, indeed, that one End of Poetry is to give Men Pleasure and Delight; but this is but a subordinate, subaltern End, which is it self a Means to the greater and ultimate one. . . . A Poet should imploy all his Judgment and Wit, exhaust all the Riches of his Fancy, and abound in Beautiful and Noble Expression, to divert and entertain others; but then it must be with this Prospect, that he may hereby engage Attention, insinuate more easily into their Minds, and more effectively convey to them wise Instructions. 'Tis below the Dignity of a true Poet to take his Aim at any inferior End. They are Men of little Genius, of mean and poor Design, that imploy their Wit for no higher Purpose than to please the Imagination of vain and wanton People.

He then condemned those poets "who use all their Wit in Opposition to Religion, and to the Destruction of Virtue and good Manners in the World." His primary concern was with the presentations on the stage. Since "few fine Conceipts, few Strains of Wit, or extraordinary Pieces of Raillery, but are either immodest or irreligious," and also "very few Scenes but have some spiteful and envious Stroke at Sobriety and Good Manners," the "Youth of the Nation have apparently receiv'd very bad impressions."

The universal Corruption of Manners and irreligious Disposition of Mind that infects the Kingdom seems to have been in a great Measure deriv'd from the State, or has at least been highly promoted by it. And 'tis great pitty that those in whose Power it is have not yet restrain'd the Licentiousness of it and oblig'd the Writers to observe more Decorum.

These charges were to become familiar through the writings of Jeremy Collier, especially in his *Short View of the Immorality and Profaneness of the English State* (1698), but Blackmore's has more pertinence because he attacked the major cause: wit. His next blast, "Satyr Against Wit" (1700), accused wit of subverting sense and religion. The poem exhibited in its various charges much of the extravagance which it attributed to wit. Blackmore and other critics rejected the validity of wit's paradoxical approach to truth.

The clergy vigorously joined in charges of immorality and irreligion. One of the most critical, Isaac Barrow, preached on the dangers of this subversive force. He thought of wit as a product of fancy: "It is wit that wageth the war against reason, against virtue, against religion; wit alone it is that perverteth so many, and so greatly corrupteth the world." He did admit, however, that "if wit may happily serve under the banner of truth and virtue," it should be used, "and good it were to rescue so worthy a faculty from so vile abuse."[14]

Perhaps the best statement of the moral and religious objection to wit was presented by Nicole Malebranche, a philosopher of the Cartesian school, whose work *A Treatise of Morality* was translated from the French in 1699. He believed that "that which is most opposite to the efficacy of the Grace of Christ, is that which in the Language of the World is call'd Wit; for the better the Imagination is furnish'd, the more dangerous it is; subtilty, delicacy, vivacity and spaciousness of Imagination, great qualities in the Eyes of Men, are the most prolifick and the most general causes of the blindness of the Mind and the corruption of the Heart."[15] The importance of psychological theory is clear in these attitudes. Those who saw possibilities in wit's use considered it as intelligence or judgment; those who condemned it considered it as imagination.

Another charge against wit through the years was that it encouraged and accompanied atheism. In an age rife with skepticism, wit was a logical scapegoat for this charge; certainly many wits exercised their intelligence in liberal religious thought. A favorite book of the Court wits, for instance, was Hobbes' *Leviathan.* But apparently, much of the so-called skepticism was merely fashionable pretense. James Buerdsell, fellow of Brasenose College, wrote in 1700 of the "prevailing Humour of Scepticism," which had become "so extremely Modish, that no Person can be that self-admir'd thing, a Wit, without it."[16] Its modishness led to the affectation of atheism among the pretenders. Speaking of certain young gallants the *Tatler,* No. 77, recorded: "I know at this time a young gentleman, who talks atheistically all day in coffee-houses, and in his degrees of understanding sets up for a free-thinker; though it can be proved upon him, he says his prayers every morning and evening."

However, the charge of atheism was based upon more substance than mere fashion, for the fashion originated not with the gallants but with the intellects whom the gallants imitated. Liberal thought consciously sought orientation in a chaotic, new world, and the term atheism was used indiscriminately to refer to many forms of new thought. Deism was one such form. The Deists revived the teachings of Socinius and applied reason to their religious belief; they were regularly called atheists, despite their name.

Men of liberal philosophy were judged popularly to be atheists, and Thomas Hobbes was one of the chief of these. The occasion of his death was observed by moralizing. One broadside elegy included an epitaph which began,

> Is Atheist-Hobbes then dead! Forbear to Cry;
> For whilst he liv'd, he thought he could not dy,
> Or was at least most filthy loath to try,

and ended,

> Here lies Tom Hobbes, the Bug-bear of the Nation,
> Whose Death hath frighted Atheism out of Fashion.[17]

The Earl of Rochester was one wit of the Restoration who symbolized godlessness. In 1680 appeared "An Elegie Humbly offered to the Memory of that Matchless Wit, and Unparallel'd Example of Sincere Penitency, the Right Honorable John, Earl of Rochester," which made much of a rumored deathbed repentance:

> The Mighty Rochester a Convert Dies,
> He fell a Poet, but a Saint shall Rise.

The elegy ended with the admonition:

> How broad soe're his Faults be shown,
> His Penitence as large was known.
> Forebear then!—let you and I
> By him, at least, learn how to Dye.[18]

Some of the great wits felt that the charge of irreligion had some basis in fact. Pope said that the wit of some men was "like a dark lanthorn, which serves their own turn and guides them their own way; but is never known (according to the scripture phrase) either to shine forth before men, or to glorify their Father who is in heaven."[19] He asserted to Caryll in 1712 (November 19) that there were several things that he "would be thought besides a wit,—as a christian, a friend, a frank companion, and a well-natured fellow, and so forth." Swift's viewpoints changed with his mood and the moment. He corrected himself in the line, "The wits, I mean the Atheists of the Age," in his "Ode to the Athenian Society" (1692). He accused them of trying to rule the pulpit as they already ruled the stage. But being a wit himself, he defended true wits against the charge:

> For as of old Mathematicians
> Were by the vulgar thought magicians;
> So academic dull ale-drinkers
> Pronounce all men of wit, free-thinkers.[20]

This was no doubt a touchy subject to Swift, who was charged often with irreligion.

Charges of irreligion continued generally through the last half of the age. Atheism was a choice topic of Blackmore when he was at his favorite whipping horse. A typical passage in *An Essay upon Wit* follows:

> It would be endless to enumerate the various Ways which the atheistical Wit and merry Libertine employ, to take off all Veneration of Religion, and expose its Adherents to publick Derision. This is certainly the greatest Abuse of Wit imaginable. In all the Errors and monstrous Productions of Nature, can any appear more deform'd than a Man of Parts, who employs his admirable Qualities in bringing Piety into Contempt, putting Vertue to the blush, and making Sobriety of Manners the common Subject of his Mirth; while with Zeal and Industry, he propagates the malignant Contagion of Vice and Irreligion, poisons his Friends and Admirers, and promotes the Destruction of his native Country? And if these foolish Wits and ingenious Madmen could reflect, they would soon be convinc'd, that while they are engag'd against Religion they hurt themselves; and that Wit and Humour thus misapply'd, will prove but a wretched compensation for their want of Vertue.

But even in the face of such criticism, the skeptical wits seem not to have disappeared. The *Esprits forts,* as Lord Chesterfield called them, were still active in 1750 (January 8) when he warned his son against accepting their irreligion. "Depend upon this truth, that every man is the worse looked upon, and the less trusted for being thought to have no religion."

Hand in hand with the charge of irreligion went that of immorality, particularly the use of bawdry and obscenity. Both were wit's older companions.[21] Cowley's "Ode: Of Wit" had recognized in 1656 the current use of obscenity:

> Much less can that have any Place,
> At which a Virgin hides her Face;
> Such Dross the Fire must purge away; 'Tis just
> The Author blush, there where the Reader must.
> (stanza 6)

Bawdry was a point of contention between Dryden and Shadwell. Flecknoe referred to Fletcher's "witty obscenity . . . which like poison infused in pleasant liquor is alwayes the more dangerous the more delightful."[22] In satiric vein authors of plays confessed to attempt to eliminate obscenity, but they desisted when the result was dullness.[23]

All of the men of wit rejected bawdry and obscenity as ends in themselves, echoing Sheffield's classic phrasing, "Bawdry barefac'd, that poor pretence to Wit," though the pretence, however poor, continued. Wolseley justified the proper use of bawdry for purposes of satire and ridicule, but apologized for Rochester's unforgivable obscenity.[24] Defoe listed in the *Review* (IV, 24) satiric conditions for capitulating to the play houses, one being that "Bawdry and Blasphemy shall no more please the Auditory —That they shall make right Judgments of Things, and never take prophaneness for Wit, clap a nasty Jest, and like the Representations of Lewdness, under the Foppish Disguises of Love and Gallantry." As Defoe knew, audiences were getting what they demanded. The popular taste for salacious entertainment receded almost imperceptibly, in spite of the increasing moral tone of society.

Steele gave much attention in his writings to the question of obscenity, never justifying its misuse but placing responsibility for such misuse where it belonged. Other than in the audience or reader, he held the responsibility to lie in certain shortcomings of the author. A "Constant Reader and Well-wisher" sent him a line of bawdry from a play, *The Funeral,* in which the "Confident Lover in the Play, speaking of his Mistress," cried out, "Oh that Harriot! To fold these Arms about the Waste of that beauteous, struggling, and at last yielding Fair!" Steele sympathized with the contributor's criticism of such lines and at the same time (being a playwright) made excuses for his craft in ironic tone (*Spectator,* No. 51):

> The Complaint of this Young Lady is so just, that the Offence is gross enough to have displeased Persons who cannot pretend to that Delicacy and Modesty, of which she is Mistress. But there is a great deal to be said in Behalf of an Author: If the Audience would but consider the Difficulty of keeping up a sprightly Dialogue for five Acts together, they would allow a Writer, when he wants Wit, and can't please any otherwise, to help it out with a little Smuttiness.

He then took the author's point of view in order to deliver the *coup de grâce:*

> I will answer for the Poets, that no one ever writ Bawdry for any other Reason but Dearth of Invention. When the Author cannot strike out of himself any more of that which he has superior to those who make up the Bulk of his Audience, his natural Recourse is to that which he has in common with them; and a Description which gratifies a sensual Appetite will please, when the Author has nothing about him to delight a refined Imagination.

In a later *Spectator* (No. 286), in a more sympathetic mood, Steele made a straightforward defense of certain words which might be considered obscene, distinguishing between the obscene and the modest word, both expressing the same action, but each making use of a different "accessary Idea." Thus, "Fornication and Adultery are modest Words, because they express an evil Action as Criminal, and so as to excite Horrour and Aversion." On the other hand, "Words representing the Pleasure rather than the Sin, are for this Reason indecent and dishonest." But to the less tolerant, this was mere quibbling in an age when every occasion was taken to relate bawdry to the matter at hand. A notable collection of wit in wide circulation as late as the 1760's listed as synonyms for *gallantry* the two words "fornication" and "adultery," defined *opportunity* as the "season of cuckoldom," and glossed the word *marriage* as "a kind of traffic carried on between the two sexes, in which both are constantly endeavoring to cheat each other, and both are commonly losers in the end."[25]

The stock answer to these changes was that the irreligion and immorality were illusions, impressions unavoidable in the techniques of wit. Such answer did not convince the average middle-class Englishman. Dryden and Wolseley could justify the wit of Restoration poetry, on the stage or elsewhere, and a moralist of the stature of Dennis could praise the comedies of Wycherley; but the fact remained that this literature, witty though it was, did demonstrate to the audience infidelity, sex play, and other immoralities. The moral instruction seemed indirect and secondary, if extant.

Modern critics may perceive fundamental moral seriousness in the most salacious plays, but to the contemporary middle-class tradesmen, merchants, and artisans the plays were inexcusably obscene and immoral, "the Nursery of all manner of Wickedness, where the Seeds of Atheism and Irreligion are sown, which Weak and Tender Minds too readily cultivate, and from thence are easily led into a Contempt of all that's Serious."[26] And for the learned moralist, England remained a "degenerate State" in which men were attracted to "those Voluptuous Objects, that please their Appetites and gratify their Senses."

No productions of Human Understanding are receiv'd with such a general Pleasure and Approbation, as those that abound with Wit and Humour, on which the people set a greater Value, than on the wisest and most instructive Discourses. Hence a pleasant Man is always caress'd above a wise one, and Ridicule and Satyr, that entertain the Laughers, often put solid Reason and useful Science out of Countenance. The wanton Temper of a Nation has been gratify'd so long with the high Seasonings of Wit and Raillery in Writing and Conversation, that now almost all Things that are not accommodated to their Relish by a strong Infusion of those Ingredients are rejected as the heavy and insipid Performances of Men of a plain Understanding and meer Masters of Sense.[27]

The triumph, such as it was, of ridicule and satire over "solid Reason and useful Science" and of the "high Seasonings" of wit and raillery over the "heavy and insipid Performances" of men of understanding and sense was destined to be short-lived.

Wit as Betrayer of Truth

One of the blows to the prestige of wit was the accumulation of arguments against its ability to illuminate truth, for this criticism not only struck at the very basis of the republic but discredited the venerable tradition of rhetoric. Several charges served to alienate truth and wit.

One of the charges was that wit's rhetorical devices were deceptive. This charge referred to "amplification, digressions, and swellings of style," which obscured the thought. To the imaginative, creative mind, such ornamentation and figurative language appeared as a primary value in writing, but to the factual or prosaic mind, this language obscured and confused. Bishop Sprat voiced this view:

> Who can behold, without indignation, how many mists and uncertainties, these specious Tropes and Figures have brought on our knowledges? How many rewards, which are due to more profitable, and difficult Arts, have been still snatch'd away by the easie vanity of fine speaking? For now I am warm'd with this just Anger, I cannot with-hold my self, from betraying the shallowness of all these seeming Mysteries; upon which, we Writers, and Speakers, look so bigg. And, in few words, I dare say; that of all the Studies of men, nothing may be sooner obtain'd, than this vicious abundance of Phrase, this trick of Metaphors, this volubility of Tongue, which makes so great a noise in the World.[28]

The delusions which the metaphorical or allegorical figures cause were pointed out by a contemporary of Bishop Sprat, Samuel

Parker, the Bishop of Oxford, who believed that metaphor and allegory were limited to similitudes, which were in turn produced by the fancy. Even "Theories in Philosophie which are expressed only in metaphorical Termes, are not real Truths, but the meer Products of Imagination, dress'd up (like Childrens babies) in a few spangled empty words." He ended his argument with a striking metaphor, the use of which would seem to belie his whole point: "Thus their wanton & luxuriant fancies climbing up into the Bed of Reason, do not only defile it by unchast and illegitimate Embraces, but instead of real conceptions and notices of Things, impregnate the mind with nothing but Ayerie and Subventaneous Phantasmes."[29]

Such arguments as these discredited the possible discovery of truth through wit; the hazards of the search seemed too great. One reaction was a form of anti-intellectualism expressed very aptly by James Arbuckle. In May, 1726, he wrote that "since the Temper and Dispositions of Men are so extremely various" and "since Objects appear so differently to different Minds," since also "it is owned almost impossible that the same Reason should make the same Impression on every Understanding," and "since the Adepts in all kinds of Science are every day making new Discoveries, and rejecting Opinions they formerly held for certain and demonstrative," then the "wisest and safest course" seemed that of being "less positive and dogmatical in our Decisions, and to put an end to those empty Wranglings and Disputes which have so long plagued Mankind, made Bigotry a Science, and Persecution a Demonstration." He added by way of conclusion that a "supposition of the Truth . . . propagated with so much Industry and with so much Profusion of false Learning, and unfeigned Zeal" would lead to the "valuable Privilege of knowing ourselves to be very unhappy."[30] In support he quoted a quatrain from Matthew Prior's ode to the late Earl of Halifax:

> If we see right, we see our Woes:
> Then what avails it to have Eyes?
> From Ignorance our Comfort flows;
> And Sorrow from our being wise.

Although this reaction was not popular, it was certainly encouraged by the indirection of rhetorical figures and by the "wranglings and Disputes" that followed the intellectual weapons of wit.

Wit found itself estranged from truth for other reasons than the so-called deceptive nature of figurative language. For one thing, the modish preoccupation with new jokes, new games, and new slang seemed to limit wit to the present and transitory values, tending thereby to cut it off from universal and traditional values. Swift, castigating the moderns, felt strongly upon this very point. His narrator in the Preface to *A Tale of a Tub* says,

> I have remarked, that nothing is so very tender as a modern piece of wit, which is apt to suffer so much in the carriage. Some things are extremely witty to-day, or fasting, or in this place, or at eight o'clock, or over a bottle, or spoken by Mr. What'd'y'call'm, or in a summer's morning: any of the which, by the smallest transposal or misapplication, is utterly annihilate. Thus, wit has its walks and purlieus, out of which it may not stray the breadth of an hair, upon peril of being lost.

This was an old grievance to Swift. In 1693 the unique language of wit was so common that he had written as follows in his poem "To Mr. Congreve,"

> Last year, a lad hence by his parents sent
> With other cattle to the city went;
> Where having cast his coat, and well pursu'd
> The methods most in fashion to be lewd,
> Returns a finish'd spark this summer down,
> Stock'd with the freshest gibberish of the town;
> A jargon form'd from the lost language, wit,
> Confounded in that Babel of the pit;
> Form'd by diseas'd conceptions, weak, and wild,
> Sick lust of souls, and an abortive child;
> Born between whores and fops, by lewd compacts,
> Before the play, or else between the acts:
> Nor wonder, if from such polluted minds
> Should spring such short and transitory kinds,
> Or crazy rules to make us wits by rote
> Last just as long as ev'ry cuckow's note.

Forty years later Chesterfield admonished his son (October 29, 1748), "Remember that the wit, humor, and jokes, of most mixed companies are local. They thrive in that particular soil, but will not often bear transplanting." He explained that every separate company had its own "cant and jargon; which may give occasion to wit and mirth within that circle, but would seem flat and insipid in any other, and there will not bear repeating." He warned his son of such repeating, because "nothing makes a man look sillier than a pleasantry not relished or not understood."

The cant and jargon of wit, largely in the social context of caricature, further isolated wit from the eternal verities. This private language was the very antithesis of the universality of the truth sought by the Republic of Wit. As Steele complained in the *Tatler*, No. 12, "Gamsters, banterers, biters, swearers, and twenty new-born insects more, are, in their several species, the modern men of wit. Hence it is, that a man who has been out of town but one half-year, has lost the language, and must have some friend to stand by him, and keep him in countenance for talking common sense." The term "common sense" has an especially sarcastic ring.

A further view of wit helped divorce wit from truth. This was the view of wit as chance, a corollary of the *je ne sais quoi*. Some of the seventeenth-century critics had considered chance as attractive. Davenant had referred to wit as "the laborious and the lucky resultances of thought," and described its delicate balance of thought and phrasing as "a Webb consisting of the subt'lest threds."[31] This particular wit was the easy, loose "Negligence of a great Genius,"[32] one of the sure evidences of genius itself. Dryden had Davenant's phrase in mind when, in speaking of Shakespeare's having the "largest and most comprehensive soul," he added, "All the images of Nature were still present to him, and he drew them, not laboriously, but luckily."[33] The naturalness chance gave to effective expression was considered desirable, even when achieved through contrivance. Thus Sheffield, in discussing Dryden's "propriety of thoughts and words," included the couplet:

No words transpos'd, but in such just cadance,
As, though hard wrought, may seem the effect of chance.[34]

Steele expressed in the *Tatler*, No. 6, the same view upon discovering the excellence of the poetry of Sappho: "She went on, and said a thousand good things at random, but so strangely mixed that you would be apt to say all her wit is mere good luck, and not the effect of reason and judgment."

However, the element of chance came to represent the haphazard, accidental way of writing which characterized the little wit. Abercromby had made a reasonable distinction in his classification of wits, opposing the habitual and the accidental wits. The accidental wits made use of "meer chance, and hazard," as observed in most women and in the more talkative men. In any instance, accidental wit followed "the sudden motions of a mutable and confused Imagination or Fancy."[35] Leonard Welsted made much of this haphazard element in *State of Poetry* (1724). One of his premises was that "a Poet often owes more to his good Fortune than to his Industry." Such good fortune he called "the Felicity of a Writer," which exists "when in the Warmth of his Imagination he lights upon a Conception, an Image, or way of turning a Thought or Phrase, with a Beauty, which he could not have attain'd by any Study, and which no Rules could have led him to."[36] This felicity Welsted called inspiration; Dryden and Pope would have called it wit. Wit, on the other hand, Welsted defined as "some uncommon Thought or just Observation, couch'd in Images or Allusions, which create a sudden Surprize through their Agreeableness, and the Lustre with which they strike the Imagination."[37] His amplification of this definition shows the degenerating concept of wit:

Now if the Account I have given of Wit, be true, it may sometimes, far from proceeding from a superior Understanding, be the effect of Luck, or mere Chance-work; or in other Words, Wit may come from very unwitty Heads; since, where People think and talk at random, as Persons of a vivacious Fancy, with little Judgment, commonly do, and where they ignorantly confound a Multitude of different Ideas, it is almost impossible, but that some of them should fall into that Position or Figure of Thought and Language, which may be Wit, or not unlike it; it is even possible, that this may frequently happen, and when it does, those, who have the least Wit, may be said to have the most.[38]

Here was a law of averages in wit; it was a random achievement which even the dullard might accidentally enjoy along with the genius.

A similar defamatory explanation of wit appeared a few years later in 1732. This view maintained that wit "as often arises from the Defect of the Mind, as from its strength and Capacity." The anonymous writer revealed the great prejudice created by social wit when he added, "This is evident in those who are Wits only, without being grave or wise."[39] The grave and the wise were not readily apparent in a literature filled with fictitious narrators, satiric irony, and other devices of indirection; neither were they apparent in wit of mere action.

Finally, the identification of wit with imagination always placed wit, to many observers, outside the reach of truth, for imagination had not been freed popularly from the necessity of control by judgment. The weakness of wit in leaving the "bounds of Reason and good Sense" was explained by Samuel Clarke in a sermon preached at St. Paul's in 1705:

. . . whatsoever things are profane, impure, filthy, dishonourable and absurd; these things they make it their business to present as harmless and indifferent, and to laugh Men out of their utmost Wit. Such Men as these, are not to be argued with, till they can be persuaded to use Arguments instead of Drollery. For Banter is not capable of being answered by Reason: not because it has any strength in it; but because it runs out of all the bounds of Reason and good Sense, by extravagantly joining together such Images, as have not in themselves any manner of Similitude or Connextion; by which means all things are alike to be rendered ridiculous.[40]

Swift voiced lack of respect for wit without knowledge,[41] and Blackmore relegated wit to light and fanciful activities: "Wit is employ'd in its own Province, when the Possessor of it exercises his Genius on the ordinary Customs and Manners of Life, either in Conversation or Comick Writing," but it "has therefore no place in the Works where severe Knowledge and Judgment are chiefly exercis'd; those superior Productions of the Understanding must be express'd in a clear and strong manner, without intervening Strains of Wit or Facetious Fancies." In the same essay, he argued the incompatibility of "Wit and Discretion."[42]

Many of these views conflicted with wit as a test of truth. Later opponents of Shaftesbury's test—Berkeley, Warburton, and others—put the exercises of wit in a separate category from those of reason.[43] Even John Brown, in his defense of Shaftesbury's test, could defend wit only with qualifications. He felt that in the "Conduct of literary Warfare" the "saturnine Complexion of the dry Reasoner" was "ill-qualified . . . to cope with this mercurial Spirit of modern Wit."[44] Such a spirit could be unreliable, he concluded in his first essay: "Upon the whole: This new Design of discovering Truth by the vague and unsteady Light of Ridicule, puts one in Mind of the honest Irishman, who applied his Candle to the Sun-Dial, in order to see how the Night went."[45]

Curiously enough, as wit was disassociated from truth, the light image, which had been used to illustrate wit's ability to discover truth, came to be used more frequently to emphasize its purely ephemeral quality. Still recognizing the sudden insight of which it was capable, this new view likened wit to the flash of lightning, which disappears as suddenly as it appears. Samuel Cobb used this image in "Of Poetry, A Poem" when referring to Waller's poetic effectiveness:

> Such Wit, like Lightning, for a while looks Gay,
> Just gilds the Place, and vanishes away.

This allusion was used more frequently with disparagement. The author of the essay "Of Wit" in *The Weekly Register* (1732) made the following damning comment, using both the old and new light images: "Wit is a State of Imagination in the Speaker, that strikes the Imagination of the Hearer with an Idea of Beauty common to both; and the immediate Result of the Comparison is the Flash of Joy that attends it; it stands in the same Regard to

Sense, or Wisdom, as Lightning to the Sun, suddenly kindled and as suddenly gone."[46] With the same idea Morris refuted Dryden's definition:

> He [Dryden] discovers no Idea of the Surprize, and Brilliancy of Wit, or of the sudden Light thrown upon a Subject. Instead of once pointing at these, he only describes the Properties of clear Reasoning, which are a Propriety of Thoughts and Words;—whereas Wit, in its sudden Flashes, makes no Pretension to Reasoning; but is perceived in the pleasant Surprize which it starts, and in the Light darted upon a subject, which instantly vanishes again, without abiding a strict Examination.[47]

Morris later contrasted wit and humor, praising humor over its adversary and making use of the same view of wit: "The Strokes of Wit are like sudden Flashes, vanishing in an Instant, and usually flying too fast to be sufficiently marked and pursued by the Audience."[48] This interpretation of wit poses the ancient duality of judgment and imagination.

In spite of the increasing interest of the eighteenth century in the imagination, wit lost status by its association with that erratic faculty, retaining some of its major weaknesses: its transitory beauty, its attractive surprise, its superficial illumination—none of which were thoroughly dependable in discovering eternal truth.

Wit as Abusive and Ill-Natured

A third general charge throughout the Age of Wit was that wit was incorrigibly abusive. This abuse, so the criticism ran, corrupted the man of wit himself and vilified his target. All of wit's intellectual arsenal were guilty of this fault, a serious violation of both ethics and decorum. Sympathy fell upon the object of wit, and stigma fell upon its source. Flecknoe's irritation showed clearly in his description of a "bold abusive Wit," who, when he found a weakness in an individual, made "a hole of a breach and a tear of a hole."[49] Wolseley was alarmed at the abuse of satire, "that most needful part of our Poetry," because "Slander" had become the wit of the little satirists.[50] Blackmore's "Satyr against Wit" directly attacked the libelous wits without mercy. He proposed in an extended metaphor a bank for the recoining of wit, and suggested St. Evremond and Rymer to supervise the processing of old "coins":

> Let these be made the Masters of Essay,
> They'll every Piece of Metal touch and weigh,
> And Tell which is too light, which has too much Allay.
> 'Tis true that when the course and worthless Dross
> Is purg'd away, there will be mighty Loss.
> Ev'n C[ongrev]e, S[outher]n[e], Manly W[ycher]ly,
> When thus refin'd will grievous Suff'rers be.
> Into the melting Pot when D[ryde]n comes,
> What horrid Stench will rise, what noisome Fumes!
> How will he shrink, when all his leud Allay
> And wicked Mixture shall be purg'd away!
> When once his boasted Heaps are melted down,
> A Chest full scarce will yield one Sterling Crown.

The contagion against which Blackmore railed had overtaken him.

Perhaps the greatest single force in the growing stigma of wit was the growth of sensibility and its accompanying benevolence. Wit fell in easily and completely with the overly critical and fickle nature of the Restoration society. Around 1690 Tillotson reported (Sermon XLII), "By a general mistake Ill-nature passeth for Wit, as Cunning doth for Wisdom," adding that the "Wit of Man doth more naturally vent itself in Satire and Censure, than in Praise and Panegyrick." The verbal scourges and thrusts remained as the age waned. John Brown expressed near the end of the age the familiar complaint of the "terrible Accession of Bitterness and Rancour." He added, however, "'Tis the Glory of our Days, that this accursed Spirit of Persecution is at least dying away. What Pity that we cannot add: it is wholly extinguished!"[51]

The popular taste for personal attack continued well into the eighteenth century. Addison's essay in the *Free-Holder* took into account the public fascination for slander and libel:

A writer who makes fame the chief of his endeavours, and would be more desirous of pleasing than of improving his readers, might find an inexhaustible fund of mirth in politics. Scandal and satire are never-failing gratifications to the public. Detraction and obloquy are received with as much eagerness as wit and humour.[52]

Because of his particular sensibilities, Addison understandably excluded personal attack from the categories of wit and humor. However, the temper of other wits lacked this discrimination. They did not allow respect for personalities or delicacy to stand in the way of their pursuit of truth. Pope's *Dunciad* went through several successful editions in his lifetime. Gay's *Beggar's Opera,* produced by John Rich, was so phenomenally successful that, as the quip went, it made Gay rich and Rich gay. It included personal satire which the audiences understood and enjoyed. Even its ambiguities were taken personally. *The Mist's Weekly Journal* for March 23, 1728, published the following eyewitness account: "I have observ'd as often as I have been present at the Beggar's Opera, that whenever the facetious Mr. Hall sings the following Words, he is received with a more than ordinary Applause."[53] The song, Air XII in Act II, went:

When you censure the Age,
Be cautious and sage
Lest the Courtiers offended should be.
If you mention vice or bribe,
'Tis so pat to all the tribe,
Each cries—That was levell'd at me.

Nothing but sheer enjoyment of the contentious atmosphere could account for this reaction. The supply of such wit was produced to meet the demand.

Both sensibility and benevolence made strong impressions upon public opinion and created powerful opposition to personal, cutting wit. In the conflict between gravity and levity, sober moral forces gained strength through the years. The popularity of the *Tatler* and *Spectator* exerted a powerful influence on the spirit of wit. In the *Tatler,* No. 60, John Hughes argued for general satire and ridicule motivated by benevolence.

> A general representation of an Action, either ridiculous or enormous, may make those wince who find too much similitude in the character with themselves to plead not guilty; but none but a witness to the crime can charge them with the guilt, whilst the indictment is general, and the offender has the asylum of the whole world to protect him. Here can then be no injustice, where no one is injured; for it is themselves must appropriate the saddle, before scandal can ride them.

This and the continuing discussion in a journal as disarming as the *Tatler* reveals the extent of the growth of sensibility. Dennis reflected the same point of view in his concern for the hurt that the unsuspecting might undergo. He argued for a less particular satire because "a general Benefit must be the chief Design of it." He said further, "The Good which it carries with it, is equally intended to all; even those who happen to be hit by it, are design'd to be oblig'd among the rest, and suffer only by Accident."[54] The benevolent spirit conditioned Lord Chesterfield's advice. One letter dated September 5, 1748, read: "Never yield to that temptation, which to most young men is very strong, of exposing other people's weaknesses and infirmities, for the sake of diverting the company, or showing your own superiority." He added the thought, "A good heart desires rather to conceal than expose other people's weaknesses or misfortunes. If you have wit, use it to please, and not to hurt."

Another criticism was directed at the character of the man of wit. His aggressive nature and critical temper were judged inferior to the good nature of the man of sensibility, a man conscious of the feelings of others. So Steele found good-natured men superior to "shallow wits, superficial critics, and conceited fops" (*Tatler,* No. 227), who "can hold nothing but faults and blemishes, and indeed see nothing that is worth seeing. Show them a poem, it is stuff; a picture, it is daubing." Steele would substitute innocence for shallow wit. The "true spirit of satire" now was to lash vice pleasantly. The *Tatler,* No. 74, contained a letter by an anonymous writer commending that journal for "raising merit from obscurity, celebrating virtue in distress, and attacking vice in another method, by setting innocence in a proper light."

Humanitarianism influenced the standards of social discourse. The *Tatler,* No. 219, described conversation among the new men of feeling as the communication of "thoughts to each other upon such subjects, and in such a manner, as would be pleasant if there were no such thing as folly in the world; for it is but a low condition of wit in one man which depends upon folly in another." Men meeting together were to be governed henceforth by a "Spirit of Benevolence" and were not "to distinguish themselves as Wits or Philosophers"; they would, therefore, "suppress every Motion that can hinder what the scripture elegantly calls *preferring one another in love.*" This meant for Addison a substitution of good nature for wit, for good nature "shows Virtue in the fairest Light, takes off in some measure from the Deformity of Vice, and makes even Folly and Impertinence supportable" (*Spectator,* No. 169). Addison did not thereby reject wit but only its ill nature, a distinction which he clarified in that same issue of the *Spectator:*

> It is grown almost into a Maxim, that Good-natured Men are not always Men of most Wit. This Observation in my Opinion, has no Foundation in Nature. The Greatest Wits I have conversed with, are Men eminent for their Humanity. I take therefore this Remark to have been occasioned by two Reasons. First, because Ill-nature among ordinary Observers passes for Wit.
>
> Another Reason why the Good-natured Man may sometimes bring his Wit in Question, is, perhaps, because he is apt to be moved with Compassion for those Misfortunes or Infirmities, which another would turn into Ridicule, and by that Means gain the Reputation of a Wit.

So benevolence prompted a re-evaluation of amusement by forcing the distinction between proper and improper jokes and risible situations. As a result, quiet amusement replaced laughter.[55] This development had serious implications for the context of caricature, for in society wit often indulged in boisterous amusement. Excessive mirth was criticized even by those who defended milder forms of wit. Arbuckle did not think that "all Wit and Mirth" should be "banished from conversation," as long as it did not become "offensive to Company." He was sure that "as People seldom laugh when they are most pleased, so they are not always pleased when they laugh most." Further, "boistrous Mirth" always indicates "Clownishness and Rusticity in all civil and well-bred Companies."[56] His view remained valid for the next half-century and longer. The position of delicate and sensitive decorum was explained in 1748 (March 9) by Lord Chesterfield:

> Having mentioned laughing, I must particularly warn you against it: and I could heartily wish, that you may often be seen to smile, but never heard to laugh while you live. Frequent and loud laughter is the characteristic of folly and ill manners: it is the manner in which the mob express their silly joy at silly things: and they call it merry. In my mind, there is nothing so illiberal, and so ill-bred as audible laughter. True wit, or sense, never yet made anybody laugh; they are above it: they please the mind, and give a cheerfulness to the countenance. But it is low buffoonery, or silly accidents, that always excite laughter: and that is what people of sense and breeding should show themselves above. . . . I am neither of a melancholy nor a cynical disposition, and am as willing and as apt to be pleased as anybody; but I am sure that, since I have had the full use of my reason, nobody has heard me laugh.

In this sort of atmosphere the imminent stultification of wit was almost assured.

It is clear, therefore, that the eighteenth century came to subordinate the intellectual incisiveness of wit to good-natured sympathy. Man was by nature good, not trained to goodness. In Steel's words (*Tatler,* No. 45), "The natural, and not the acquired man, is the companion. Learning, wit, gallantry, and good breeding, are all but subordinate qualities in society, and are of no value, but as they are subservient to benevolence, and tend to a certain manner of being or appearing equal to the rest of the company." The appeal was to the heart, not to the head; the intellectualizing upon vices and follies, along with rhetorical brilliance, had become passé. Dennis had argued effectively for the emotional appeal in his Remarks on *Prince Arthur* in 1696:

As no Pleasure can be very great, if it is not surprising, so no Surprize can be very great if it is not pathetick. . . . Indeed, a Poet ought always to speak to the Heart. And the greatest Wit in the World, when he ceases to do that, is a Rhimer and not a Poet. For a Poet, that he may be sure to instruct, is oblig'd to give all the delight that he can. . . . Now nothing that is not pathetick in Poetry, can very much delight: For he who is very much pleas'd, is at the same time very much mov'd; and Poetical genius . . . is itself a Passion. A Poet then is oblig'd always to speak to the heart. And it is for this reason, that Point and Conceit, and all that they call Wit, is to be fore ever banish'd from true Poetry; because he who uses it, speaks to the head alone.[57]

The appeal for the pathetic signalled the appearance of another cult—that of the "good Heart." Sentimentality in the form of public weeping became common. Follies were even encouraged, according to Goldsmith in his discussion of "weeping sentimental comedy": "If they [the characters] happen to have faults or foibles, the spectator is taught not only to pardon, but to applaud them, in consideration of the goodness of their hearts: so that folly, instead of being ridiculed, is commended, and the comedy aims at touching our passions without the power of being truly pathetic."[58] If we grant only partial seriousness to Goldsmith, the development he cites was a subversion not only of good sense but of wit. Certainly in such an atmosphere the spirit of wit was doomed.

The Stigma of Wit in Jonathan Swift's Poem "Verses on the Death of Dr. Swift"

Few will deny that Jonathan Swift was the greatest wit of the age. And certainly no one can argue that he was not most loyal to his role in the Republic of Wit, in spite of an awareness of the ill will engendered by such a role. Anthony Henley had warned him in July, 1709, of what he might expect from the viciousness of his attacks upon his enemies: "Therefore I would advise you to fall upon old Joan, eat, do I live to bid thee, eat Addison: and when you have eat everybody also, eat my Lord

Lieutenant—he is something lean—God help the while; and though it will, for aught I know, be treason, there will be nobody left to hang you, unless you should think fit to do yourself that favour." So Swift was duly warned.

Swift's motivation was a combination of a serious search for truth[59] and a desire for personal prestige.[60] As for fame, he had few illusions. "Take care the bad poets do not outwit you," he wrote to Pope in November, 1725, "as they served the good ones in every age, whom they have provoked to transmit their names to posterity. Maevius is as well known as Virgil, and Gildon will be as well known as you, if his name gets into your verses: and as to the difference between good and bad fame, it is a perfect trifle." In April, 1731, when Pope had turned grave, Lord Bathurst concluded a letter to Swift with the admonition, "So, in this farce of life, wise men pass their time in mirth, while fools only are serious. Adieu. Continue to be merry and wise; but never turn serious, or cunning." Swift added his own postscript: "It is too late for me to turn serious now."

Committed to wit as he was, Swift still recognized the stigma which antagonized his enemies and thwarted his ambitions. "Verses on the Death of Dr. Swift," finished near the end of 1731 though not published until 1739, expresses his awareness of the stigma. He obviously enjoyed writing the poem, for he wrote John Gay in December, 1731, "I have been several months writing near five hundred lines on a pleasant subject, only to tell what my friends and enemies will say on me after I am dead. I shall finish it soon, for I add two lines every week, and blot out four and alter eight."

The subtitle reads "Occasioned by Reading the Following Maxim in Rochefoucauld," which translated asserts, "In the adversity of our best friends, we find something that doth not displease us." Early in the poem, Swift illustrated the operation of the maxim among friends.

> We all behold with envious Eyes,
> Our Equal rais'd above our Size;
> Who wou'd not at a crowded Show,
> Stand high himself, keep others low?

I love my Friend as well as you,
But would not have him stop my View:
Then let him have the higher Post;
I ask but for an Inch at most.

If in a Battle you should find,
One, whom you love of all Mankind,
Had some heroick Action done,
A Champion kill'd, or Trophy won;
Rather than thus be over-topt,
Would you not wish his Lawrels cropt?

Dead honest Ned is in the Gout,
Lies rackt with Pain, and you without:
How patiently you hear him groan!
How glad the Case is not your own!

What Poet would not grieve to see,
His Brethren write as well as he?
But rather than they should excell,
He'd wish his Rivals all in Hell.

After castigating mankind for its perfidy and selfishness in the very face of friendship, Swift searched his own relationships with close friends for signs of these same human weaknesses.

In Pope, I cannot read a Line,
But with a Sigh, I wish it mine:
When he can in one Couplet fix
More Sense than I can do in Six:
It gives me such a jealous Fit,
I cry, Pox take him, and his Wit.

Why must I be outdone by Gay,
In my own hum'rous biting Way?

Arbuthnot is no more my Friend,
Who dares to Irony pretend;
Which I was born to introduce,
Refin'd it first, and shew'd its Use.

St. John, as well as Pultney knows,
That I had some repute for Prose;
And till they drove me out of Date,
Could maul a Minister of State:

If they have mortify'd my Pride,
And made me throw my Pen aside;
If with such Talents Heav'n hath blest 'em
Have I not Reason to detest 'em?

To all my Foes, dear Fortune, send
Thy Gifts, but never to my Friend:
I tamely can endure the first,
But, this with Envy makes me burst.

Swift next contemplated his possible death in the near future.

The Time is not remote, when I
Must by the Course of Nature dye:
When I foresee my special Friends,
Will try to find their private Ends:
Tho' it is hardly understood,
Which way my Death can do them good;
Yet, thus methinks, I hear 'em speak.

And so his friends considered the prospect of his approaching demise:

See, how the Dean begins to break:
Poor Gentleman, he droops apace,
You plainly find it in his Face:
That old Vertigo in his Head,
Will never leave him, till he's dead:
Besides, his Memory decays,
He recollects not what he says;
He cannot call his Friends to Mind;
Forgets the Place where last he din'd:
Plyes you with Stories o'er and o'er,
He told them fifty Times before.
How does he fancy we can sit,
To hear his out-of-fashion'd Wit?
. . . .

For Poetry, he's past his Prime,
He takes an Hour to find a Rhime:
His Fire is out, his Wit decay'd,
His Fancy sunk, his Muse a Jade.
I'd have him throw away his Pen;
But there's no talking to some Men.

Next, Swift described his last breaths and the first thoughts of the bedside watchers as he slipped away.

> "Behold the fatal Day arrive!
> How is the Dean? He's just alive.
> Now the departing Prayer is read:
> He hardly breathes. The Dean is dead.
> Before the Passing-Bell begun,
> The News thro' half the Town has run.
> O, may we all for Death prepare!
> What has he left? And who's his Heir?
> I know no more than what the News is,
> 'Tis all bequeath'd to publick Uses.
> To public Use! A perfect Whim!
> What had the Publick done for him!
> Meer Envy, Avarice, and Pride!
> He gave it all:—But first he dy'd.
> And had the Dean, in all the Nation,
> No worthy Friend, no poor Relation?
> So ready to do Strangers good,
> Forgetting his own Flesh and Blood?"

The news of Swift's death finally reached the citadel of the nation, the Queen's Court.

> Kind Lady Suffolk in the Spleen,
> Runs laughing up to tell the Queen.
> The Queen, so Gracious, Mild, and Good,
> Cries, "Is he gone? 'Tis time he shou'd.
> He's dead you say; why let him rot;
> I'm glad the Medals were forgot.
> I promis'd them, I own; but when?
> I only was the Princess then;
> But now as Consort of the King,
> You know 'tis quite a different Thing."

And what of his personal friends?

> Here shift the Scene, to represent
> How those I love, my Death lament.
> Poor Pope will grieve a Month; and Gay
> A Week; and Arbuthnot a Day.
> . . . .

My female Friends, whose tender Hearts
Have better learn'd to act their Parts.
Receive the News in doleful Dumps,
"The Dean is dead, (and what is Trumps?)
Then Lord have Mercy on his Soul.
(Ladies 'll venture for the Vole.)
Six Deans they say must bear the Pall.
(I wish I knew what King to call.)
Madam, your Husband will attend
The Funeral of so good a Friend?"
"No Madam, 'tis a shocking Sight,
And he's engag'd To-morrow Night!
My Lady Club wou'd take it ill,
If he shou'd fail her at Quadrill.
He lov'd the Dean. (I lead a Heart.)
But dearest Friends, they say, must part.
His Time was come, he ran his Race;
We hope he's in a better Place."

The card game continued. In a few months, Swift predicted, his works would be forgotten.

One year is past; a different Scene;
No further mention of the Dean;
Who now, alas, no more is mist,
Than if he never did exist.
Where's now this Fav'rite of Apollo?
Departed; and his Works must follow:
Must undergo the common Fate;
His Kind of Wit is out of Date.

Seeking a position for comparative objectivity in evaluating the work of the dead wit, Swift continued:

Suppose me dead; and then suppose
A Club assembled at the Rose;
Where from Discourse of this and that,
I grow the Subject of their Chat:
And, while they toss my Name about,
With Favour some, and some without;
One quite indiff'rent in the Cause,
My Character impartial draws.

From this perspective, he allowed himself the liberty of assessing his career as a wit. Of his serious moral purpose he wrote:

As with a moral View design'd
To cure the Vices of Mankind:
His Vein, ironically grave,
Expos'd the Fool, and lash'd the Knave:
To steal a Hint was never known,
But what he writ was all his own.

With insight into the stigma of his role, he included the lines:

Had he but spar'd his Tongue and Pen,
He might have rose like other Men:
But, Power was never in his Thought;
And, Wealth he valu'd not a Groat.

The closing verses are especially revealing:

Perhaps I may allow, the Dean
Had too much Satyr in his Vein;
And seem'd determin'd not to starve it,
Because no Age could more deserve it.
Yet, Malice never was his Aim;
He lash'd the Vice but spar'd the Name.
No Individual could resent,
Where Thousands equally were meant.
His Satyr points at no Defect,
But what all Mortals may correct;
For he abhorr'd that senseless Tribe,
Who call it Humour when they jibe:
He spar'd a Hump or crooked Nose,
Whose Owners set not up for Beaux.
True genuine Dulness mov'd his Pity,
Unless it offer'd to be witty.
Those, who their Ignorance confess'd,
He ne'er offended with a Jest;
But laugh'd to hear an Idiot quote,
A Verse from Horace, learn'd by Rote.

. . . .

He gave the little Wealth he had,
To build a House for Fools and Mad:

And shew'd by one satyric Touch,
No Nation wanted it so much:
That Kingdom he hath left his Debtor,
I wish it soon may have a Better.

Swift defended his wit against such charges as malice, personal invective, and—in deference, no doubt, to benevolence and the cult of the good heart—harm of the innocent, the helpless, and the ignorant. He admitted a strong satiric vein but justified it in the belief that the age deserved satire. And certainly no one knew better than he that if he had spared his tongue and pen, he "might have rose like other men." As Lord Bathurst wrote him in 1739, Swift had "often told truth of persons, who would rather [he] had abused them in the grossest manner."

However, the poem contains no retraction nor rejection of his wit or of the role it should play in the republic. He remained adamant in his efforts in behalf of truth and virtue. The nearest Swift ever came to apology was in a variation of the above poem, "The Life and Character of Dean Swift." Long considered spurious, it was presumably altered from the original for the sake of surreptitious publication and was published in 1733. The concluding lines, put in the mouth of a defender, read:

'Tis plain, his Writings were design'd
To please, and to reform Mankind;
And, if he often miss'd his Aim,
The World must own it, to their Shame;
The Praise is His, and Theirs the Blame.

Then, since you dread no further Lashes,
You freely may forgive his Ashes.

The Man of Wit as an Object of Ridicule

By the last decade of the Age of Wit, the effects of the stigma were evident upon the status of the man of wit per se. He could not maintain his respected position in society while his product suffered under these charges and his role was stigmatized. Something of the general attitude toward wit is indicated in "A Modern Glossary," circulated at the time, which defined wit as "profaneness, indecency, immorality, scurrility, mimickry, buffonery; abuse of all good men, and especially of the clergy."[61] This listing reveals the great influence of the social caricature of wit on its stigma.

The changing economic and social pattern of English culture also aided in the demise of wit's authority. Society had undergone a quiet revolution in the midst of the Age of Wit. With the increasing wealth and importance of the middle classes, cultural dominance shifted from the landed to the merchant class. The new leadership in both Church and State, faced with an irresponsible Catholic king in 1688, established their political power and reinforced their economic supremacy with two new advantages: a Bank of England and a Protestant succession. Thus bolstered, they sought further cultural adjustments.[62] The one adjustment pertinent to wit was the search for a new literature expressive of the middle classes, a literature possessing conventional virtues. Such literature had to be serious, moral, and profitable.

This revolution in taste underlay many of the charges and reactions against wit. The criteria of judgment ceased to be aristocratic and learned, becoming bourgeois and practical. One sees this change reflected in Pope's *Dunciad* (I–III), where the action consists of the "progress of dulness" from the city to Westminster (symbolizing the Court). This progress is most specific in Book III.[63] The triumph of the dunces would mark the end of the rule of the ancients and of wit (IV, 21–24), as well as of the rule of the Court. In actuality the city gradually triumphed, and with it middle-class morality and sentiment. The man of wit became anachronistic along with the courtier.

Perhaps most influential in placing this stigma upon the man of wit was the growing spirit of romanticism. Broadly speaking, this new spirit represented certain changes in perspective, which conditioned future attitudes toward wit—a turning from matters of the head to matters of the heart, or from "intellection" to feeling. The initial reaction of the individual to the implications of dynamic organicism was introspection and indulgence in the imagination. In exploring the pleasures of the imagination, romanticism disassociated imagination from wit, for the nature and methods of wit were incompatible with romanticism. Where wit would laugh vices and follies out of existence, the early romanticism would applaud them understandingly. Sensibility took the barbs from the man of wit and tolerated the weaknesses and faults he opposed.

So alien did wit become that the young men of intelligence and learning no longer aspired to become wits. The title "man of wit" ceased to challenge the best efforts of capable intellects. Edward Young, a poet and contemporary of Swift and Pope (seven years older than Pope and a personal friend), was one of the most brilliant men of his day and particularly adept in conversation. When he had occasion to converse with Voltaire during the latter's visit to England in 1722, observers of the meeting were in agreement that Young's wit was the most scintillating. Though he rejected the role of wit and became a poet of major importance in the newer spirit of the approaching age, he nevertheless had much to say on the subject. In the second of his "Two Epistles to Mr. Pope, Concerning the Authors of the Age" (1730), Young continued the idealism of the republic of letters, using the classical metaphor in the opening lines:

> All write at London: shall the rage abate
> Here, where it most should shine, the Muses' seat?
> Where, mortal or immortal, as they please,
> The learn'd may choose eternity or ease?
> Has not a royal patron [George I] wisely strove
> To woo the Muse in her Athenian grove?

Young's purpose was to "give some needful precepts how to write and live" in the literary community. He showed throughout the poem the prejudice which existed against the literary wit. For example,

Wits are a despicable race of men,
If they confine their talents to the pen:
When a man shocks us, while the writer shines,
Our scorn in life, our envy in his lines.

(ll. 71–75)

Never considering himself a "wit," he rejected wit as unessential to the poet:

Nature has shown, by making it so rare,
That wit's a jewel which we need not wear:
Of plain sound sense life's current coin is made;
With that we drive the most substantial trade.

(ll. 81–85)

Young's sympathy with the new man of feeling is apparent in his view of satire:

Let Satire less engage you than applause:
It shows a gen'rous mind to wink at flaws.
Is genius yours? be yours a glorious end,
Be your king's, country's, truth's, religion's friend.

(ll. 153–157)

Equating satire and wit, he would admit them only within the confines of benevolence:

If satire charms, strike faults, but spare the man:
'Tis dull to be as witty as you can.

(ll. 161–162)

In this reversal of former values, wit was now evidence of dullness. In a final metaphor in his "Epistle," Young expressed again the ironic reversal:

As turns a flock of geese, and on the green
Poke out their foolish necks in awkward spleen
(Ridiculous in rage!) to hiss, not bite,
So war their quills when sons of Dullness write.

Public opinion turned rapidly against the man of wit. The special attributes which had distinguished him from his fellow men now became his humiliation. When it was suspected and then argued that his wit might arise as often from weakness as from strength, his prestige was seriously impaired. The anonymous author of the essay "Of Wit" wrote in 1732 that wit

> . . . as often arises from the Defect of the Mind, as from its Strength and Capacity. This is evident in those who are Wits only, without being grave or wise. Just, solid, and lasting Wit is the Result of fine Imagination, finished Study, and a happy temper of Body. As no one pleases more than the Man of Wit, none is more liable to offend; therefore he shou'd have a Fancy quick to conceive, knowledge, good Humour, and Discretion to direct the whole. Wit often leads a Man into Misfortunes, that his Prudence wou'd have avoided; as it is the Means of raising a Reputation, so it sometimes destroys it. He who affects to be always witty, renders himself cheap, and, perhaps, ridiculous.[64]

Such a defect of the mind was believed to be a result of the delusion of imagination. The belief that wit could be ridiculous, even foolish, continued. Contemporaries agreed with John Gilbert Cooper in "Taste: An Epistle to a Young Critic" (1755): "'Tis true! 'tis pity!/But 'tis not every lunatic that's witty."

Another special attribute of the wit, his quick tongue, made him unpleasant company, unpredictable, and not a little sinister in a polite, benevolent society. Lord Chesterfield wrote (October 12, 1748) of "professed" wits and poets, whose company "is extremely inviting to most young men who if they have wit themselves, are pleased with it." However, "a wit is a very unpopular denomination, as it carries terror along with it: and the people in general are as much afraid of a live wit, in company, as a woman is of a gun, which she thinks may go off of itself, and do her mischief." He did admit that the company of wits was worth seeking, but only if visited in moderation and judgment.

It remained for Oliver Goldsmith to describe the final degraded position of the man of wit in society in facetious wittiness befitting his subject. In *An Inquiry into The Present State of Polite Learning* (1759), he reported,

> Since the days of a certain prime minister [Sir Robert Walpole] of inglorious memory, the learned have been kept pretty much at a distance. A jockey, or a laced player, supplies the place of the scholar, poet, or the man of virtue. Those conversations, once the result of wisdom, wit and innocence, are now turned to humbler topics, little more being expected from a companion than a laced coat, a pliant bow, and an immoderate friendship for—a well served table.
>
> Wit, when neglected by the great, is generally despised by the vulgar. Those who are unacquainted with the world, are apt to fancy the man of wit as leading a very agreeable life. . . . Very different is his present situation. He is called an author, and all know that an author is a thing only to be laughed at. His person, not his jest, becomes the mirth of the company. At his approach the most fat unthinking face brightens into malicious meaning. Even alderman laugh, and revenge on him the ridicule which was lavished on their forefathers. (Chap. X)

So by 1750, the biter was being bitten.

Summary

The impact of the stigma of wit, together with its caricature, continued for decades. Once an unavoidable word, wit almost disappeared from conversation and writing. Examination of such a sensitive body of material as the Whig journal *World* reveals only an occasional and casual allusion, often derogatory in nature. Thus, wit was judged in No. 70 for May 2, 1754, to be a mere drug, having practically no value. And in the poem "The Insensible" in No. 156, "hapless Wit darts all her stings in vain." But just as indicative of its status, wit was avoided in discussions of subjects which earlier would have required its use. In No. 104, dated December 26, 1754, a serious tone for the Christmas issue was rejected as inappropriate to the tradition of "public papers," thus raising the question of the nature of the journal. Its contents were called "papers of Pleasantry," and in the discussion that followed, which included an examination of the "Pleasantries of the town," the word wit was not once used.

Instead, the writer used such phrases as "innocent mirth and levity," "novelty," and "the colouring of humour." In fact, humor had replaced wit, as in the following passage:

> In writings of humour, figures are sometimes used of so delicate a nature, that it shall often happen that some people will see things in a direct contrary sense to what the author and the majority of readers understand them. To such the most innocent irony may appear irreligion or wickedness. But, in the misapprehension of this figure, it is not always that the reader is to blame. A great deal of irony may seem very clear to the writer, which may not be so properly managed, as to be safely trusted to the various capacities and apprehensions of all sorts of readers. In such cases the conductor of a paper will be liable to various kinds of censure, though in reality nothing can be proved against him but want of judgment.

Here, the common association of wit with rhetoric and all of the accompanying criticism of ironic ambiguity, obscenity, and undisciplined imagination are avoided. In the struggle between wit and humor, humor clearly won, for it became the respectable term.

Another factor in the decline of wit least often found in eighteenth-century literature was the simultaneous decline of rhetoric as the medium for truth. A vivid description of decadent wit is found in Richard Bentley's poem "Epistle to Lord Melcombe."[65] Lamenting the destruction of fable before the onslaught of fact and the consequent rejection of figurative language, he expressed dismay at the searing of the mythic kingdoms of the imagination by the penetrating light of mathematic and empirical minds. He began by addressing himself to lost poetry and vanquished wit, which he associated very closely; he then recalled the earlier ages when "the great abyss of Fable open stood," when

> All Irrealities came forth reveal'd
> By pow'rful Fancy into fact congeal'd.

But in his day, great "progress" has been made. His sarcastic tone continues:

The world grown old, its youthful follies past,
Reason assumes her reign, tho' late, at last.
By slow degrees, and labouring up the hill,
Step after step, yet seeming to stand still,
She wins her way, wherever she advances:
Satyr no more, nor Fawn, nor Dryad dances.
The groves, tho' trembling to a natural breeze,
Dismiss their horrors, and shew nought but trees.
Before her, Nonsense, Superstition fly;
We burn no Witch, let her be e'er so dry;
A woman now may live, tho' past her prime
So hallow'd and so gracious is the time.

In this matter-of-fact world, poetry has no place, and the poet faces annihilation:

Bankrupt of deities, with all their train,
And set to work without his tools in vain,
Not genius—crampt (but what can genius do
When it's tied down to one and one make two?)
How can poor poet stir? In such a case
We must do something to supply their place.

With the death of poetry died rhetorical effectiveness:

Fall'n cherub Simile, who erst divine,
Cloath'd with transcendent beauty didst outshine?
Plain angel Poesy, now art thou lost!
Sunk in Oblivion's pit! from what height toss'd!

Thus to plain Narrative confin'd alone,
Figure, Description, Simile quite gone;
The whole affair evinc'd which we contend,
The thing has had its day, and there's an end.

The theme of primitivism is evident in the poet's concept of the inverted river of verse and rhyme which "dwindles as it flows." Nevertheless, Bentley did not anticipate the complete demise of wit.

[For] while we're on this subject, 'tis worth thinking,
How little salt has kept this world from stinking;
'Tis the same wit, at different times alive,
Sunk at Whitehall, to rise up at Queenhithe.

Henry Home, Lord Kames, wrote objectively of wit in his *Elements of Criticism* (1671). His purpose, like that of Corbyn Morris, was to return to the original view of wit as rhetoric, limiting though this confinement was in respect to wit's former richness. He stripped it of the accretions of the past hundred years—its identity with truth, with secret grace, with fashions, and with behavior. Thus his initial sentence: "Wit is a quality of certain thoughts and expressions: the term is never applied to an action nor a passion, and as little to an external object."[66] He then introduced a new attribute, ludicrousness: "The term *wit* is appropriated to such thoughts and expressions as are ludicrous, and also occasion some degree of surprise by their singularity." "Ludicrous" was used earlier by Butler in his *Analogues* (II, vi), 1736, to describe a rhetorical turn. His remarks were decidedly derogatory. Ludicrousness incited laughter by its incongruity. Kames asserted that wit makes "ludicrous combinations of things that have little or no natural relation," having no foundation in nature and being a fabrication of the imagination. The inconsequential nature of wit is obvious in his discussion of repartee, which he admitted "may happen to be witty." But, he continued, "it cannot be considered as a species of wit, because there are many repartees extremely smart, and yet extremely serious." The implication is that wit is never serious.

The degraded concept of wit continued into the nineteenth century. William Hazlitt, in the essay "On Wit and Humour" (1819), wrote that "mere wit, opposed to reason and argument, consists in striking out some casual and partial coincidence which has nothing to do . . . with the nature of things." It adds "littleness to littleness" and heaps "contempt on insignificance by all the arts of petty and incessant warfare." Hazlitt quoted a comment of the Duke of Buckingham, "Laws are not, like women, the worse for being old," as an example of "a harmless truism and the utmost malice of wit united." He logically associated wit and humor in common attributes as he saw them: indolence, vanity, weakness, and insensibility.

The return to rhetoric in the middle of the eighteenth century—in other words, the stripping of wit to its early significance as rhetoric—gave wit the validity it had previously possessed, but rendered it bare and vitiated. The eclipse of rhetoric itself from the eighteenth century through the first two decades of the twentieth century obscured its crucial meaning.

Recent developments, however, have altered this eclipse. The poetry of wit, inundated by the poetry of emotion in the Romantic decades, has re-emerged. Important in this emergence have been the rhetorical achievements in startling metaphor by Emily Dickinson and Gerard Manley Hopkins; the rediscovery in this century of the metaphysical poets of the seventeenth century; and the intellectual displays of William Butler Yeats, Ezra Pound, T. S. Eliot, William Empson, and W. H. Auden in their intent examination of the manners and ethos of our time. These and other developments have resulted in a "re-emergence of rhetoric,"[67] revitalizing a rich body of poetic techniques and intellectual weapons. It may be that truth for our time will be conceptualized through the figurative power of rhetorical wit. Metaphors still retain their power to "devour any kind of experience."[68]

The atmosphere for general wittiness has not yet reappeared. Our century, still living, as Matthew Arnold said, between two worlds—one dead, the other powerless to be born—is too full of doubts, ambiguities, and disillusion, too absorbed with a new synthesis of knowledge to view itself with witty detachment. We have for the most part lost our sense of humor and satire in the grimness of our situation. For wit at its best, a society must possess a large and steady confidence which became in the Age of Wit an unparalleled optimism. It is the worse for us that wit is not one of the mirrors we successfully use, a mirror that the intellectual giants—the men of wit—held so unrelentingly to their own time, to the great gain of western culture.

Explanatory Notes

Explanatory Notes

Chapter 1 The Enigma of Wit

1. For various published studies touching upon facets of wit in the age, see the following: A. Alvarez, *The School of Donne* (London, 1961), chap. 6 on "The Game of Wit"; W. G. Crane, *Wit and Rhetoric in the Renaissance: The Formal Basis of Elizabethan Prose Style* (New York, 1937); Scott Elledge, "Cowley's Ode 'Of Wit' and Longinus on the Sublime: a Study of one Definition of the Word Wit," *MLQ*, IX (1948), 185–198; William Empson, "Wit in the Essay on Criticism," *HR*, II (Winter, 1950), 559–577; T. H. Fujimura, *The Restoration Comedy of Wit* (Princeton, N.J., 1952); E. N. Hooker, "Pope on Wit: The 'Essay on Criticism,'" in R. F. Jones *et al.*, *The Seventeenth Century* (Stanford, Calif. 1951), pp. 225–246; Ian Jack, *August Satire: Intention and Idiom in English Poetry, 1660–1750* (Oxford, England, 1952); Maurice Johnson, *The Sin of Wit: Jonathan Swift as a Poet* (Syracuse, N.Y., 1950); Robert M. Krapp, "Class Analysis of a Literary Controversy: Wit and Sense in Seventeenth Century English Literature," *Science and Society*, X (Winter, 1946), 80–92; J. B. Leishman, *The Monarch of Wit* (London, 1951) on the poetry of Donne; C. S. Lewis, *Studies in Words* (Cambridge, England, 1960), chap. 4 on "Wit"; John Loftis, *Comedy and Society from Congreve to Fielding* (Stanford, Calif., 1959), pp. 27–32; Maynard Mack, "'Wit and Poetry and Pope': Some Observations on his Imagery," in *Pope and His Contemporaries: Essays Presented to George Sherburn*, eds. J. L. Clifford and L. A. Landa (Oxford, England, 1949), pp. 20–40; R. L. Morris, "Addison's Mixt Wit," *MLN*, LVII (1942), 666–668; Martin Price, *Swift's Rhetorical Art: A Study in Structure and Meaning* (New Haven, Conn., 1953), chap. 3 on "The Method of Wit"; R. L. Sharp, *From Donne to Dryden: The Revolt Against Metaphysical Poetry* (Chapel Hill, N.C., 1940); Stuart M. Tave, *The Amiable Humorist* (Chicago, Ill., 1960), pp. 16–67; W. Lee Ustick and H. H. Hudson, "Wit, Mixt Wit, and the Bee in Amber," *HLB*, No. 8 (October, 1935), pp. 103–130;

George Williamson, "The Rhetorical Pattern of Neo-Classical Wit," *MP*, XXXIII (1935), 55–81, and *The Senecan Amble: A Study in Prose Form from Bacon to Collier* (Chicago, Ill., 1951), especially chaps. 9, 10, and 11; J. H. Wilson, *The Court Wits of the Restoration* (Princeton, N.J., 1948); W. K. Wimsatt, Jr., "Rhetoric and Poems: The Example of Pope," *English Institute Essays,* 1948, ed. D. A. Robertson (New York, 1949), pp. 179–209; W. K. Wimsatt, Jr. and Cleanth Brooks, *Literary Criticism* (New York, 1957), chap. 12 on "Rhetoric and Neo-Classic Wit"; Introductions to *Series One: Essays on Wit,* Augustan Reprint Society.

2. Thomas Burke, *The Streets of London* (London, 1940), p. 61.

3. On this point see L. B. Namier, "Monarchy and the Party System," in *Personalities and Powers* (London, 1955), pp. 13–38. Caroline Robbins in *The Eighteenth Century Commonwealth* (Cambridge, Mass., 1959) writes, "The party system without which popular parliamentary government cannot work was not accepted in any modern sense of the term by many within the political English community. Its discipline would have been irking; its theory, though implicit in some discussions and in some arrangements, was yet to be absorbed into any important sector of public opinion" p. 321.

4. For two of many lists of earlier synonyms of wit, see Walter Carleton, *A Brief Discourse Concerning the Different Wits of Men* (London, 1669), pp. 9–10; also David Abercromby, *A Discourse of Wit* (London, 1685), pp. 6–7.

5. "Sermon against Foolish Talking and Jesting," *Theological Works* (Oxford, England, 1830), I, 386.

6. "Concerning Humour in Comedy," *Critical Essays of the Seventeenth Century*, ed. Joel E. Spingarn (Oxford, England, 1908–1909), III, 242–243, hereafter cited as Spingarn.

7. "Discourse of the English Stage," Spingarn, II, 94.

8. "An Account of the Ensuing Poem, Annus Mirabilis," *Essays of John Dryden*, ed. W. P. Ker (Oxford, England, 1926), I, 14–15, hereafter cited as Ker.

9. *Theological Works*, I, 386–387.

10. "The Author's Apology for Heroic Poetry and Poetic Licence Prefixed to 'The State of Innocence and Fall of Man,'" Ker, I, 190.

11. "Preface to *Valentinian, A Tragedy*," Spingarn, III, 21.

12. Augustan Reprint Society, Series One, No. 1 (1946), p. 191.

13. "A Dissertation Concerning the Perfection of the English Language, The State of Poetry, etc.," *Critical Essays of the Eighteenth Century, 1700–1725*, ed. Willard H. Durham (New Haven, Conn., 1915), p. 392, hereafter cited as Durham.

14. Corbyn Morris's Introduction to *An Essay towards Fixing*

the True Standards of Wit, Humour, Raillery, Satire, and Ridicule, 1744, Augustan Reprint Society, Series One, No. 4 (1947), p. i, hereafter cited as Morris, *Fixing the True Standards.*

15. Quoted by J. L. Clifford in Introduction to Morris's *Fixing the True Standards,* Augustan Reprint Society, Series One, No. 4 (1947), p. 4.

16. "Abraham Cowley," *Lives of the English Poets.* Introduction by Arthur Waugh (London, 1961), I, 29.

Chapter 2 The Rhetoric of Wit

1. [John Bodenham], *Politeuphuia, or Wits Common-Wealth: or a Treasury of Divine, Moral, Historical and Political Admonitions, Similes and Sentences. For the Use of Schools. Newly Corrected and Enlarged* (London, 1722), p. 156.

2. This debasing of rhetoric has received various reactions. J. W. H. Atkins deplores it, *History of English Literary Criticism: The Renaissance* (London, 1951), p. 69; Craig La Driers justifies it, "Rhetoric and 'Merely Verbal' Art," *English Institute Essays 1948* (New York, 1949) p. 148.

3. See D. L. Clark, *Rhetoric and Poetry in the Renaissance* (New York, 1922), p. 33, and Crane, *Wit and Rhetoric,* p. 3.

4. Clark presents evidence to show that this change had come about by the late Middle Ages, *Rhetoric and Poetry,* pp. 47, 51, 54.

5. *Elizabethan Critical Essays,* ed. G. Gregory Smith (Oxford, 1904), I, 256, hereafter cited as Smith.

6. Quintilian, *Institutio Oratoria,* trans. H. E. Butler. Loeb Classical Library (London, 1933–36) IX, 1. Crane gives some evidence of simplification in *Wit and Rhetoric,* p. 59.

7. Crane, *Wit and Rhetoric,* pp. 59–60.

8. "The Author's Apology," Ker, I, 190.

9. *An Essay on Criticism: As It Regards Design, Thought, and Expression. In Prose and Verse* (London, 1728), p. 43.

10. *Elements of Criticism* (1761), ed. James R. Boyd (New York, 1883), p. 207ff.

11. *Mysterie of Rhetoric Unveil'd,* as quoted in Williamson, "Rhetorical Pattern," p. 75.

12. Samuel Butler, "A Quibbler," *Characters and Passages from Note-Books,* ed. A. R. Waller (Cambridge, England, 1908), p. 90.

13. The basic studies in this change are those of Morris W. Croll: "'Attic Prose' in the Seventeenth Century," *SP,* XVIII (1921), 79–128, and "The Baroque Style in Prose," *Studies in English Phil-*

ology (University of Minnesota, 1929), pp. 427–55. An excellent and more recent study is George Williamson's *The Senecan Amble.*

14. Croll changed his designation of this style from "Attic" to "Baroque." Williamson detects three distinct styles: the curt style of Lipsius, the loose style of Montaigne, and the obscure style of Bacon in *Senecan Amble,* p. 187.

15. *Facetiae Musarum Deliciae: or, The Muses Recreation,* 1656. *Wit Restor'd,* 1658. *Wit's Recreations,* 1640. *New Edition* (London, n.d.), II, 305.

16. *The Works of George Herbert,* ed. F. E. Hutchinson (Oxford, England, 1945), p. 77.

17. John Lyly, *Alexander and Campaspe,* III, ii.

18. *The New Foundling Hospital for Wit. Being a Collection of Fugitive Pieces in Prose and Verse, Not in Any Other Collection. With Several Pieces Never Before Published* (London, 1784), VI, 189.

19. *A Collection of Letters and Essays (Hibernicus' Letters) on Several Subjects, lately Publish'd in the Dublin Journal* (London, 1729), p. 89.

20. Henry Parrot, *Mastive,* quoted by J. William Hebel and H. H. Hudson, eds., *Poetry of the English Renaissance, 1509–1660* (New York, 1946), p. 529.

21. *The Most Elegant and Wittie Epigrams of Sir J. Harrington. Digested into Foure Books,* as quoted in *Sixteenth-Century English Poetry,* ed. N. E. McClure (New York, 1954), p. 578.

22. Preface to *Parnassi Puerperium,* as quoted in Ustick and Hudson, "Mixt Wit," p. 106.

23. Samuel Johnson attributes metaphysical wit to "Marino and his followers"; see "Life of Cowley" *Works,* I, 16; for study of Marino's influence, see Ruth Wallerstein, *Studies in Seventeenth Century Poetic* (Madison, Wisconsin, 1950), pp. 159–160.

24. "Of Poetry," Spingarn, III, 99–100.

25. *Printed Poems on Several Occasions. Originals and Translations. Printed in the Year 1694.* The poem in full is reproduced in Ustick and Hudson, "Mixt Wit," p. 120.

26. W. B. Smith, "What is Metaphysical Poetry?" *SR,* XLII (1934), 263.

27. William Winstanley, *Lives of Most Famous English Poets,* as quoted by J. J. Parry, ed., *Poems and Amyntas of Thomas Randolph* (New York, 1917), p. 18.

28. "The Metaphysical Poets," *Selected Essays, 1917–1932* (London, 1932), p. 273.

29. *Arte of English Poesie,* Bk. III, chap. 19.

30. For study of this influence, see Richard F. Jones, "Science and English Prose Style in the Third Quarter of the Seventeenth

Century," in R. F. Jones *et al., The Seventeenth Century,* pp. 75–110.

31. Thomas Blount, *The Academy of Eloquence* (1656). For the view of the Royal Society, see Bishop Sprat's preference for the statement of things "almost in equal number of words," p. 216.

32. This general scientific point of view and the moral and literary views which follow are important attitudes toward rhetorical wit, as expressed in the literature of the period. Of course, generalities about a poet or a poem may be misleading. It does not follow, however, that failure to "consider differences of intention and kind" necessarily make such generalities as these invalid, which Ian Jack argues in *Augustan Satire,* pp. 147–153. The three views described are clearly evident. As with many opinions on style, the words used (i.e. the form) often belie the views expressed (i.e. the content), lending further evidence of the prevalent discrepancy between theory and practice.

33. For exposition of this moral force, see R. F. Jones, "The Attack on Pulpit Eloquence in the Restoration: An Episode of the Development of the Neo-Classical Standard for Prose," in R. F. Jones *et al., The Seventeenth Century,* pp. 111–142.

34. Quoted by D. F. Bond, " 'Distrust' of Imagination in English Neo-classicism," *PQ,* XIV (January, 1935), 57–58.

35. Quoted by Jones, "Attack on Pulpit Eloquence," pp. 118–119.

36. See Jackson I. Cope, "Seventeenth Century Quaker Style," *PMLA,* LXXI (September, 1956), 725–754.

37. "A Discourse on Criticism and of Poetry," *Poems on Several Occasions* (1707), ed. L. I. Bredvold in Augustan Reprint Society, Series two, No. 1 (1946), p. 205.

38. Preface to *Valentinian,* Spingarn, III, 22.

39. Defence of the Epilogue," Ker, I, 173.

40. "An Essay of Dramatic Poesy" (1668), Ker, I, 80. For other recognition and justification of Shakespeare's use of false wit, see Nicholas Rowe, *Some Account of the Life of Mr. William Shakespeare* in Augustan Reprint Society, Extra Series No. 1 (1948), p. xxiii; also Lewis Theobald, Preface to *Works of Shakespeare* in Augustan Reprint Society, Publication 19 (1949), p. xvi.

41. "An Essay on True and Apparent Beauty in Which from Settled Principles is Rendered the Grounds for Choosing and Rejecting Epigrams," trans. J. V. Cunningham (1683), in Augustan Reprint Society, Series Four, No. 5 (1950), p. 16.

42. Preface to *Theatrum Poetarum,* Spingarn, II, 266.

43. "Dramatic Poesy," Ker, I, 52–53.

44. (Part III, sect. iv) in *Characteristicks of Men, Manners, Opin-*

ions, Times, etc. (London, 1732). All subsequent references will be to parts and sections of essays in this collection.

45. *Spectator,* No. 409.

46. "Abraham Cowley," I, 15.

47. *Characters,* p. 90.

48. "A Discourse of Satire," Ker, II, 107–108. Dryden had earlier recognized the accomplishment of Waller in "Epistle Dedicatory of *The Rival Ladies,*" Ker, I, 7.

49. Dedication to *Aeneis,* Ker, II, 219.

50. "Reflections Critical and Satyrical, upon a Late Rhapsody call'd, *An Essay upon Criticism,*" *The Critical Works of John Dennis,* ed. Edward N. Hooker (Baltimore, Md., 1939, 1943. 2 vols.), I, 408, hereafter cited as *Dennis.*

51. *Theater,* No. 12, as quoted in *Dennis,* II, 487 (note to p. 209).

52. Freedom from the rules of decorum is one preconception of the word "Gothic" which antedated the first Gothic revival in the eighteenth century. This preconception has been defined by A. O. Lovejoy as a lack of "rational 'simplicity and plainness' and the introduction of ornament without use or structural necessity." See "The First Gothic Revival and the Return to Nature," *RES,* XLVII (November, 1932), 419–446.

53. "Of Poetry," Spingarn, III, 95.

54. (Part II, sect. i) in *Characteristicks.*

55. *Collection of Letters and Essays,* p. 89.

56. "An Essay on the Operas after the Italian Manner," *Dennis,* I, 39.

57. "To H—— Esq.; Of Simplicity in Poetical Compositions, in Remarks on the 70th Spectator, 1711," *Dennis,* II, 32.

58. *The Art of Sinking in Poetry: Martinus Scriblerus'* ΠΕΡΙ ΒΑΘΟΓΣ, ed. Edna L. Steeves (New York, 1952), p. 35ff.

59. It must be noted at this point that most of the theoretical criticism of the age discussed only the genres which demanded a high style. Conversely, the most admired poems were generally examples of genres requiring a low or middle style: Dryden's satires, Pope's Horatian poems, and any of Swift's poems. Therefore, the problem of disparity is more complex than is evident at first glance. There is obviously much work to be done on the three styles and on the influence of Ramist rhetoric, which apparently conditioned these styles.

60. *Humane Nature: or The Fundamental Elements of Policie,* chap. 10, sect. 4.

61. *Occasional Reflections,* as quoted by W. G. Crane, *Wit and Rhetoric,* p. 210.

62. *An Account of the English Dramatick Poets: John Dryden, Esq.*, Spingarn, III, 126.

63. "Rhetoric and Poems," p. 206.

64. "Abraham Cowley," *Works*, I, 33.

65. See his "Rhetorical Pattern of Neo-Classical Wit," p. 55.

Chapter 3 The Psychology of Wit

1. The word psychology was unknown, of course, in the Age of Wit, psychological speculation being at that time a part of philosophical thought.

2. For discussions of these neoclassical antitheses, see R. L. Brett, "The Aesthetic Sense and Taste in the Literary Criticism of the Early Eighteenth Century," *RES*, XX (1944), 199–200, and Gretchen G. Pahl, Introduction to Augustan Reprint Society, Series Four, No. 2 (1949), p. 3.

3. Brett, "Aesthetic Sense and Taste," p. 200.

4. For a summary of Renaissance psychology, see Lawrence Babb, *The Elizabethan Malady: A Study of Melancholia in English Literature from 1580 to 1642* (East Lansing, Mich., 1951), chap. 1.

5. *Essays on the Characteristics* (London, 1751), p. 12.

6. *Table Talk* (London, 1868), p. 66.

7. *History of the Royal Society of London*, edited with critical apparatus by Jackson I. Cope and Harold W. Jones (St. Louis, Missouri, 1958), p. 43.

8. *Diary and Correspondence of John Evelyn, F.R.S., to which is subjoined the Private Correspondence between King Charles I and Sir Edward Nicholas and between Sir Edward Hyde, afterwards Earl of Clarendon, and Sir Richard Browne*, ed. William Bray (London, n.d.), pp. 369–370.

9. "A Supplementary Journal to the Advice from the Scandal Club," *The Review* (September, 1704), ed. Arthur W. Secord, Facsimile Text Society (New York, 1938), III, 20.

10. *Dennis*, II, 234.

11. *Spectator*, No. 463.

12. *Oxford English Dictionary*, s.v. "wit" and "understanding."

13. Part I, sect. I, member 2, subsect. 10.

14. Charles E. Spearman, *Psychology Down the Ages* (London, 1937), I, 116.

15. *Politeuphuia, or Wits Common-Wealth*, p. 9 *et passim.*

16. Bodenham, p. 13.

17. [Henry Barker], *The Polite Gentleman: or Reflections upon*

the Several Kinds of Wit, viz. In Conversation, Books, and Affairs of the World. Done out of the French (London, 1700), p. 156.

18. Barker, p. 32. His discussion of wit in terms of humors is found beginning on page 97.

19. Barker, p. 13.

20. "A Letter Concerning Enthusiasm" (sect. ii), *Characteristicks.*

21. *Leviathan, or the Matter, Forme and Power of a Commonwealth Ecclesiasticall and Civil,* ed. A. R. Waller (Cambridge, 1904), part I, chap. 8. All subsequent quotations will be from this edition.

22. *Humane Nature,* chap. X, sect. 4.

23. Burton, *Anatomy of Melancholy,* Part I, sect. I, member 3, subsect. 10.

24. *Brief Discourse,* pp. 18–19.

25. (London, 1685), pp. 31–34 *et passim.*

26. Preface to *Theophila, or Loves Sacrifice, A Divine Poem* (London, 1652), p. A_2.

27. See end of quotation on page 88.

28. Preface to *The Passion of Byblis, Dennis,* I, 2.

29. Preface to *Miscellanies in Verse and Prose, Dennis,* I, 6.

30. *An Essay on Wit,* Augustan Reprint Society, Series One, No. 1 (1946), pp. 191–192.

31. Hobbes, *Leviathan,* Part I, chap. 7.

32. *Humane Nature,* chap. X, sect. 4.

33. *An Essay Concerning Human Understanding* in *The Philosophical Works of John Locke,* ed. J. A. St. John (London, 1899. Vol. One), Bk. II, chap. xi, p. 2.

34. Samuel Wesley, *Epistle to a Friend concerning Poetry,* Augustan Reprint Society, Series Two, No. 2 (1947), p. 3.

35. *Leviathan,* Part I, chap. 8.

36. "On s'est trompé lorsqu'on a cru que l'esprit et le jugement étoient deux choses différentes: le jugement n'est que la grandeur de la lumière de l'esprit; cette lumière pénètre le fond des choses; elle y remarque tout ce qu'il faut remarquer, et apperçoit celles qui semblent imperceptibles. Ainsi il faut demeurer d'accord que c'est l'étendue de la lumière de l'esprit qui produit tous les effets qu'on attribue au jugement" (*Maximes et Réflexions Morales du Duc de la Rochefoucauld,* Maxim XCVII).

37. *Dennis,* I, 405.

38. John Bullitt and W. J. Bate, "Distinctions Between Fancy and Imagination in Eighteenth-Century English Criticism," *MLN,* LX (1945), pp. 8–15.

39. *Of Wisdom,* I, xiii (1707 ed.), quoted in Bond, "The Neo-

Classical Psychology of the Imagination," *ELH,* IV (December, 1937), pp. 246–7.

40. Samuel Daniel, "A Defence of Rhyme," Smith, II, 366.

41. Henry Reynolds, *Mythomystes,* Spingarn, I, 154.

42. *Defense of Poesy* (1595).

43. Francis Bacon, *Advancement of Learning,* Spingarn, I, 5.

44. See Bond's study "'Distrust' of the Imagination."

45. *Leviathan,* Part I, chaps. 1–2.

46. W. J. Bate, *From Classic to Romantic: Premises of Taste in Eighteenth-Century England* (Cambridge, Mass., 1946), p. 57.

47. "An Elegie Humbly offered to the Memory of that Matchless WIT, and Unparallel'd Example of Sincere Penitency, the Right Honorable John, Earl of Rochester," in *A Century of Broadside Elegies,* ed. John Draper (London, 1928), p. 137.

48. Carleton, *Brief Discourse,* p. 28.

49. "An Essay upon Poetry," Spingarn, II, 287.

50. Abercromby, *Discourse of Wit,* p. 6.

51. Temple, "Of Poetry," Spingarn, III, 80.

52. Gabriel Harvey in *Pierce's Supererogation,* Smith, II, 249–250.

53. *Leviathan,* Part I, chap. 8.

54. Robert Boyle, *Occasional Reflections,* as quoted in Ustick and Hudson, "Mixt Wit," p. 111.

55. *An Essay upon Wit,* p. 193.

56. Morris, *Fixing the True Standards,* p. xi.

57. See C. D. Thorpe's study, "Addison and Some of His Predecessors on 'Novelty,'" *PMLA,* LII (December, 1937), 1114–1129.

58. Carleton, *Brief Discourse,* pp. 20–21, and Barker, *Polite Gentleman,* p. 47.

59. *Polite Gentleman,* p. 34.

60. *Leviathan,* Part I, chap. 8.

61. Preface to Homer's *Odysses,* Spingarn, II, 70.

62. This quotation and those on the following pages are taken from Barker, *Polite Gentleman.* Exceptions will be annotated.

63. Babb, *Elizabethan Malady,* p. 8.

64. Nathaniel Field, *A Woman Is a Weathercock,* IV, i.

65. "Of Poetry," Spingarn, III, 104–105.

66. Burton, *Anatomy of Melancholy,* Part I, sect. I, member 2, subsect. 7.

67. *Discourse Upon the Mechanical Operation of the Spirit* (1710), sect. I.

68. *Brief Discourse,* p. 127.

69. *Brief Discourse,* pp. 112–113.

70. *Brief Discourse,* pp. 132–133.

71. *Sixtynine Enigmatical Characters, all exactly drawn to the Life*, ed. Edward N. Hooker, Augustan Reprint Society, Series One, No. 2 (1946), pp. 106–108.

72. Hooker, "Pope on Wit," p. 237. However, this "wall" can be found much earlier than Locke's essay, where Hooker says it occurred first.

73. See Crane, *Wit and Rhetoric*, p. 14. C. S. Lewis sees this opposition in Quintilian's countering of *ingenium* with *judicium;* see his *Studies in Words*, p. 91.

74. See Ben Jonson, *Discoveries*, in Spingarn, I, 23, and "To the Memory of My Beloved the Author, Mr. William Shakespeare, and What He Hath Left Us" (1623).

75. *Discourse of the English Stage*, Spingarn, II, 94.

76. See Bond, "Neo-Classical Psychology of the Imagination," p. 261.

77. *Essay Concerning Human Understanding*, Bk. II, chap. XI, para 2.

78. Preface to *The Works of Shakespeare*, Augustan Reprint Society, Publ. No. 19 (1949), p. lvi.

79. *Spectator*, No. 62.

80. Morris, *Fixing the True Standards*, pp. xiii–xv.

81. *Essay Concerning Human Understanding*, Bk. II, chap. II, para. 2.

82. *An Account of the Life and Writings of Mr. Abraham Cowley*, Spingarn, II, 130.

83. "Advice to an Author" (Part III, sect. ii) in *Characteristicks*.

84. Preface to *The Humorists*.

85. "Of Poetry," Spingarn, III, 81.

86. Durham, pp. 24–25.

87. For one study of the satire involved, see D. W. Jefferson, "*Tristram Shandy* and the Tradition of Learned Wit," *Essays in Criticism*, I (July, 1951), pp. 225–248. Jefferson's concept of wit, however, is limited.

Chapter 4 The Truth of Wit

1. "Le vray bell esprit . . . est inséparable du bon sens; et c'est se méprendre, que le confondre avec je ne scay quelle vivacité qui n'a rien solide. Le jugment est comme les fonds de la beauté de l'esprit: ou plutost le bel esprit est de la nature de ces pierres précieuses, qui n'ont pas moins de solidité, que d'éclat. Il n'y a rien de plus beau qu'un diamant bien poli et bien net; il éclat de tous costez, et dans toutes ses parties. . . . . C'est un corps solide que

brille; c'est un brillant qui a de la consistence et du corps." Dominique Bouhours, *Les Entretiens d'Ariste et d'Eugène,* 1671.

2. The concern for propriety in expression was traditional. Quintilian discussed several kinds of propriety, both in words and in thoughts (*Institutio Oratoria,* VIII, ii).

3. "Essay upon Poetry."

4. Preface to *Valentinian.*

5. *Les Entretiens d'Ariste et d'Eugène,* translated by John Dennis in "Reflections," *Dennis,* I, 405.

6. "Epistle Dedicatory," of *The Rival Ladies,* Ker, I, 8.

7. "Account of the Ensuing Poem *Annus Mirabilis,* Ker, I, 14.

8. *Ker,* I, 138ff.

9. For the general argument, see R. Jack Smith, "Shadwell's Impact upon John Dryden," *RES,* XX (1944), 29–44.

10. Preface to *Albion and Albanius,* Ker, I, 270.

11. "Reflections Critical and Satirical," *Dennis,* I, 405.

12. M. M. Mahood, "The Fatal Cleopatra: Shakespeare and the Pun," *Essays in Criticism,* I (July, 1951), 193.

13. Preface to Homer's *Odysses,* Spingarn, II, 70.

14. Letter to Wycherley, Dec. 26, 1704.

15. Introduction to *Fixing of True Standards,* p. xi.

16. Students of the period differ widely on Hobbes's opinion of these terms. Spingarn was of the opinion that Hobbes distinguished between wit and judgment, *Critical Essays,* I, xxix. Williamson quotes Spingarn and supports his view, concluding that "in Hobbes supremacy of judgment is already patent," *The Donne Tradition: A Study in English Poetry from Donne to the Death of Cowley* (Cambridge, Mass., 1930), p. 214. Crane and Bond disagree. Crane maintains that Hobbes "is clearly distinguishing judgment from fancy, not from wit," *Wit and Rhetoric,* pp. 13–14; and Bond agrees, "Neoclassical Psychology of Imagination," p. 259. A sounder explanation is offered by Elledge, who thinks that Hobbes changed his mind and yielded to current usage in 1651, admitting that "men give fancy 'alone the name of wit,'' "Cowley and Longinus," p. 195. Ustick and Hudson admit a change in Hobbes' point of view but describe it as the separating of judgment from wit by identifying wit with fancy, "Mixt Wit," p. 108; this is substantially the view of Spingarn and Williamson. Easily overlooked are the facts that Hobbes reserved to each faculty an important function, that judgment (from his point of view and that of the age) was most reliable, and that his argument or emphasis varied with the kind of thinking or writing which concerned him at the moment.

17. Letter IV, 1721–1722, in *Dennis,* II, 223.

18. *Discourse of the English State* (1664), Spingarn, II, 94.

19. "An Essay upon Poetry" (1682), Spingarn, II, 294.

20. *Dennis,* I, 411. See also Pope's revision of lines 500–503 in heading quotation to Chapter I.

21. For an account of esteem for Cowley through the years, see A. H. Nethercot, "The Reputation of Abraham Cowley 1660–1800," *PMLA* XXXVIII (1923), pp. 588–641.

22. "An Essay upon Poetry," Spingarn, II, 289.

23. Quoted by Morris in his introduction to *Fixing the True Standards,* p. ix.

24. Nicole, *True and Apparent Beauty,* p. 6.

25. Spingarn, III, 80–81.

26. "Of Style," Durham, p. 82.

27. Dedication to *Spanish Friar,* Ker, I, 247.

28. Ker, II, 194.

29. *Spectator,* No. 223.

30. Preface to Homer's *Odysses.*

31. "An Essay upon Poetry."

32. Preface to *Valentinian.*

33. Hobbes, *Humane Nature,* chap. X, sect. 4.

34. *Dennis,* I, 7.

35. "Preface to Miscellanies in Verse and Prose," *Dennis,* I, 7.

36. *A Discourse of Wit* (London, 1685), p. 7.

37. *O.E.D.,* IV, 458.

38. *A Discourse of Wit,* p. 8.

39. Abercromby, p. 12. With this statement, Abercromby would seem to side with Gassendi in the latter's controversy with Descartes over the status of animals.

40. Abercromby, p. 22.

41. Preface to *Valentinian,* Spingarn, III, 4.

42. Charles Kerby-Miller, ed., *Memoirs of Martinus Scriblerus* (New Haven, Conn., 1950), p. 31.

43. *Desfence of the Essay of Dramatic Poesy* (1668), Ker, I, 121.

44. Compare Dryden's sentiments with the following lines from the *Defense of Poesy.* "Only the poet, disdaining to be tied to any such subjection, lifted up with the vigor of his own invention, doth grow in effect another nature, in making things either better than nature bringeth forth, or, quite anew, forms such as never were in nature, as the Heroes, Demigods, Cyclops, Chimeras, Furies, and such like: so as he goeth hand in hand with nature, not enclosed within the narrow warrant of her gifts, but freely ranging only within the zodiac of his own wit."

45. Quoted by Hooker, "Pope on Wit," p. 241.

46. *History of the Royal Society,* p. 419.

47. Quoted by Hooker, "Pope on Wit," p. 242.

48. *The Works of the Most Reverend Dr. John Tilletson, Late Lord Archbishop of Canterbury: Continuing Fifty Four Sermons and Discourses, on Several Occasions. Together with the Rule of Faith. Being All that were Published by his Grace Himself, And now Collected into one Volume* (London, 1728. Ninth Edition), pp. 32–33; hereafter cited as *Works.*

49. The argument over this test, which lasted through much of the century, has been presented by A. O. Aldridge, "Shaftesbury and the Test of Truth," *PMLA*, LX (March, 1945), 129–156.

50. *Works*, p. 33.

51. The semantic phenomenon of using such words as criticism, wit, raillery, ridicule, and humor as synonyms is discussed in section "The Intellectual Media of Wit." Wit was, in effect, the generic term. Shaftesbury defined raillery, for instance, as "this Species of Wit"; see "Wit and Humour" (Part I, sect. i) in *Characteristicks.*

52. "A Letter Concerning Enthusiasm" (sect. ii).

53. Aldridge believes "that Shaftesbury does not propose ridicule as a test of truth," but merely started debate over the social utility of ridicule, stating further that Berkeley was the first to apply the actual phrase "test of truth" to ridicule, "Shaftesbury and the Test of Truth," p. 129.

54. "Wit and Humour" (Part I, sect. i) in *Characteristicks.*

55. "Wit and Humour" (Part I, sect. v).

56. *Essays on the Characteristics*, p. 5.

57. *Essays on the Characteristics*, p. 7.

58. *Essays on the Characteristics*, p. 8. Italics mine.

59. The seeming confusion of such key words is reflected in recent studies. S. M. Tave, for instance, interprets ridicule in one passage to mean "something far more benevolent than satiric" and as something like "good humour" and in a later comment as "a highly distasteful species of wit." *Amiable Humorist*, pp. 35 and 37. For a discussion of the semantic identity of these words, see page 197 of this study.

60. See his Introduction to *Gulliver's Travels, A Tale of a Tub, Battle of the Books*, etc. (Oxford, 1933), p. iii.

61. "Life of Cowley," *Works*, I, 14.

62. For explanation, see W. B. C. Watkins, "Dr. Johnson on the Imagination: A Note," *RES*, XXII (April, 1946), 131.

Chapter 5 The Grace of Wit

1. See chap. 2.
2. See Introduction to *Dennis*, II, lxxx.

3. *Essay concerning Critical and Curious Learning* (1698).
4. "The Tragedies of the Last Age," Spingarn, II, 185.
5. "An Essay upon Poetry," Spingarn, II, 287.
6. "The Grounds of Criticism in Poetry," *Dennis,* I, 335. Italics mine.
7. Durham, pp. 22 and 55.
8. "Of Genius," Augustan Reprint Society, Series Four, No. 2. (1949), p. 19.
9. For a concise treatment, *see* Hooker's Introduction to *Dennis,* II, lxxix–xci.
10. "A Discourse upon Comedy, in Reference to the English Stage," Dunham, pp. 258–259.
11. *Review,* VIII, No. 60.
12. Bond, "The Neo-Classical Psychology of the Imagination," *ELH,* IV, 245.
13. Bodenham, *Politeuphuia,* p. 49.
14. Ker, I, 106.
15. Ker, p. 128.
16. Ker, p. 146.
17. Ker, p. 146.
18. *The Author's Apology* (1667), Ker, I, 179.
19. "Discourse on Criticism," Augustan Reprint Society, Series Two, No. 1 (1946), p. [5].
20. *Brief Discourse,* p. 25.
21. O.E.D. s.v. "Genius" includes as a fifth definition the following: "native intellectual power of an exalted type, such as is attributed to those who are esteemed greatest in any department of art, speculation, or practice; instinctive and extraordinary capacity for imaginative creation, original thought, invention, or discovery." The first example is from Fielding's *Tom Jones,* 1749. Evidence indicates that, through its association with wit, genius assumed this meaning almost one hundred years earlier.
22. *Some Account of the Life of Mr. William Shakespeare,* Augustan Reprint Society, Extra Series, No. 20, 1 (1948), p. xxiii.
23. "Complete Art of Poetry," Durham, p. 56.
24. See *Dennis,* I, 451.
25. "Essay upon Poetry," Spingarn, II, 286.
26. "Of Poetry," Spingarn, III, 80.
27. "Complete Art of Poetry," Durham, p. 34.
28. See Elledge, "Cowley and Longinus," p. 193.
29. "Author's Apology for Heroic Poetry and Poetic Licence" (1677), Ker, I, 179–180.
30. Barker, *Polite Gentleman,* p. A_2.
31. "An Essay on Wit," p. 201.

32. "An Essay on Wit," p. 194.
33. As quoted by Hooker in Introduction to *Dennis,* II, lxxxi.
34. "Of Style," Durham, p. 82.
35. As quoted by Hooker in Explanatory Notes to *Dennis,* I, 451.
36. *Discourse of Wit,* p. 27.
37. Bodenham, *Politeuphuia,* s.v. "poetry" and "wit."
38. Preface to *Tyrannic Love.*
39. "State of Poetry," Durham, p. 391.
40. "Dramatic Poesy," Ker, I, 82–83.
41. Spingarn, II, 94.
42. *De Carmine Pastorali.* Prefixed to Thomas Creech's translation of the *Idylliums of Theocritus,* Augustan Reprint Society, Series Two, No. 3 (1947), p. 51.
43. As quoted by Hooker, "Pope on Wit," p. 240.
44. Spingarn, II, 20–21.
45. "Of Wit," *A Farrage of several Pieces,* quoted by Ustick and Hudson, "Mixt Wit," p. 112.
46. *A Satyr upon a Late Pamphlet Entitled, A Satyr Against Wit,* quoted in Hooker, "Pope on Wit," p. 241.
47. Longinus, *On the Sublime,* sect. II.
48. Elledge has noted this association in "Cowley and Longinus," p. 186.
49. Nicole, *True and Apparent Beauty,* p. 6.
50. *A Tale of a Tub,* eds. A. C. Guthkelch and D. N. Smith (Oxford, England, 1920), p. 44.
51. *Tale of a Tub,* pp. 46–47.
52. *Art of Sinking in Poetry,* p. 6.
53. *Art of Sinking,* p. 10.
54. *Art of Sinking,* p. 21.
55. Augustan Reprint Society, Publication No. 43 (1953), pp. 2–3.
56. See Brett, "Aesthetic Sense and Taste," p. 200.
57. S. H. Monk has discussed the history of secret grace as a critical term in "A Grace Beyond the Reach of Art," *JHI,* V (1944), 131–150.
58. Preface to Homer's *Odysses.*
59. Preface to *An Evening's Love.*
60. *English Theophrastus,* p. 282.
61. "Of Poetry," Spingarn, III, 83–84.
62. Preface to *Valentinian,* Spingarn, III, 1.
63. (Part IV, sect. ii), *Characteristicks.* For further elaboration of the Platonic "Idea of Perfection" and the concept of secret grace, see Shaftesbury's "Advice to an Author" (Part III, sect. iii), *Characteristicks. Scai* was the older spelling of *sais.*

64. Joseph Spence, *Anecdotes*, ed. S. W. Singer (London 1820), p. 142.

65. *The Immortality of the Soule*, ii, p. ix.

66. Spingarn, II, 165.

67. (Part III, sect. ii). Notice the similarity of meaning here between "romantic" and "Gothic," page 60.

68. For other contemporary attitudes of "romantic," i.e. as pastoral scenes and descriptions, its pre-romantic popularity in the Gothic romance, and its ultimate analysis and condemnation in the nineteenth century, see Arthur Johnston, *Enchanted Ground: The Study of Medieval Romance in the Eighteenth Century* (London, 1964), particularly chap. 8.

Chapter 6 The Republic of Wit

1. See Morse Peckham's "Towards a Theory of Romanticism," *PMLA*, LXVI (March, 1951), pp. 5–23.

2. "An Anatomie of the World." For implications of the phrase in the seventeenth century, see V. I. Harris, *All Coherence Gone* (Chicago, Illinois, 1949).

3. Carl Becker, "Climates of Opinion," *The Heavenly City of the Eighteenth Century Philosophers* (New Haven, Conn., 1932).

4. I am indebted to Professor Lewis P. Simpson of Louisiana State University for the use of his unpublished study of the literary community, entitled, "The End of the Literary World: Notes on the Symbolism of the Literary Community."

5. See Petrarch's *Letters to Ancient Authors.*

6. Letter to Sir Horace Mann, 1742.

7. Quoted by Hooker, "Pope on Wit," p. 229.

8. *History of the Royal Society*, p. 419.

9. *New Foundling Hospital*, VI, 104.

10. Carleton, *Brief Discourse*, p. 41.

11. *Essay on Criticism*, p. 44.

12. *New Foundling Hospital*, VI, 159.

13. See Hooker's Introduction to *Dennis*, II, liii.

14. Prologue to *The Libertine.*

15. Preface to *All for Love.*

16. *English Theophrastus*, p. 6.

17. *Poems on Several Occasions*, p. [5].

18. E. N. Hooker says "by the 1690's." See his Introduction to Augustan Reprint Society, Series One, No. 2 (1946), p. 3.

19. "The Neo-Classical Theory of the Formal Verse Satire in

England, 1700–1750," unpublished dissertation (University of North Carolina, 1939), p. 41.

20. *The Author's Apology,* Ker, I, 182.

21. *Broadside Elegies,* p. 137.

22. Preface to *Valentinian.*

23. *Review,* I, No. 76.

24. "Original and Progress of Satire," Ker, II, 92–93.

25. Preface to *Valentinian,* Spingarn, III, 14.

26. *Review,* I, No. 76.

27. *Collection of Letters and Essays,* p. 72.

28. *Fixing the True Standards,* p. 37.

29. Preface to *An Evening's Love,* Ker, I, 143.

30. "Of Poetry," Spingarn, III, 101.

31. *Essay upon the Ancient and Modern Learning,* Spingarn, III, 71–72.

32. See J. W. Draper's study, "The Theory of the Comic in Eighteenth Century England," *JEGP,* XXXVII (1938), 207–223.

33. The difficulties of the early eighteenth century with this question of the proper subjects for laughter have been treated to an extent by Hooker in "Humour in the Age of Pope," *HLQ,* XI (1948), 361–385.

34. *Fixing the True Standards,* p. 13.

35. Life and Writings of Cowley," Ker, II, 130.

36. *Diary,* p. 25.

37. *Gray's-Inn Journal,* No. 25.

38. *Diary,* p. 307.

39. "Ode to the Athenian Society" (1692).

40. "Wit and Humour" (Part I, sect. iii), *Characteristicks.*

41. Augustan Reprint Society, Series One, No. 2 (1946), p. 14.

42. Spingarn's Introduction to *Critical Essays of the Seventeenth Century* (I, lviii–lxiii) traced the opposition between wit and humor through Swift's discussion in the *Intelligencer,* No. 3 (1728); more recently Henry L. Snuggs examined the varying interpretations of humor by Dryden, Shadwell, and Congreve, "The Comic Humours: A New Interpretation," *PMLA,* LXII (1947), 114–122; a third study by Edward N. Hooker relates the change in humor to the changing attitudes toward satire and laughter, with attention to the changing character of what was known in society as the "Humorist;" see "Humour in the Age of Pope," *HLQ,* XI (1948), 361–385. See also Stuart M. Tave, *The Amiable Humorist* (Chicago, Ill., 1960).

43. Preface to *An Evening's Love,* Ker, I, 139.

44. Ker, I, 143, and Shadwell, *Complete Works,* I, 189.

45. Spingarn, III, 242–244.

46. *Irish Intelligencer* (1728), No. 3.

47. Act I, scene i, as quoted by Louis F. Cazamian, *The Development of English Humor* (Durham, N.C., 1952), p. 394. Cazamian traces very carefully the changes in meaning of humor in the latter half of the seventeenth century; see especially pages 393–394.

48. *History of the Royal Society*, p. 417.

49. Cazamian attributes the change to the fact that "the especially important part played by the 'humor' . . . more or less grew humorous, as we should say, through a growing discovery of the significance of his own oddity," and also to the increasing association of humor with "a mode of pleasantry." *English Humor*, p. 393.

50. "Wit and Humour" (Part I, sect. iii), *Characteristicks.*

51. D. W. Jefferson uses the term "learned wit" to denote "several related kinds" of wit, but its essence was "scholastic" in ingenuity, becoming more diffuse as it developed in later centuries. It is certainly rhetorical, involving a combination of erudition and deductive logic. See Jefferson's "*Tristram Shandy* and the Tradition of Learned Wit."

52. See Arrowsmith's *The Reformation* (1673); Etherege's *The Man of Mode* (1676); and Otway's *The Souldiers Fortune* (1683).

53. *Polite Gentleman*, p. 79.

54. "Letters upon Several Occasions," *Dennis*, II, 383.

55. Preface to *Shakespeare's Works*, p. liii.

56. "An Essay on Criticism," ll. 36–37. See also Pope's letter to Swift on February 16, 1733.

57. Gay, *Present State of Wit*, p. 1.

58. Robert Wolseley, Preface to *Valentinian.*

59. An open conflict between men of wit and men of sense did not develop along such clear-cut lines as suggested by R. M. Krapp ("Class Analysis of a Literary Controversy"). The charges made by Blackmore and Defoe against men of wit were significant but minor, since all critics considered themselves men of sense. Krapp's association of men of sense with the middle class and of men of wit "usually" with the aristocracy is also inaccurate and misleading.

60. *History of the Royal Society*, p. 113.

61. See study of James R. Wilson, "The Narrators of Jonathan Swift," unpublished dissertation (Oklahoma University, 1953).

62. Preface to *Prince Arthur*, 1695, Spingarn, III, 229.

63. Spingarn, III, 18. Italics mine.

64. "Defence of the Essay of Dramatic Poesy," Ker, I, 121.

65. "Wit and Humour" (Part IV, sect. iii), *Characteristicks*, I, 142. See also "Advice to an Author" (Part III, sect. iii).

66. "Wit and Humour (Part I, sect. i).

67. See also Temple's discussion in "Of Poetry," Spingarn, III, 80.

68. Robert Wolseley, Preface to *Valentinian.*

69. Pope, "An Essay on Criticism," ll. 179–180.

70. Pope in a letter to Elijah Fenton, *Works of Pope,* III, 128.

71. *The Present State of the Republic of Letters* (London, 1728), I, i.

72. Letter "To Sir Richard Steele, Declaring the Reasons for which I publish'd the two Volumes of Select Works," *Dennis,* III, 173–174.

73. Unless otherwise noted, the parenthetical notations refer to part and/or section numbers of essays in Volume One of the *Characteristicks* (London, 1732).

74. However, in practice he felt *A Tale of a Tub* to be "that detestable writing of that most detestable author." See his letter to Pierre Coste from Naples on July 25, 1712.

75. "Advice to an Author" (Part II, sect. iii).

76. "Defence of the Epilogue," Ker, I, 163.

77. "Epistle to Lord Melcombe," *New Foundling Hospital,* VI, 98.

Chapter 7 The Caricature of Wit

1. See "Ode to the Athenian Society" (1692).

2. "Defence of the Epilogue," Ker, I, 174.

3. *History of the Royal Society,* p. 44.

4. "Of Style," Durham, p. 80.

5. For special consideration of Swift's essay, its antecedents, and Augustan conversation in general, see Herbert Davis, "The Conversation of the Augustans," in R. F. Jones *et al, The Seventeenth Century,* pp. 181–197.

6. "Of Poetry," Spingarn, III, 101.

7. "An Essay upon Publick Spirit," *Dennis,* II, 397.

8. Lines translated by John Dennis and quoted by Oldmixon, *An Essay on Criticism,* p. 87.

9. "Defence of the Epilogue."

10. *Review,* IV, No. 99.

11. Epilogue to *The Unhappy Favorite* (1681), by John Banks.

12. Preface to *Valentinian,* Spingarn, III, 3–4.

13. "An Essay upon the Ancient and Modern Learning," Spingarn, III, 72.

14. "Complete Art of Poetry," Durham, p. 35.

15. Durham, p. 53.

16. "Of Poetry."

17. *Selected Writings of the Ingenius Mrs. Aphra Behn,* eds. John Balcomb and Robert Phelps (New York, 1950), p. 13.

18. *Discourse of Wit,* p. 214.

19. For a recent study of correspondence and letter writing in general, see W. H. Irvine, *The Province of Wit in the English Letter Writers* (Durham, N.C., 1955).

20. *New Foundling Hospital,* VI, 170.

21. See *Tatler,* No. 60, for one instance.

22. "Of Poetry: A Rapsody," 1733.

23. For a recent study of these gentlemen, see J. H. Wilson, *The Court Wits of the Restoration* (Princeton, N.J., 1948).

24. J. H. Wilson, p. 18.

25. "The Preface of the Author," *The Battle of the Books.*

26. Dedication to the *Aeneis.*

27. "An Essay on Criticism," l. 40.

28. *Discourse of Wit,* pp. 41–42.

29. Preface to *Valentinian,* Spingarn, III, 9–10.

30. *English Theophrastus,* p. 7.

31. *Discourse of Wit,* pp. 42–43.

32. *Hudibras Redivivus,* as quoted in Howard W. Troyer, *Ned Ward of Grubstreet: A Study of Sub-Literary London in the Eighteenth Century* (Cambridge, Mass., 1946), p. 93.

33. *Essay on Criticism,* p. 88.

34. Preface to *The Sullen Lovers.*

35. Letter IV: "A Defence of Mr. Wycherley's Characters in the Plaindealer," *Dennis,* II, 233.

36. "Upon the dramatic poems of Mr. John Fletcher."

37. *Spectator,* No. 151.

38. Quoted by L. C. Knights, *Explorations: Essays in Criticism Mainly on the Literature of the Seventeenth Century* (New York, 1947), p. 150.

39. One such account, labeled "An Allegory on the Game of Quadrille" and said to have been written by William Congreve, follows:

Substance of an Information Taken Before One of His Majesty's Justices of the Peace.

That four Ladies of Quality, whom the deponent does not care to name, repair mightily to a certain convenient house, to meet four gallants, of the highest rank, whom the deponent would not name, but so far described, that two of them were of a swarthy, and two of a ruddy complexion (but he believes they are abominably painted); the gallants are called, by these Ladies, by the fond names of Hercules, Cupid, Pitts, and the Gardener.

After a plentiful service of the most costly fish, they begin to play their tricks like the tumblers in Bartholomew Fair, upon a carpet; strip is the word, and it has been known, that they have lately stripp'd a Gentleman who lately came into the house.

At first they begin very civilly, as Madam, by your leave, or so, which the Lady is so good as seldom to refuse.

By a certain established rule of precedency, every Lady has, in her turn, the choice of her gallant, and some have been so unreasonable, that after they have had three, they have called for a fourth.

Afterwards, it is shameful to relate the tricks that are played by the lewd pack; sometimes they are thrown on their backs, sometimes on their bellies, and thus they make beasts of one another; now hickledy pickledy, and by and by you may see them a-top of one another.

Their discourse is of a piece with their practice—The deponent has often heard them talk of their A——, with as much ease as they do of their hands.—I have a black one, says one, and names the thing directly.—Mine is better than yours, says another, and names it.—Must I be laughed at, only because I have a red one, says the third.

It is a constant rule, that if a Lady is called upon, she must show all.

What is monstrous; it has been known that after a Lady has had six—she has asked a Gentleman if he could no more—and it has been known, that when the Ladies have been tired with their gallants, they have called for fresh ones.—In short, those Ladies have spent not only their pin-money, but their husbands' estates, upon Hercules, Cupid, Pitts, and the Gardener; and when they want ready money, they commonly pawn their most valuable jewels. (*New Foundling Hospital for Wit*, VI, 78—80.)

40. "Prologue to the King and Queen at the Opening of their Theatre" (1683), *Rare Prologues and Epilogues, 1642–1700*, ed. Autrey Nell Wiley (London, 1940), pp. 144–145.

41. Letter to Rev. William Tisdall, December 16, 1703.

42. See James R. Wilson, "The Narrators of Jonathan Swift."

43. *An Essay upon Wit*, p. 197.

44. Such a conclusion is made by Hooker in his Introduction to Augustan Reprint Society, Series One, No. 2 (1946), p. 4.

45. *The Present State of Wit*, p. 6.

46. Preface to *An Evening's Love*, 1671.

47. "The Author's Apology," Ker, I, 170.

48. Preface to *Troilus and Cressida*, 1679, Ker, I, 209–210.

49. Preface to *The Fables*, Ker, II, 263.

50. As quoted in Gardner, *Prologues and Epilogues of Dryden*, p. 336. Italics mine.

Chapter 8 The Stigma of Wit

1. "Reflections upon An Essay upon Criticism," *Dennis,* I, 413.
2. Preface to *The Fables,* Ker, II, 263.
3. A summary of the correspondence on this subject is made by Hooker, "Pope on Wit," pp. 231–233.
4. Henry Fielding makes the same substitution of invention for wit as the counterbalance to judgment in the make-up of genius (*Tom Jones,* IX, I).
5. Swift's letter to Charles Wogan (August 2, 1732).
6. *Brief Discourse,* p. 23.
7. Sheffield, "An Essay upon Poetry," Spingarn, II, 287.
8. Shadwell, Preface to *The Humorists.*
9. Shaftesbury, "Advice to an Author" (Part III, sect. ii), *Characteristicks.*
10. "Preface to *Troilus and Cressida,* Ker, I, 221–222.
11. "A Satyr Against Wit."
12. *English Theophrastus,* p. 8.
13. *The British Academy,* Augustan Reprint Society, Series Six, No. 1 (1948), p. 13.
14. "Sermon against Foolish Talking and Jesting," *Theological Works,* I, 393–394.
15. Quoted in Hooker, "Pope on Wit," p. 228.
16. Quoted in Hooker, "Pope on Wit," p. 228.
17. *Broadside Elegies,* p. 134.
18. *Broadside Elegies,* p. 137.
19. "Thoughts on Various Subjects," *Works of Pope,* V, 561.
20. "To Dr. Delany on the Libels Written Against Him" (1729).
21. See William Cartwright's lines on "old fashioned Wit" above, page 246.
22. *Discourse of the English Stage,* Spingarn, II, 94; see also his "Of one that Zanys the Good Companion," Augustan Reprint Society, Sesies One, No. 2 (1947), pp. 9–10.
23. See page 87.
24. Preface to *Valentinian,* Spingarn, II, 24–25.
25. *New Foundling Hospital,* VI, 159 ff.
26. Anonymous, *Some Thoughts Concerning the Stage in a Letter to a Lady,* Augustan Reprint Society, Series Three, No. 2 (1947), pp. 4–5.
27. Blackmore, *An Essay upon Wit,* pp. 189–190.
28. *History of the Royal Society,* p. 112.
29. *A Free and Impartial Censure of the Platonick Philosophie,* (1666), as quoted in Bond, " 'Distrust' of Imagination," p. 57.

30. *Collection of Letters and Essays*, p. 46.
31. Preface to *Gondibert*.
32. Wolseley, Preface to *Valentinian*.
33. *An Essay of Dramatic Poesy*, 1668, Ker, I, 79–80.
34. "An Essay upon Poetry," 1682, Spingarn, II, 288.
35. *Discourse of Wit*, pp. 31–32.
36. Durham, p. 368.
37. Durham, p. 329.
38. Durham, p. 330.
39. "Of Wit," *The Weekly Register*, No. 119, Augustan Reprint Society, Series One, No. 2 (1946), p. 861.
40. Quoted by Hooker, "Pope on Wit," p. 229.
41. "The Preface of the Author," *The Battle of the Books*.
42. *An Essay upon Wit*, pp. 195.
43. See Aldridge, "Shaftesbury and the Test of Truth," pp. 143 ff for each man's point of view.
44. Brown, *Essays on the Characteristics*, p. 9.
45. Brown, p. 107.
46. Augustan Reprint Society, Series One, No. 2 (1946), p. 861.
47. Morris, Introduction to *Fixing the True Standards*, p. xi.
48. Morris, p. 24.
49. *Sixtynine Enigmatical Characters*, pp. 107–108.
50. Preface to *Valentinian*, Spingarn, III, 13.
51. *Essays on the Characteristics*, pp. 3–4.
52. No. 45, Augustan Reprint Society, Series One, No. 1 (1946), pp. 327–328.
53. Quoted by W. E. Schultz, *Gay's Beggar's Opera: Its Content, History, and Influence* (New Haven, Conn., 1923), p. 180.
54. "Essay upon Publick Spirit," *Dennis*, II, 396.
55. This development has been discussed variously: see particularly E. N. Hooker, "Humour in the Age of Pope," and J. W. Draper, "Theory of the Comic in Eighteenth Century England."
56. *Collection of Letters and Essays*, pp. 72, 74.
57. *Dennis*, I, 127.
58. "Essay on the Theatre; or, a Comparison Between Sentimental and Laughing Comedy" (1773).
59. Letter to Charles Wogan, *Correspondence of Jonathan Swift*, ed. F. E. Ball (London, 1910–1914), IV, 329.
60. Letter to Pope (April 5, 1729).
61. *New Foundling Hospital*, VI, 161.
62. Robert M. Krapp summarizes the implications of this change in "Class Analysis of a Literary Controversy," pp. 81–93.
63. Aubrey L. Williams discusses the historical significance of this shift in his *Pope's Dunciad: A Study of its Meaning* (Baton

Rouge, La., 1955), p. 31. But he overlooks the symbolic significance in the status of the Republic of Wit, a significance borne out by the "opposed realms of value" which supported the shift: the classical and contemporary versus the epical and the duncical (p. 48). The leader of the dunces is called "The Antichrist of Wit" and the Goddess of Dullness is antithetical and yet analogous to Venus, who symbolized a chief characteristic of wit, *venustas.*

64. *Weekly Register,* No. 119, p. 861.

65. *New Foundling Hospital,* VI, 98ff.

66. Kames, *Elements of Criticism,* s.v. "wit."

67. Maynard Mack, "The Muse of Satire," *The Yale Review,* XLI (1951), pp. 80–92.

68. T. S. Eliot, "The Metaphysical Poets," *Selected Essays, 1917–1932* (London, 1932), p. 273.

Index

*Index**

* Terms found in the Table of Contents (i.e. *rhetoric, true wit, false wit, dullness, decorum, satire, ridicule,* etc.) are not included in the Index.